30

Bi

R‹

X118745660   BPR

Resistance

Resistance

RECLAIMING

AN

AMERICAN

TRADITION

Jeff Biggers

COUNTERPOINT
Berkeley, California

Grateful acknowledgment for reprinting materials is made to the following: "Amrita: Immortal" © 2016 by Kara Hoving

Library of Congress Cataloging-in-Publication Data
Names: Biggers, Jeff, 1963– author.
Title: Resistance : reclaiming an American tradition / Jeff Biggers.
Description: Berkeley, CA : Counterpoint Press, 2018.
Identifiers: LCCN 2017057937 | ISBN 9781640090477
Subjects: LCSH: Passive resistance—United States. | Multiculturalism—United States. | Social movements—United States. | Social justice—United States.
Classification: LCC HM1281 .B545 2018 | DDC 303.48/40973—dc23
LC record available at https://lccn.loc.gov/2017057937

Jacket designed by Jason Gabbert
Book designed by Jordan Koluch

COUNTERPOINT
2560 Ninth Street, Suite 318
Berkeley, CA 94710
www.counterpointpress.com

Printed in the United States of America
Distributed by Publishers Group West

10 9 8 7 6 5 4 3 2 1

Per Carla, per sempre
For my billie boys, Massimo and Diego, and their future
For my folks, Mam and Paps, makers of our radical roots

In memory of
Ella Baker
and
William Sloane Coffin, Jr.

That's starting to be history now.
Right now we're in a whirlpool of paradigms
Beatitudes and messes. With uprisings
come upwellings of old-fashioned ideas re-shined and green-stamped
ideas brewed for ages before popping out and hailed in headlines
Where did this come from?
And others swirl down into the depths
Forgotten stories of our foremothers
who thrust us up as collective memory dragged them down.
But we were not seeking recognition, we sought only change
And still we seek, forever galvanized
Bringing ourselves to the tables, turning power plays into
compromises reaching our hands out to the bottom where we've been
    instead of
clawing our way up to the top, building change, casting seeds, setting
small fires wherever we can make it, let them spread instead of
waiting for one giant fix to make or break it.
Sustaining the things that make life worth living instead of
worth money, living in ways that
make sense instead of—that other stuff.

—Kara Hoving, "Amrita: Immortal"
Climate Narrative Project

Contents

Hope Resists

If I fall, I will fall five-feet four-inches forward in the fight for freedom.
—Fannie Lou Hamer, "Sick and Tired of Being Sick and Tired," 1964

THESE ARE THE TIMES THAT try our souls, as Thomas Paine would say.

On the day of President Donald Trump's landmark decision to withdraw the United States from the Paris Climate Accord in the summer of 2017, my twelve-year-old son Massimo asked me if there was any hope for action on climate change. His real question: Was there any hope for his future?

It took me a while to muster the words to answer my son's question. He had heard me rattle on for years about the realities of climate change, the possibilities of regenerative cities, and the unending struggle for civil rights. But these stories suddenly seemed distant—even illusory—against the rollbacks of Trump's policies on multiple fronts, not only climate action.

Instead of a lecture on climate change, I wanted to tell my son about a moment of doubt, sitting in a jail cell in Washington, DC, in 1985, after I had been arrested in a sit-in at the South African embassy. We had joined a year-long campaign of civil disobedience, as part of the Free South African Movement, to draw attention to the American support of the brutal apartheid system of white supremacy and segregation. As a twenty-one-year-old, I realized that African National Congress leader Nelson Mandela had spent more time in prison at Robben Island, Pollsmoor Prison, and Victor Verster Prison than I had been on the planet.

My cellmate was Rev. William Sloane Coffin, my boss at the Riverside Church in New York City, where I served as his personal aide. A World War II intelligence officer and former CIA agent, Coffin had led civil disobedience campaigns against the Vietnam War as the chaplain at Yale. But it was his role in one of the first Freedom Rides in the summer of 1961, following the courageous lead of young African American activists, that had transformed Coffin's fervent belief in the role of nonviolent resistance.

Coffin smiled at the youthful frustration in my voice. I told him our protests seemed futile, even hopeless. The apartheid system seemed unshakeable. He looked at me with the same hesitation I offered my son. He told me what he had learned sitting in jail in Alabama.

"Hope resists," he said, shifting on the concrete bench. "Hopelessness adapts."

Calling it our "duty rightly," Revolutionary forefather Thomas Paine had urged Americans, in one of the most hopeless moments before the American Revolution in 1776, to "take our children in our hand, and fix our station a few years farther into life." The seeds of our democracy, he reminded the disconsolate, would take root from an American resistance. Paine did not offer a promise but a challenge to the American colonies. "The sun never shined on a cause of greater worth," he wrote in *Common Sense*.

Every generation must decide how that sun will illuminate the challenges of our own times. The language may alter, but the tribulation remains the same: "The sun shines today also," Ralph Waldo Emerson reminded his generation of abolitionists in a dark moment of slavery in 1836; "Pray for the dead and fight like hell for the living," Irish immigrant and labor leader Mary "Mother" Jones told a crowd of striking coal miners seeking fair wages and better working conditions in West Virginia in 1912.

In my own lifetime, Mississippi freedom leader Fannie Lou Hamer reminded civil rights activists in 1965 that the only way to end segregation in Mississippi was to "bring out to the light all that has been under the cover all these years." Joining thousands of Mexican American students in the streets of Los Angeles on a spring day in 1968, Chicano leader Carlos Muñoz, Jr., saw the historic walkouts at the nation's largest public school system as a counterpart to the civil rights movement—and a new chapter in an American tradition of resistance. In leading a successful two-year campaign of civil disobedience to halt fracking and the storing of liquid petroleum gas at Seneca Lake in New York, scientist Sandra Steingraber invoked the words in 2017 of poet Ella Wheeler Wilcox: "To sin by silence, when we should protest / Makes cowards out of men."

More than a decade after she launched the "Me Too" movement to empower millions to speak out on sexual violence and harassment, activist Tarana Burke was recognized, among many other "silence breakers," as the *Time* "Person of the Year" in 2017. At the historic March for Our Lives rally in Washington, DC, on March 24, 2018, Emma González read the names of fellow Florida students killed in the February 14 shooting, stood in silence, and then challenged the nation to "fight for your lives before it is someone else's job."

On February 11, 1990, freed from twenty-seven years in prison in South Africa, Nelson Mandela saluted multiple generations of resistance from the balcony of the Cape Town city hall: "Today, the majority of South Africans, black and white, recognize that apartheid has no future. It has to be ended by our decisive mass action. We have waited too long for our freedom."

To be sure, I could not be glib or disingenuous about the powerful idea of "resistance" today. My son is also an Italian citizen, where *la resistenza italiana,* as he knew well from his grandparents' experience during World War II and plaques on corners of town piazzas, referred to armed liberation and brutal guerilla warfare against German occupation and fascist forces.

Yet, as a chronicler of American social movements, and as a participant in what historian Howard Zinn called the "unreported resistance," I knew a deeper story of American resistance needed to be brought out of the shadows. In my earlier books, I have traced the history of rebellion along the Appalachian mountains and our nation's first frontier, from indigenous and pre–Revolutionary War insurrections to the abolitionist, labor, and civil rights movements; I have explored my own family's 200 years of struggle in the American heartland, taking part in militant anti-slavery efforts, union labor battles for coal miners, and present-day environmental movements; I have reported on the cycles of resistance by indigenous, Mexican American, and rooted communities against anti-immigrant and white supremacist interlopers in the American Southwest; I have chronicled the life struggles of a pioneering woman journalist's battle over freedom of speech in the early nineteenth century and the resistance work of a Southern writer and agitator in the mid-twentieth century, who had been wanted "dead or alive" for his subversive organizing in the mills, mines, and racist institutions of the white ruling class.

I have set out to write this book for my son, in the context of our American story today; not to write an exhaustive history of social justice movements, but to respond to his question by reconsidering how the arc of everyday resistance, and not just random episodes of rebellion, has shaped our American experience in moving those challenges forward— not backward. To remind him, and perhaps myself, that any hope for the future depends on our ability to reclaim the narrative of a long continuum of resistance that has been the foundation of our country and the bulwark against the very forces that have threatened our democracy since its founding.

Resistance

Let Us Now Praise Resistance

Let them call me rebel and welcome, I feel no concern from it;
but I should suffer the misery of devils, were I to make a whore of
my soul by swearing allegiance to one whose character is that of
a sottish, stupid, stubborn, worthless, brutish man.
                                  —Thomas Paine, *The American Crisis,* 1776

PETITION AND RESISTANCE, THOMAS PAINE explained to his readers in the aftermath of the American Revolution. "It left to the Americans no other modes of redress than those which are left to people under despotic governments."

Resistance—the word conjures black and white images of beret-capped French fighters taking on German Nazis in occupied Paris or Sophie Scholl, the young White Rose resister carted off to to the guillotine in Germany; or the chilling defiance of the "Tank Man" in Tiananmen Square in Beijing, standing in front of a column of tanks in 1989.

In virtually every case, *resistance* implies a foreign concept, an assortment of freedom fighters in countries aflame, in chaos or riven by conflict, an occupying force, or an oppressive dictatorship. It somehow resounds like a battle cry from someone else's past: *No pasaran,* as Dolores Ibarruri, *la Pasionaria,* warned Spaniards in Madrid of the fascist threat under General Francisco Franco in 1936: "The whole country cringes in indignation at these heartless barbarians." In the other-world parlance of the U.S. Department of Defense: "Resistance is an organized effort by some portion of the civil population of a country to resist the legally established government or an occupying power and to disrupt civil order and stability."

Overlooked in this ominous depiction might be our country's best-kept secret: in dealing with the most challenging issues of every generation, resistance to duplicitous civil authority and its corporate enablers has defined our quintessential American story.

Resistance, as an American credo, blossomed from the seed-time of our American Revolution as a universal right, not simply some random act to "disrupt civil order and stability" or fleeting moments of dissent or vague calls for freedom, as often defined. Resistance, over the centuries, has endowed a "public commons" for "we the people" to have a voice in framing the defining issues in our most trying times. And while those defining issues have remained unresolved, in many respects— expanding the protection of life, liberty, and the pursuit of happiness for all; defending the right of free speech and freedom of the press as inalienable—they have taken new forms in an age of nuclear weapons and climate change.

With the rise of a reckless presidential administration and conservative movement set on dismantling constitutional safeguards and protections, never have the benchmarks of our democracy been so threatened or left in the small hands of a single demagogic leader.

Never, perhaps we should say, since the days of our country's founding.

In 1782, as peace negotiations began in Paris between representatives of the United States and the British Crown, Paine sat down to write a response to the Abbé Raynal in France, who had published his own long-distance version of the American Revolution. Anguished that the Frenchman had reduced the "justifiable resistance" to a nationalistic spat over tea and taxes, Paine characterized his letter as one "in which the Mistakes in the Abbé's Account of the Revolution of America are Corrected and Cleared Up."

A letter from Paine was no small event. He may have once identified himself as the Secretary in the Foreign Department of Congress, but Paine's numerous revolutionary pamphlets had ensured his legacy as the literary instigator of the American resistance. The very name of our nation—the United States of America—first appeared in Paine's handwriting. He was the nation's most widely read author—though not its bestselling one, for all of Paine's freely distributed works had gone viral, in modern terms, but did not leave a single penny in his pocket. Even the envious founding father John Adams bitterly admitted to Thomas Jefferson: "History is to ascribe the American Revolution to Thomas Paine."

In Paris, an American traveler reported, Paine's translated work was "everywhere." His *Letter to the Abbé Raynal* had "sealed his fame," the traveler added. "Even those who are jealous of, and envy him, acknowledge that the point of his pen has been as formidable in politics as the point of the sword in the field."

Far from being an armchair revolutionary, Paine had insisted on taking a role on the front lines. "As I was with the troops at Fort Lee, and marched with them to the edge of Pennsylvania, I am well acquainted with many circumstances, which those who live at a distance know but little or nothing of," he had written from the camps of George Washington's Revolutionary forces.

But the misinformation about military tactics and strategies did not interest Paine now. His extraordinary letter to the Abbé sought to define the transformative impact of the resistance movement on Americans in the aftershock of their triumph. "Our style and manner of thinking have undergone a revolution more extraordinary than the political revolution of the country," he explained to the French. "We see with other eyes; we hear with other ears; and think with other thoughts, than those we formerly used. We can look back on our own prejudices, as if they had been the prejudices of other people. We now see and know they were prejudices and nothing else; and, relieved from their shackles, enjoy a freedom of mind, we felt not before."

High-minded perhaps, but hardly delusional, Paine claimed this new way of thinking had "opened itself toward the world" and brought Americans into the world of nations. He didn't trumpet the military triumph of Washington and his French allies; nor did Paine make an inventory of the natural resources and wealth now at American disposal. The future of the United States of America—and consequently the world—rested in the hands of "science, the partisan of no country, but the beneficent patroness of all," which served as the great "temple where all may meet."

Paine's message to the Abbé reflected the ongoing negotiations in Paris—and a clear admonition to its leaders. Instead of pursuing that "temper of arrogance," he warned, "which serves only to sink" a country in esteem, and "entail the dislike of all nations," Paine called on all leaders to find a way for the world to live in peace.

"The philosopher of one country sees not an enemy in the philosopher of another: he takes his seat in the temple of science, and asks not who sits beside him."

Two hundred and thirty-five years after Paine's historic analysis of the American Revolution and the role of science in uniting world concerns in Paris, President Donald Trump announced the withdrawal of the United States from the historic Paris climate accord on June 1, 2017. A self-proclaimed billionaire real estate tycoon and reality TV star, Trump had bare-knuckled his way into office as a repudiation of President Barack Obama, losing the popular vote but winning an election victory over former Secretary of State Hillary Clinton through electoral votes. He rejected science and fact-based assessments on climate change, defending a corporate energy lobby of coal, oil, and gas that had produced most of the nation's carbon emissions. In the process, Trump also repudiated global cooperation, breaking with all 196 nations (including war-torn Syria, which would eventually sign the accord in the winter of 2017) that had negotiated the accord over several years.

His actions did not only sink him in the esteem of and entail the dislike of nations. Trump had "committed an error for the interests of his country, his people and a mistake for the future of our planet," French Prime Minister Emmanuel Macron charged. "The time in which we could fully rely on others is a bit in the past," added German Chancellor Angela Merkel.

Trump's withdrawal from the global "temple" epitomized an "America First" agenda that sought to do more than simply roll back regulations and laws on environmental protection. "Our withdrawal from the agreement represents a reassertion of America's sovereignty," Trump proclaimed. "One by one, we are keeping the promises I made to the American people during my campaign for President," he added. "And believe me, we've just begun."

Gutting civil rights enforcements, including workplace protections for LGBTQ citizens and transgender Americans in the military, ramping up anti-immigrant hysteria against Muslims, and sweeps and deportations of undocumented residents, marginalizing journalists and the media, and seizing data and social media records of government critics, the Trump administration had ushered in one of the most authoritarian regimes in American history.

Notably, the language of Trump's America First narrative—with his emphasis on always being first, the best, the biggest, regardless of the facts—reflected Paine's warning of "brutish" leadership, which now took form in a new world of social media. Trump commanded the whiplash barrages of 140–280 characters on Twitter, casting aspersions, insults, threats, and misleading statements at all hours of the day and night, as if issued from a throne to a hall of sycophantic minions.

Paine's analysis of imperial conceit also foretold such a display of reckless power; in 1776, he chastised "the Royal Brute of Great Britain" for making "havoc of mankind" with his impertinent decisions, and warned he would pay a price.

In the shadow of America's formation at the Paris treaty, Paine's flagging of arrogance and despotism took on a new meaning in the twenty-first century.

So did a historical framework of American resistance, dating back to the American Revolution and its antecedents, that issued more warnings than rules; it alerted the pretenders to the throne that while authoritarian spasms of power might attempt to bury the freedom of a people, the seeds of resistance in a nation would continue to flourish.

This framework set the American Revolution in motion, like any resistance movement, as a continuous questioning of democratic relevancy, a circular road of defense for certain inalienable rights—not a one-time act of demarcation. The Declaration of Independence announced on July 4, 1776, that the American resistance was not a one-day affair, but the beginning of a messy, divisive, and unresolvable process that would seed democracy—not establish it—and generate centuries of unintended consequences.

This culture of resistance served a writ of rebellion to some of the first policies of President George Washington in the 1790s. It has confronted every presidential administration since, including Trump's predecessor, President Barack Obama, with the rise of numerous resistance movements like Black Lives Matter, the historic gathering of indigenous nations on the Standing Rock Sioux reservation against the Dakota Access Pipeline, and the sanctuary city movement for undocumented residents.

The rise of Trump, who lost the popular vote by more than 2.8 million votes, added an extra gear to its drive.

In one of his first tweets as the president of the United States, Trump mocked the estimated four million Americans in the Women's March on January 21, 2017, which overflowed the streets from Washington, DC, to Des Moines, Iowa, to Los Angeles, California. "Watched protests yesterday but was under the impression that we just had an election!" Trump wrote on Twitter. "Why didn't these people vote?"

They did. Nevertheless, they resisted. Thousands carried signs: "A Woman's Place Is in the Resistance." Or rather, in the front of the resistance. One year later, a record number of women had launched campaigns for local, state, and federal offices.

"Thy ev'ry action let the goddess guide," African American poet Phillis Wheatley had written prophetically to Washington in 1775, on the emergence of an armed resistance to British rule. The nation's commander in chief responded to the recently liberated Wheatley, who had been enslaved since childhood, as "your obedient humble servant."

Mary Katharine Goddard, the courageous Baltimore printer, like most women of her time, did not receive the same historical acclaim for her role as a humble servant, as well. Goddard defiantly published the "authenticated" copy of the Declaration of Independence as an act of treason on a similarly cold January day in 1777. *When a long train of abuses and usurpations, pursuing invariably the same Object evinces a design to reduce them under absolute Despotism, it is their right, it is their duty, to throw off such Government.*

Goddard's name rested below John Hancock's famous signature as the bedrock of colonial American resistance. A fearless woman did not just give a name to the resistance; she provided its return address.

RESISTANCE HAS BEEN ENTRENCHED IN the American experience since the first imprint on soil was shaped by an invading force or corporation that claimed the right to name it.

In Jamestown, Virginia, the first permanent settlement founded by English merchants, Polish artisans rebelled in 1619 against their exclusion from voting in the first legislative assembly in the American colonies. The "Polonian" immigrants, who had been recruited for their glass-blowing and craft skills, carried out the first labor strike in the colonies. In resistance against the Virginia Company, the stock-owned corporation chartered in London, which had granted voting rights to the House of Burgess for all white, landowning English males, the Poles brought the daily operations to a standstill. Within days, the Poles won enfranchisement, and were "made as free as any inhabitant."

Angelo and "twenty and odd Negroes" did not share such freedom in 1619, as the first enslaved Africans to be purchased by the Jamestown residents. Acts of running away, among other forms of resistance, became so frequent that the Virginia colonial government issued edicts that admitted a subversive number of planters and enslaved workers had "given them assistance and directions how to escape." Revolts in Virginia eventually followed.

Within three years, Powhatan leader Opechancanough's unexpected attacks on the *tassantassas*, or "strangers," at Jamestown in 1622 effectively ended the corporate control of Virginia, and ushered in a new regime appointed by King James I. The indigenous uprising devastated the colony, but it also brought equally ruinous consequences for the Powhatan, whose armed resistance to English encroachment would define a century of conflict along the eastern colonies.

What remained of Native America resisted. And always has.

These roots of resistance, before and after the American Revolution, would deepen in commitment and sharpen in experience, unsparing in their reach, even among the emerging country's own leaders. Prior to serving as president in 1789, General George Washington cringed at the storm of resistance so soon after the Independence movement. He was "mortified" that Europe would see Americans as "ridiculous and contemptible." Outraged by the policies of eastern Massachusetts aristocrats and their machinations on behalf of speculators, farmers and former Revolutionary soldiers in the western part of the state took up arms in 1786 to shut down courts over debt and confront a corrupt state government and, according to historian Leonard Richards, "its attempt to enrich the few at the expense of the many."

"Shay's Rebellion" in 1786, as those farmers and former Revolutionary soldiers were eventually named, testified to this inherent nature of resistance in democracy. Blasting an aristocracy of "overgrown plunderers," the Chief Justice of the Court of Common Pleas of Berkshire County, William Whiting, sided with the resisters in an extraordinary letter on the role of dissent in the emerging democracy: "Therefore whenever any incroachments are making either upon the liberties or properties of the people, if redress cannot be had without, it is Virtue in them to disturb the government." Charged with sedition himself, Whiting's stance served as a clarion call for "the People at large" and their "indispensable duty to watch and guard their Liberties, and to crush the very first appearances of incroachments upon it."

Why call it resistance—and not protest, dissent, radicalism?

Resistance, as a medical term, is the process of warding off harmful disorders, or disease, both intrinsic and extrinsic. The Resistance—with a capital—has traditionally achieved the same in our political and civic lives; as an organized social movement, small or large, it defies an aberrant force and its collaborators that have occupied the public commons and imperiled expressions of democracy.

The phenomenon of the Trump ascendancy and its apparatus is therefore unique, but it is not without precedent. Nor should it be considered normal but pathological—a demagogic abuse of power, a toxic intrusion on civic life, an aversion of justice, and a corruption of constitutional touchstones that threaten our very ways of life. The response of resistance to crises instigated by Trump draws from a deeply rooted American tradition. Consider these examples:

No issue vexed the architects of the Constitution more than the handing over of executive power to a single powerful person beholden to the interests of an aristocracy. Thomas Jefferson feared the monarchical intentions of fellow founding fathers, like Alexander Hamilton; John Adams pushed for an assembly of aristocrats to somehow limit an oligarchical power grab.

No one was more concerned about an aristocratic stranglehold on power than George Mason, the "forgotten founder," a slave-owning aristocrat from Virginia, who authored that state's influential Declaration of Rights passed in June of 1776.

It was Mason's prophetic writing that put the "happiness" into our nation's credo of "life, liberty and the pursuit of happiness."

As one of three visionary leaders who refused to sign the Constitution in 1787 in Philadelphia, drawing the wrath of the colonial elite, Mason denounced the Constitution's lack of a Declaration of Rights (or Bill of Rights), challenged a president's unrestrained power of granting pardons for treason, criticized the absence of any declaration to preserve the liberty of the press, and finally, called out the general legislature's inability to prohibit the further importation of slaves for twenty more years.

"This government will set out a moderate aristocracy," Mason charged in 1787. "It is at present impossible to foresee whether it will, in its operation, produce a monarchy, or a corrupt, tyrannical aristocracy; it will most probably vibrate some years between the two, and then terminate in the one or the other."

All these fears and clashes over such an abuse of power have been revived today. Representing "a historic level of wealth that's at least fifty times greater than the Cabinet that George W. Bush led," as CBS News reported, Trump's pursuit of economic policies, such as the $1.5 trillion tax cut bill he signed in the last days of December 2017, continues the dynasties of wealth that Mason predicted. "You all just got a lot richer," Trump told members of his Mar-a-Lago club on Christmas Eve in 2017, where he spent the holidays. Proclaimed by Trump as the "Winter White House," the club upped initiation fees to $200,000, with annual dues at $14,000. "If you're a billionaire with your own company and are happy to use your private jet so you can 'commute' from a low-tax state," Andrew Ross Sorkin wrote in the *New York Times*, "the plan is a godsend."

It all sounded vaguely reminiscent of the Gilded Age, a riff on Mark Twain's satirical novel of late nineteenth–century greed, corruption, monopolies, and the abuse of labor and immigrants which was followed by the great Panic of 1893, and a rising Progressive Era of muckrakers, agitators, and innovators like Ida B. Wells, Mother Jones, John Dewey, and Upton Sinclair.

In a nation where the "richest one tenth of one percent of Americans now owns almost as much wealth as the bottom 90 percent," as former Labor Secretary Robert Reich has noted, "six out of the ten wealthiest Americans alive today are heirs to prominent fortunes."

Trump's policies, in the view of the conservative *Chicago Tribune*, "carry water for America's growing aristocracy of the ultra-rich." "And I love all people, rich or poor, but in those particular positions," Trump once told a rally in Iowa, about shaping his cabinet, "I just don't want a poor person."

Resistance to such a monarchical stranglehold on power has been a crucible of the free press since the earliest days of our nation.

From 1798 to 1800, journalists fended off accusations of leaks and "fake news" similar to those that have appeared constantly on Trump's Twitter account, when President John Adams invoked the powers of the Sedition Act. Concocted under the guise of wartime threats from France, the controversial act allowed the thin-skinned President— mockingly referred to as "his Rotundity"—to prosecute any journalists or other Americans who "write, print, utter or publish, or cause it to be done, or assist in it, any false, scandalous, and malicious writing against the government of the United States, or either House of Congress, or the President."

In his campaign for presidency, Trump floated a similar type of law—though one which suited his money-making ethos: Trump claimed he would "open up our libel laws so when [newspapers] write purposely negative stories ... we can sue them and make lots of money."

"The real scandal here is that classified information is illegally given out by 'intelligence' like candy," Trump tweeted on February 15, 2017, blasting the media for publishing assertions of his administration's collusion with Russian meddling in the 2016 election. "Very un-American!"

This was an old story: William Duane, editor and publisher of the *Philadelphia Aurora*, had already published accounts about electoral collusions of former enemies of the Americans in 1798—then with the British, not the Russians of today, who had allegedly spent over $800,000 to influence the mid-term elections and buy off Adams's support. The *Aurora* had also chastised Adams for appointing family members and in-laws to government positions as personal secretaries and diplomats in Berlin.

Another Duane exclusive went viral, bringing down the wrath of the Adams government. The newspaper revealed a plot by Federalist members of Congress to secretly change the electoral vote rules, potentially altering the outcome for the next election. Hounded by Adams under the Sedition Act, Duane went into hiding and joined other courageous journalists who had defiantly resisted the authoritarian law.

The first and most consequential defense of the Constitution and Bill of Rights, according to Thomas Jefferson, did not come from its venerable architects in Congress, but the indefatigable efforts of imprisoned journalists who "arrested the rapid march of our government toward monarchy."

Adams did not only wield the power to cast accusations of treason; he also gained the power to deport any non-citizen he deemed dangerous, thanks to the Alien Act of 1798. Its ominous repercussions haunt Trump's immigrant policies today.

The borders between immigration policies at the beginning of our nation and now in the twenty-first century also follow a troubling reality. First Lady Eleanor Roosevelt's visit to a Japanese American internment camp in Arizona in 1943 forewarned Trump's select crackdown on immigration in 2017. "To undo a mistake is always harder than not to create one originally," she warned, "but we seldom have the foresight."

With the announcement of one of Trump's first executive orders in the White House, "Protecting the Nation from Foreign Terrorist Entry into the United States"—the "Muslim travel ban" in the campaign words of the President—today's resistance possessed such historical foresight. While the American Civil Liberties Union (ACLU) and other legal advisors set up in the terminals to assist affected families, protests erupted at airports across the nation. Standing behind a backdrop of signs, "We are all immigrants" and "No ban, no wall," U.S. Rep. Nydia Velazquez spoke out at the John F. Kennedy Airport in New York City in the first days of the presidency in 2017. "Mr. President, look at us. This is America. What you have done is shameful. It's un-American."

No one would have understood this better than Fred Korematsu, an American citizen who resisted orders in 1942 to report to an internment camp with other Japanese and Japanese Americans. While his conviction would lead to a landmark Supreme Court ruling upholding his imprisonment, Korematsu waged a decades-long battle for vindication, finally resulting in the U.S. Circuit Court vacating his conviction in 1983. A federal commission that same year concluded: "The broad historical causes which shaped these decisions were race prejudice, war hysteria and a failure of political leadership."

Trump's first three attempts at a travel ban were struck down in the federal courts; the U.S. Supreme Court partially restored a ban whose racial and religious connotations recalled anti-immigrant policies dating back to the Alien Act of 1798, the Chinese Exclusion Act of 1882, World War I, and the subsequent internment of Japanese Americans during World War II. The children of undocumented immigrants, born on foreign soil and brought to the United States as toddlers, understood this history better than anyone who could trace their genealogy back to the woodpile of the Pilgrims.

"You met with Trump and you call that resistance?" young Dream Act activists chanted in the fall of 2017, crashing a press conference held by House Minority Leader Nancy Pelosi in San Francisco. "This is what the resistance looks like."

Outraged that Pelosi and fellow Democrat leader Sen. Charles Schumer had met with Trump over his decision to rescind the Deferred

Action for Childhood Arrivals (DACA) program, which had granted legal status for children of undocumented immigrants, these resistance leaders charged the Democrats with using them as "bargaining chips" in negotiations with Trump over his plan to build a wall on the U.S.-Mexico border and deport or pursue punitive measures against the roughly 11 million undocumented immigrants in the United States.

The resistance for immigrant rights dated back to one of the key indictments in the Declaration of Independence; King George III was accused of "obstructing the Laws for Naturalization of Foreigners; refusing to pass others [laws] to encourage their migrations hither."

"Immigrant youth has been at the forefront protesting, heckling, and carrying out direct actions against Obama and the Democratic Party, regardless of the unpopularity of such tactics," Sandy Valenciano wrote in an op-ed following Pelosi's press conference. "DACA was achieved through fearless organizing and resistance by undocumented people."

This race-baiting policy by Trump overlapped domestic policies affecting African Americans. At a campaign rally for a Republican candidate in Alabama in September 2017, Trump chastised protesters against police brutality and racism, singling out African American NFL football player Colin Kaepernick, who had knelt during the national anthem. "Get that son of a bitch off the field right now," Trump said, in a Southern state that had been ground zero for nonviolent civil disobedience campaigns in the civil rights movement in the 1950s and 1960s. "If a player wants the privilege of making millions of dollars in the NFL or other leagues," Trump followed up on Twitter, "he or she should not be allowed to disrespect our Great American Flag (or Country) and should stand for the National Anthem. If not, YOU'RE FIRED. Find something else to do!"

Three months later, Alabama defied Trump and upended electoral politics when it elected Democrat Doug Jones to the U.S. Senate in a special election to replace Trump's Attorney General Jeff Sessions. Jones served as a U.S. Attorney who had successfully prosecuted former members of the Ku Klux Klan for their involvement in the bombing of a Birmingham church that took the lives of four African American girls in 1963.

To Trump's obsessive tweets over the Sunday football protests,

Rev. William Barber, who had led the "Moral Mondays" movement against the regressive policies of the North Carolina legislature, would tweet back from the pulpit: "NFL players who #TakeAKnee are sons of Justice, taking their place in the river of resistance that has brought us thus far on our way."

"Rooted in the experiences of Black people in this country who actively resist our dehumanization," Black Lives Matter had already taken a leading role in the resistance since the movement's founding in 2013, after the acquittal of George Zimmerman for the murder of seventeen-year-old Trayvon Martin in Florida.

"Protest is patriotic," singer John Legend responded to the President. "If we quell protest in the name of patriotism, we are not patriots. We are tyrants." Legend linked the National Football League protests to the Boston Tea Party, the suffragists, and anti-war movements. "They are a demand that we Americans make this country's reality match its proud symbolism. They are an attempt to educate the public that criminal justice—mass incarceration, lengthy sentences, police brutality—is the civil rights issue of our time."

This very civil rights issue of our time came to a head in Charlottesville, Virginia, in the summer of 2017, when self-proclaimed Nazis, Klansmen, and tiki-torch-bearing "alt-right" white supremacists led a violent march to a statue of Confederate general Robert E. Lee.

"Black Lives Matter is not a trend," co-founder Alicia Garza told an audience, in the aftermath of Charlottesville's reckoning. "Our movement has led the resistance to white supremacy and white supremacists. We made sure that we didn't just talk about statues, but we pointed out that there are living monuments to the Confederacy in the White House and in our Congress."

"REPROACH AND CENSURE IN THE strongest possible terms are necessary," began the letter from the entire board of the President's Committee on the Arts and Humanities, referencing the murder of a young American woman by a white supremacist who plowed his car into the Charlottesville crowd. Addressed to President Trump, the letter chas-

tised the "administration's refusal to quickly and unequivocally condemn the cancer of hatred."

*Elevating any group that threatens and discriminates based on race was
un-American.*

Speaking truth to power was never easy.

Ignoring your hated rhetoric would have made us complicit.

Supremacy, discrimination and vitriol are not American values.

The Committee's letter of resignation called on the President to do
the same: Resign.

And in a hidden message to the rest of the nation, the first letter of
each sentence displayed an artist's touch. R-E-S-I-S-T.

"WE MUST NOT DELUDE OURSELVES with an idea that the past is recov-
erable," historian Bernard DeVoto wisely warned other writers. "We are
chained and pinioned in our moment ... What we recover from the past
is an image of ourselves, and very likely our search sets out to find nothing other than just that."

History does not provide a blueprint for our own times. But it does
belie our arrogance in thinking we are the first generation to face certain
challenges. "History, as nearly no one seems to know, is not merely something to be read," James Baldwin wrote in his essay "Unnameable Objects, Unspeakable Crimes." "The great force of history comes from the
fact that we carry it within us, are unconsciously controlled by it in many
ways, and history is literally present in all that we do. It could scarcely be
otherwise, since it is to history that we owe our frames of reference, our
identities, and our aspirations."

Resistance, within this framework, shines a light on five areas on
that quintessential stage of history, which have transcended the narrow
definition of civil unrest that many in power fear.

First, resistance is always seen differently in the eyes of those who
hold power. The gray areas between resistance and nonviolent civil disobedience, and then violent civil unrest, are even blurrier in our historical interpretations. Watershed moments in history tend to define such
acts of civil disobedience in our resistance credo; according to historian

Alfred Young, the fabled Boston Tea Party of 1773, which only benefited a handful of merchants, was not framed in positive terms until the 1830s, given its association with property damage and an unlawful mob. Benjamin Franklin, one of the true godfathers of the American Revolution, called on the rebellious Bostonians to pay for the destroyed tea.

Perhaps a better comparison could be found in our own times. Instead of a handful of Bostonians dressed up as "Mohawks," a historic alliance of First Nations and indigenous peoples gathered at Standing Rock on the Sioux Nation throughout 2016, engaged in a historic civil disobedience campaign that challenged the Dakota Access Pipeline for the same transgressions of outside market forces as the Bostonians in 1773. Water played a role, too; "water protectors" challenged a violation-ridden pipeline that could carry half a million barrels of crude oil and burst at any time, contaminating the Missouri River and drinking-water supply.

Second, resistance defies claims of a single American way; and reminds us that there are many American ways, often conflicting and sometimes deceiving. This is particularly true of resistance movements themselves; splintered by nature, the small and vital acts of resistance, often those of a single person, have their own sources of inspiration. They follow a different timeline in everyone's life. At their best, resistance movements flow like many rivers into an ocean or historic watershed event.

Today's "Resistance," like all resistance movements, has its own issues over nuance. Some view it strictly in terms of electoral politics; others stand arm-in-arm at the intersection of civil rights and justice; a new era of resisters, newcomers to politics and activism, see it specifically as a repudiation of the crass Trump branding of the American way, a calling-out of complicity of men who shamelessly "grab them by the pussy," a rejection of Washington as the revolving door of Wall Street financial brokers.

Within days of Trump's ascendancy to the White House, business periodicals headlined "Google, Starbucks, and Lyft" as the "new voice of the resistance." Teenage reality TV personality Kylie Jenner triggered a hornet's nest of social media mockery when she cast off her fashion model attire in a Pepsi commercial, took to the streets in a generic rebel-without-a-cause march framed as a Black Lives Matter protest, and then handed a Pepsi to a cop at the barricades in a breathless moment of history. The Resistance wasn't drinking it. Pepsi yanked the ad within hours.

By the end of the spring, defeated presidential candidate Hillary Clinton took the public stage and announced that she, too, had joined "the Resistance."

If we take Paine's broader vision of a "more equal" democracy—including the forces of resistance that Presidents George Washington and John Adams abhorred and never trusted—we can begin to construct a fuller picture of history, especially for those left out in its official rendition. The cycles of resistance plow the soil of history, exposing the strata of stories below the surface. It also digs up a lot of bones.

As a response to erasure and historicide—the intentional destruction or oversight of history—a republic of resistance has served as a de facto "truth and reconciliation" commission for multiple viewpoints of history, especially in times when our nation—and its leaders—need to be held accountable for the unfulfilled aspirations of the American Revolution for all Americans.

Case in point: Local newspapers in South Carolina refused to even acknowledge the Stono Rebellion in 1739—the largest revolt of enslaved African people in the colonies—until months after plantation owners had quelled other dissent. Then, only hushed accountings emerged of the scores of enslaved rebels, marching along the Stono River, hoisting banners with slogans of liberty and laying waste to plantations and their owners, as if such conjuring of history would manifest itself again in rebellion. According to historian Jack Shuler, "the narrative that Stono represents has always been in the hearts and minds of many Americans," and it created a ripple effect throughout the South. "For a moment, the Stono rebels sliced open—literally and figuratively—the public sphere in South Carolina, speaking directly to the philosophical concerns of many Enlightenment figures: What does it mean to be human? What does it mean to be free? The rebels responded to both these questions."

Third, resistance is a tradition of building blocks; a continuum of action that may not have dislodged injustice in its own time, but whose

revolutionary founders left behind the framework and tools for a subsequent generation to take up, and ultimately carry out its vision. We can
stand back and admire certain laws and protections now—child labor
laws, voter enfranchisement for all, an eight-hour work day, clean water,
for example—and appreciate the irreversible process of resistance that
not only guaranteed their formation, but fought off the innumerable attacks that once kept them from rising.

Fourth, resistance, as it has unfolded over the centuries, has claimed
a "public commons" for "we the people" to have a voice in shaping the defining issues in our most trying times—beyond the thirty-nine wealthy
white men who signed our Constitution. This means beyond elections.

Delivering the Fourth of July address to fellow mechanics and crafts-
men in New York City in 1797, George James Warner invoked the "bold
resistance" of the American Revolution to remind his audience that voting was not enough. "Wherever the wealthy by the influences of riches,
are enabled to direct the choice of public officers, there the downfall of
liberty cannot be very remote." It took more than elections to ensure
life, liberty, and the pursuit of happiness for all and to defend the right of
free speech and freedom of the press as inalienable. The fragile border-
line between an aristocratic form of government and a representative democracy still required resistance in what historian Robert Martin calls
"counterpublic spaces."

Finally, writing in *Common Sense*, Paine seeded the American Revolution with a fundamental belief in resistance as an agency of renewal:
"We have it in our power to begin the world over again." It was perhaps
his most revolutionary act; to reenvision so-called "norms" or business-
as-usual processes that resulted in a kind of inexorable paralysis of action
for a better way. "A long habit of not thinking a thing wrong, gives it a
superficial appearance of being right, and raises at first a formidable outcry in defense of custom," he wrote in his famous debunking of the divine rights of the monarchy. "But the tumult soon subsides. Time makes
more converts than reason."

The early American seeds for climate resistance movements, for example, drawing on the pioneering environmental campaigns of scientist
Barry Commoner, among others, are now taking root with decentralized

plans for renewable energy, regenerative agriculture, and new urban designs for cities of resistance in an age of climate change.

It just may take more time than we can ever imagine. "Ojibwe legends speak of a time when our people will have a choice between two paths," internationally renowned author and White Earth activist Winona LaDuke once wrote. "One path is well worn and scorched, but the second path is not well traveled and it is green."

The task of today's resistance will be to build on our histories to make the second path.

"THE REVOLT AGAINST BRUTALITY BEGINS with a revolt against the language that hides that brutality," author Rebecca Solnit had warned in an essay, "Call climate change what it is: violence."

As the author of several landmark books, including *Hope in the Dark: Untold Histories*, *Wild Possibilities*, and *Men Explain Things to Me*, Solnit had become indispensable, through her treasury of work and daily presence on social media, in elucidating the complexities of the various resistance movements, and their unique strands in history. "Change is often unpredictable and indirect," she told the *New York Times* in the summer of 2017. "We don't know the future. We've changed the world many times, and remembering that, that history, is really a source of power to continue and it doesn't get talked about nearly enough."

It was time to call our response what it should be: the resistance, against the fundamental policies driving climate change, environmental injustice, and the denial of basic civil rights.

Within days of Trump's climate announcement, California and New York, along with a dozen other states, announced the formation of the United States Climate Alliance to uphold the American benchmarks of the global agreement; mayors across the nation affirmed their commitment to the Paris accord.

Doomsday scenarios about the climate abounded in the aftermath of Trump's announcement. Released one day before world leaders celebrated the historic Paris accord, the annual UN Environmental Program "Emission's Gap" report had concluded that the warming limit of 1.5 degrees Celsius—the death knell for the "vulnerable nations" already threatened by rising tides—would likely remain out of reach. "If we don't [act]," the report forewarned in the winter of 2015, "we will mourn the loss of biodiversity and natural resources. We will regret the economic fallout. Most of all, we will grieve over the avoidable human tragedy; the growing numbers of climate refugees hit by hunger, poverty, illness and conflict will be a constant reminder of our failure to deliver."

The White House declaration to withdraw from the Paris climate accord made it imperative for local and regional climate action movements to shift from being a trend to rising as leaders in a new era of cities of resistance.

"The spirit of resistance to government is so valuable on certain occasions, that I wish it to be always kept alive," Thomas Jefferson had written in the 1790s, during a period of civil unrest. "It will often be exercised when wrong, but better so than not to be exercised at all. I like a little rebellion now and then. It is like a storm in the atmosphere."

It was a storm in an age of climate change now—and a spirit of resistance launched long before Trump walked through the front doors of the White House. In the fall of 2014, a Massachusetts prosecutor dropped the charges of conspiracy and disturbing the peace against two activists who had blocked a cargo ship loaded with coal. "I had to give strong consideration to the cause that led to the act of civil disobedience," Bristol County District Attorney Sam Sutter announced at a press conference. "And I agree that climate change is one of the greatest crises the planet has ever faced and that we have to act more boldly now."

Climate hope, to paraphrase Jefferson in our own times, needed to be refreshed from time to time with climate resistance.

Not just climate resistance, of course—resistance on every front.

I

We the People, Resist

The Constitution itself. Its language is "we the people"; not we the white people. Not even we the citizens, not we the privileged class, not we the high, not we the low, but we the people. Not we the horses, sheep, and swine, and wheel-barrows, but we the people, we the human inhabitants. If Negroes are people, they are included in the benefits for which the Constitution of America was ordained and established. But how dare any man who pretends to be a friend to the Negro thus gratuitously concede away what the Negro has a right to claim under the Constitution?
—Frederick Douglass, "The Constitution of the United States: Is It Pro-Slavery or Anti-Slavery?" Glasgow, Scotland, March 26, 1860

A WEEK BEFORE THE INAUGURATION of President Donald J. Trump in 2017, "Writers Resist" literary readings took place across the country, from the New York City Public Library, across the Appalachians, prairies and plains to the Town Hall in Seattle, to resist, according to the *New York Times*, "the dark power of words" of an incoming president who echoed "the appeals of some demagogues of the past century."

"These are the times that try women's souls," read Mariam Keita, a fifteen-year-old Gambian-American Muslim student and poet in Iowa City, who had agreed to join me on the Englert Theatre stage. One of the leaders of local high school protests against Trump that would soon be featured on the front page of the *New York Times*, Mariam made Thomas Paine's words come alive for a new generation, especially as a reminder of the role of women in the forefront of resistance.

Paine declared the "universal empire is the prerogative of the writer." He added for good measure: "The Republic of Letters is more ancient than monarchy."

"In establishing American independence," concurred David Ramsey, a South Carolina physician and early American historian, in 1789, "the pen and the press had merit equal to that of the sword."

Shortly after Trump's election, former Wall Street executive Amy Siskind started an online "Weekly List" to track the changes in government norms and categorize the avalanche of Trump's statements, policies, and machinations in the media. "Experts in authoritarianism advise to keep a list of things subtly changing around you, so you'll remember," posted Siskind, an LGBTQ advocate and founder of the New Agenda rights group. Within weeks, her list on Medium had gone viral, gaining millions of readers.

Paine, among others, chronicled the daily tribulations like an omniscient narrator, and also envisioned the United States before it came into existence; they wrote unabashed accounts of history in the making, at once aspirational, confessional, and grand. They embraced their roles as resistance writers and storytellers, poets and journalists, pamphleteers and letter writers; they went beyond agitation or muckrakes or declarations to tell deeper stories of what contemporary writer Grace Paley called the "still small possibility for justice."

In response, their success in both reaching a wide audience and shaping an emerging American narrative created a space for even more writers to read their words to the public commons. Call it the poetry slam at the birth of a nation—outside the halls of power, resounding in the town squares and dockyards, proclaimed in the shade of backwoods and farms, posted on liberty trees. With or without the permission of the brokers of literary authority, every story of these writers of the resistance essentially probed and proffered their visions of one fundamental question about our nation: Just who is "we the people"?

We the people—the first words of the stirring preamble of the American Constitution remain one of the most hallowed lines ever written and certainly one of our country's most illusory and unresolved avowals.

On January 21, 2010, the U.S. Supreme Court added additional in-laws to the "people" in its decision *Citizens United v. Federal Election Commission*: corporate personhood. Granting corporations the same First Amendment protections for political campaign expenditures, the decision gave "we the people" a new meaning.

In dissent, Supreme Court Justice John Paul Stevens spoke for another kind of resistance: "... corporations have no consciences, no beliefs, no feelings, no thoughts, no desires. Corporations help structure and facilitate the activities of human beings, to be sure, and their 'personhood' often serves as a useful legal fiction. But they are not themselves members of 'We the People' by whom and for whom our Constitution was established."

As we will see, the storyline of resistance has transfigured this fault line of identity over two centuries. It has expanded its meanings of presence and absence, reminding us who has been left in and out of this American story, who has provided its bedrock and blood, and who has been vanquished by its glory. Instead of being tablets of commandments in stone, this new American narrative has unfolded like a book opened at both ends, in a constant state of revisions over centuries; edited, grafted, rewritten, deleted, and recovered for its very contradictions and the paradox of a nation, real or imagined, still unfolding.

The story of resistance has never had the same ending—or beginning.

In the days following the Women's March and Trump inauguration, an op-ed in the *New York Post* mocked such a storyline for our modern times. "The 'resistance' decided to pretend the loss of an election amounts to oppression and have adopted the language of revolution to rally themselves," the op-ed argued. "That incendiary language didn't just get adopted by a few on the fringe, but by many on the left, including some in the news and entertainment media."

As the "most incendiary and popular pamphlet of the entire revolutionary era," according to historian Gordon Wood, Paine's *Common Sense* riled his adversaries in a similar fashion. It, too, received a mocking reception from the loyalist side of the throne. Dismissing the impact of *Common Sense*'s exploding readership, writing under the pseudonym Cato, the Provost of the College of Philadelphia huffed that "little notice" had been taken of Paine's screed, despite the "vanity of the author." He concluded that nine-tenths of the people of Pennsylvania "yet abhor the doctrine" of Independence.

The cowering former governor of Massachusetts, Thomas Hutchinson, shared the *Post*'s judgment of fulsome claims to revolution in a letter to the English Crown in 1776: "Gratitude, I am sensible, is seldom to be found in a community, but so sudden a revolt from the rest of the Empire . . . is an instance of ingratitude no where to be paralleled."

The American colonists, as Trump would refer to Americans in Puerto Rico in the aftermath of the devastating Hurricane Maria in the fall of 2017, were "ingrates."

Hutchinson accused the resistance writers of being pathetic fishermen of "subjects for controversy in opposition to Government," with the sole intent "to irritate and inflame the minds of the people, and dispose them to revolt." Poor losers, as Trump would write on Twitter. Sad.

To be fair, even after the British attack on American militia members at Lexington and Concord, Massachusetts, on a spring day in 1775, the vast majority of inhabitants in the colonies still had misgivings about resistance as a conduit to independence. Some refused to risk their property and fortunes to the uncertain fate of rebellion; others thought armed resistance was hopeless against the Crown's overwhelming armies. Loyalty to the divine rights of the English empire did not shake off easily. Long-distance proclamations by committees were easy; the dirty work of resistance, at this point, had been in the hands of indigenous people, enslaved African Americans, breakaway communities in the frontier woods of North Carolina and southwest Virginia, or the "motley crews" who had brawled with British troops at Golden Hill in New York City and on King Street in Boston. John Adams had called them a "motley rabble of saucy boys, negroes and molattoes, Irish teagues, and outlandish Jack Tarrs."

The "shot heard around the world" at Lexington and Concord may have announced the opening salvo of the American Revolution, but it failed to muster more than excited but fleeting support for George Washington's fledgling army. It divided the wished-for country into factions. A "desultory civil war," as an early American biographer wrote, would soon desolate the thirteen colonies. What is considered a deep-seated creed today—*We the people*—was considered a fanatical concept at its inception.

In an attempt to forge an American unity, Thomas Paine upended this national malaise with his writings—first *Common Sense*, then a series of "Crisis" pamphlets. Transformed by the British assault in Massachusetts, he sought to transform a new nation. The incident at Lexington and Concord forced him to "reject the hardened, sullen tempered Pharaoh of England for ever; and disdain the wretch." In a line: "The cause of America made me an author."

Urged by fellow Patriots in Philadelphia to draw up a response to the times, mindful of its treasonous risks, Paine began to write *Common Sense* with the fervency of a true believer. "I offer nothing more than simple facts, plain arguments, and common sense," he declared in the first lines of his unsigned pamphlet, which rolled from the printer's shop on January 10, 1776.

That seemingly harmless sentence, of course, was loaded with meaning. Two centuries before German author Bertolt Brecht urged his hungry commoners to "reach for the book: it is a weapon," Paine would dramatically reshape the media of his times as the main weapon of the resistance. As the editor of the *Pennsylvania Magazine*, Paine was no stranger to the printing press. Yet, far from churning out an impartial news rag in uncertain times, he had quickly established a new audience and infused its issues with poetry, song, essays, and tales that claimed the printing press as the open mike of the public commons. His poem "Liberty Tree" became a popular song; following the Lexington and Concord conflict, he published a subversive allegory, "Observations of the Military Characteristics of Ants," where brutal red ants deny the "natural rights" of brown ants, who must now defend themselves.

The immediacy of social media notwithstanding, Paine's words, like those of other resistance leaders, were not limited to the page, but passed along and shared; he relinquished any private rights or royalties, offering his words as part of the "cause." As if written to be read aloud to the great unread at taverns, cafes, squares, barns, cabins, and the camps of soldiers, over 100,000 copies of *Common Sense* circulated around the colonies, making it the first bestselling publication in early American history. It remains one of the most-read American texts of all time.

Paine forged a new political language, according to historian Eric Foner. Rooting his words in common experience, with clear and straightforward prose, "he did not simply change the meaning of words, he created a literary style designed to bring his message to the widest possible audience."

Paine's writing also broke the stranglehold of a self-appointed colonial elite over the official declarations of the day. As a landless commoner, his audacious writing was an act of resistance even among his own allies: uncompromising as a modern blog, with the edgy wit and precision of a Twitter thread. John Adams feared it was a "disastrous meteor" that could be too "democratical."

Writing in *Wired* magazine in 1995, Jon Katz declared this innovative deployment of feisty, unrelenting, and self-published media, freed of any corporate restraint, made Paine the "moral father of the Internet." In effect, Paine had electrified an American network of resistance with his anonymous and pithy offerings.

One of the first acts of resistance against the Trump administration, in fact, shared Paine's communication strategy through the media of the day, Twitter. Within hours of the 2017 inauguration in January, Trump officials shut down the National Park Service Twitter account after it had posted embarrassing side-by-side aerial photos of President Obama's much larger inaugural crowd in 2009. When White House officials required government employees at the Environmental Protection Agency, among other departments, to remove climate change research, bilingual websites, and various online pages available to the public, dozens of rogue twitter accounts appeared in defiance of the orders. They immediately gained hundreds of thousands of followers. Online was the new underground. Some Twitter accounts included:

@altUSEPA, The "Unofficial Resistance" team of U.S. Environmental Protection Agency;

@ResistanceNASA, We are a #Resist sect of the National Aeronautics and Space Administration.

@AltStateDpt, The News & opinion on the State of the #Resistance.

Censorship was not Paine's only preoccupation; he faced potential charges of treason, a boots-on-the-ground advance of British troops, and frustrating inaction of a Congress that had lulled the American public into a grievous stupor with their tepid official statements.

Consider the demoralizing counternarrative of Paine's day—the tortuous "Olive Branch" prose of the Continental Congress, issued in the months before the publication of *Common Sense*: "We, therefore, beseech your Majesty, that your royal authority and influence may be graciously interposed to procure us relief from our afflicting fears and jealousies," the declaration read, "that your Majesty be pleased to direct some mode, by which the united applications of your faithful colonists to the throne, in pursuance of their common councils, *may be improved into a happy and permanent reconciliation*" (emphasis added).

Reconciliation? A tavern renaissance man who loved science as much as literature, Paine responded with a line from Milton's *Paradise Lost*: "Never can true reconcilement grow where wounds of deadly hate have pierced so deep."

John Hancock's famous signature may have rested at the bottom of the Declaration of Independence, but it did so as well with numerous pleas to the British Crown for reconciliation.

On July 8, 1775, only days after charging the British with butchering our countrymen and "wantonly" burning down Charlestown, Hancock presided over the groveling language issued by a frightened Continental Congress:

Attached to your Majesty's person, family, and government, with all devotion that principle and affection can inspire, connected with Great Britain by the strongest ties that can unite societies, and deploring every event that tends in any degree to weaken them, we solemnly assure your Majesty, that we not only most ardently desire the former harmony between her and these colonies may be restored, but that a concord may be established between them upon so firm a basis as to perpetuate its blessings, uninterrupted by any future dissensions, to succeeding generations in both countries, and to transmit your Majesty's Name to posterity, adorned with that signal and lasting glory, that has attended the memory of those illustrious personages, whose virtues and abilities have extricated states from dangerous convulsions, and, by securing happiness to others, have erected the most noble and durable monuments to their own fame.

We beg leave further to assure your Majesty, that notwithstanding the sufferings of your loyal colonists, during the course of the present controversy, our breasts retain too tender a regard for the kingdom from which we derive our origin, to request such a reconciliation as might in any manner be inconsistent with her dignity or her welfare. These, related as we are to her, honor and duty, as well as inclination, induce us to support and advance; and the apprehensions that now oppress our hearts with unspeakable grief, being once removed, your Majesty will find your faithful subjects on this continent ready and willing at all times, as they ever have been, with their lives and fortunes, to assert and maintain the rights and interests of your Majesty, and of our Mother country.

It got worse. In the summer of 1775, the Second Continental Congress sent off a "Declaration of the Causes and Necessity of Taking Up Arms" and then immediately backstepped on the cause of Independence, as if regretting it had clicked the send button on an email. With Washington standing in an awkward situation with his loaded muskets, the Congress begged: "Lest this declaration should disquiet the minds of our friends and fellow-subjects in any part of the Empire, we assure them that we mean not to dissolve that union which has so long and so happily subsisted between us, and which we sincerely wish to see restored."

Within months, Paine's pamphlet skewered this kind of equivocation of the colonial elite and its exclusively wealthy white males in Congress. Their submissive pleas rang hollow in the face of attack on Americans in New England. "It is the good fortune of many to live distant from the scene of sorrow," he chided Congress. "The evil is not sufficiently brought to *their* doors to make *them* feel the precariousness with which all American property is possessed."

Holding the colonists accountable as much as any Tory, Paine effectively forced the fence-sitters to take a side. "If you still can shake hands with the murderers," he warned, "then you are unworthy of the name of husband, father, friend, or lover, and whatever may be your rank or title in life, you have the heart of a coward, and the spirit of a sycophant."

To the "men of passive tempers [who] look somewhat lightly over the offences of Britain, and, still hoping for the best, are apt to call out, 'Come, come, we shall be friends again, for all this,'" Paine delivered a long-awaited denouement with a definitive stroke: "Since nothing but blows will do, for God's sake let us come to a final separation."

The resistance found its voice. And Paine's personalized refrain against the "royal brute" of England and his colonial enablers inspired a chorus of indignation, and emboldened a daring movement for Independence.

For the two military commanders in the field, General George Washington and General Charles Lee, Paine single-handedly crossed the enemy lines and raised the flag of separation: "A masterly, irresistible performance," Lee gushed, "the coup-de-grâce to Great Britain." Washington called it an "unanswerable reasoning" for separation, "working a wonderful change in the minds of many men."

Frightfully conceited and thin-skinned, Paine did not suffer fools: "To argue with a man who has renounced the use and authority of reason, and whose philosophy consists in holding humanity in contempt, is like administering medicine to the dead, or endeavoring to convert an atheist by scripture." While Paine might have thrived on Twitter, he probably would have been blocked and unfriended by many on Facebook.

At the same time, Paine knew the limits of his words. He called it "folly to argue against determined hardness." With British troops, Hessian mercenaries, and Loyalist factions descending on his adopted Philadelphia, the Patriots in disarray, he knew "eloquence may strike the ear, and the language of sorrow draw forth the tear of compassion, but nothing can reach the heart that is steeled with prejudice."

Paine temporarily turned in his pen, grabbed a musket, and marched to the front lines in New Jersey. He served as an aide-de-camp to General Nathanael Greene, filing dispatches on the military maneuvers. He also donated all the proceeds from his writings to the cause—a generous gift, to be sure, that would never be repaid in kind.

At the age of thirty-seven, Thomas Paine carried more baggage than most travelers who had immigrated from England. Even before our nation came into being, he embodied the words of novelist Alfredo Véa: "America is best seen through the eyes of an immigrant." A trail of debts and bankruptcy nagged him, the legacy of dismissals from government appointments as a tax collector, a failed career as a stay-maker and shop-keeper, and two childless marriages that had unraveled. His first wife died tragically in labor with her first child; his second marriage dissolved into a loveless business arrangement that collapsed, as well. The couple separated, Paine sold off his possessions to avoid debtor's prison, and then he disappeared into London, haunting the taverns, attending lectures on science and philosophy, and plotting his departure to the New World. There was a genius about Paine, who had been esteemed by fellow excise men and welcomed into the political parlors, that could not find a door of opportunity in England.

Paine had arrived at the Philadelphia docks in 1774 on a stretcher in a virtual coma, having fallen ill from typhoid on the ship from England. A letter of introduction from Benjamin Franklin, who had briefly met him in London, ensured his safe passage to a house of recovery. Within a short period of settlement, Paine turned his own personal reinvention in the upheaval of the colonies into a reinvention of America's destiny, as well. After a floundering attempt to tutor children, he found work at a new magazine.

Paine, of course, did not emerge out of a vacuum of rebellion. His adopted home of Philadelphia struggled over its own power shift to an emerging radical faction. In the years following the Stamp Act of 1765, according to historian R. A. Ryerson, as various factions squabbled over tactics, a new resistance movement came of age in Philadelphia. Drawn from a broader assortment of mechanics and laborers, movement leaders felt that "neither the city's merchants as a body, nor any established elite, nor any branch of the provincial government would go far to defend them."

By the time the Boston Tea Party rebellion erupted over the Tea Act in 1773, this younger and bolder resistance movement in Philadelphia had organized enough support to force the tea agents to backstep on to their ships and set their humiliated sails for home. While the elder Benjamin Franklin and his supporters may have chastised the vandals in Boston, this new resistance movement celebrated it. Within months, defying moderate power brokers, Philadelphia's far more radical movement against reconciliation had grown dramatically in numbers, claiming a more representative range of Quakers, Presbyterians, Baptists, Lutherans, and Anglicans.

As a lapsed Quaker who had dabbled among the Methodists and soon-to-be-despised Deists, the well-versed Paine stylistically turned biblical rage into an American jeremiad and dissent into conviction. He invoked Bible passages to reach a growing evangelical audience.

In the four parts of *Common Sense*, Paine displayed the language of effrontery to the Crown with a biting edge. "He who dares not offend cannot be honest," he would respond to his American critics. While the colonial elite left the room, Paine willingly picked a fight.

"There is something exceedingly ridiculous in the composition of monarchy," he mockingly wrote, in a dramatic deconstruction of royal worship. Paine personified the resistance's figure of shame: the Royal "brute" of England. In his place, Paine the commoner countered that "in America the law is King."

Paine reduced Great Britain to a failed state, a dot on an imaginary atlas, and placed it aside the flourishing colonies in a geography lesson: "Small islands not capable of protecting themselves are the proper objects for kingdoms to take under their care; but there is something very absurd in supposing a continent to be perpetually governed by an island."

Nonetheless, that island and its forces dominated the American forces in the harsh December days in 1776, when Washington's ragtag army had been routed in New York City, and thousands of militiamen walked away from the front lines in New Jersey. Facing mutinies, one Revolutionary colonel pleaded with Washington to "give up the cause."

"I think the game will pretty well be up," Washington wrote in a letter, "as from disaffection and want of spirit and fortitude, the inhabitants, instead of resistance, are offering submission and taking protection from Howe [the British general] in Jersey."

The fickle majority of American colonists, once excited at the Declaration of Independence, had dwindled to a courageous minority in the resistance. The reasons for inaction were the same as in any resistance movement, today or in 1776: the concerns over daily bread, family safety, and a lack of grit or courage for the cause of freedom that presented too many risks. "I tremble for Philadelphia," Washington admitted.

Whether Washington made a personal appeal to Paine to put down his gun and pick up his plume, it was clear to military advisors that without a return of American volunteers and a reanimation of the Continental Army, the American Revolution would collapse. The annals of history, of course, from Hannibal's speech to his forces crossing the Alps, to General Dwight D. Eisenhower's exhortation before the Normandy Invasion during World War II, recount the speeches of military leaders galvanizing their forces before a historic victory. The famously hushed Washington relied on Paine to salvage the American Revolution.

In a "passion of patriotism," Paine would recall, having walked through enemy lines to reach his home in Philadelphia, the author of *Common Sense* embarked on a resistance campaign of literary warfare. On December 19, 1776, Paine published the first of sixteen *American Crisis* pamphlets that would revamp the spirits of the demoralized American army and convince a new wave of volunteer reinforcements to return to the battlefield. On December 23, Washington commanded his troops to gather as an official read Paine's *Crisis* aloud.

> These are the times that try men's souls. The summer soldier and the sunshine patriot will, in this crisis, shrink from the service of their country; but he that stands by it now, deserves the love and thanks of man and woman. Tyranny, like hell, is not easily conquered; yet we have this consolation with us, that the harder the conflict, the more glorious the triumph.

Two days later, the American forces crossed the icy Delaware River, crept through the snow-swept woods, and launched a surprise attack on the British and Hessian troops in Trenton, New Jersey, gaining a critical victory to stave off the British advance. The American Revolution got its groove back.

"Without the pen of the author of *Common Sense*," John Adams begrudgingly admitted, "the sword of Washington would have been raised in vain."

Rarely in history has the extraordinary power of writing galvanized such an armed resistance. Paine was a living icon in his own age, an eighteenth-century romantic figure as reviled and revered as Argentinian revolutionary Ernesto "Che" Guevara in the 1960s; Paine would go on to play a key role in the French Revolution. While he was tried in absentia for treason in Britain, his *Rights of Man* book on the natural rights of people over monarchy would become a global literary phenomenon and upend England's social order.

Intentional or not, the conviction of Paine's writing underscored the role of writers in the resistance. He was a truth teller, contentious and bold, and adamant about holding accountable the brokers of authorized versions of history, calling out their hypocrisy, omissions, and mistruths—and the betrayal of an American credo of "we the people."

Paine had not cornered the market on this literary tradition, of course. And his own select vision, especially in recognizing a more perfect vision of "we the people," would be challenged in the process.

WHEN SHE PRINTED THE DECLARATION of Independence in her Baltimore shop, Mary Katharine Goddard was no stranger to civil disobedience; writing in her family newspaper in the summer of 1775, she had already challenged the wavering Continental Congress of wealthy white men in the aftermath of the first military exchanges with the British at Lexington and Concord, Massachusetts: "The ever memorable 19th of April gave a conclusive answer to the questions of American freedom. What think ye of Congress now? That day . . . evidenced that Americans would rather die than live slaves!"

That Goddard ran ads for fugitive-slave catchers on the very same pages of her *Maryland Journal and Baltimore Advertiser* testified to the savage inequalities of the American resistance movement for Independence. The Declaration hailed the "merciless Indian Savages" as accomplices of the enemy. In removing an anti-slavery clause from an earlier draft, the Declaration censored freedom's call for one out of five Americans who were people of color and African descent. Nor did "All men are created equal" include Goddard and all women.

To be sure, Abigail Adams warned John Adams to not put unlimited power into the hands of husbands, all of whom "would be tyrants if they could." In vain, Abigail had appealed to Adams to remember "the ladies" in the Constitution. "If particular care and attention is not paid to the Ladies, we are determined to foment a rebellion and will not hold ourselves bound by any laws in which we have no voice, or Representation." It would take another three quarters of a century before women meeting at the Seneca Falls Convention in 1848 would rewrite our historical texts with a fuller account: "We hold these truths to be self-evident: that all men *and women* are created equal; that they are endowed by their Creator with certain inalienable rights." The grievances were real: "He has compelled her to submit to laws, in the formation of which she had no voice."

It would take even longer to recognize African Americans and all people of color. "Your celebration is a sham," abolitionist leader Frederick Douglass would proclaim seventy-five years later, at a Fourth of July celebration. "Your boasted liberty, an unholy license; your national greatness, swelling vanity; your sounds of rejoicing are empty and heartless; your denunciation of tyrants, brass fronted impudence; your shouts of liberty and equality, hollow mockery."

The original draft of the Declaration of Independence, as written by Jefferson, was unsparing in its indictments—for a broader version of "we the people," including those who were enslaved.

> . . . he has waged cruel war against human nature itself, violating its
> most sacred rights of life & liberty in the persons of a distant people
> who never offended him, captivating & carrying them into slavery in
> another hemisphere, or to incur miserable death in their transporta-

tion thither. This piratical warfare, the opprobrium of infidel powers, is the warfare of the CHRISTIAN king of Great Britain. Determined to keep open a market where MEN should be bought & sold ...

It did not take much convincing for the drafters to defer to the slave-owning delegates from South Carolina and Georgia, and capitulate to the bottom lines of revenue-over-human-rights in the accounting books of Northern merchants invested in the transatlantic slave trade. Jefferson did not simply remove the anti-slavery clause: he turned Africans and African Americans, like indigenous people, into the enemy of the people. The code words for slaves: domestic insurrection.

He [the King] has excited domestic insurrections amongst us, and has endeavoured to bring on the inhabitants of our frontiers, the merciless Indian Savages, whose known rule of warfare, is an undistinguished destruction of all ages, sexes and conditions.

Jefferson, like all the Southern delegates, had enslaved hundreds of Americans all of his life; he inherited fifty-two slaves at the age of twenty-one. The eloquent hypocrisy of Thomas Jefferson filled reams of letters and public statements on the inhumanity of human bondage, even as he oversaw a massive plantation of enslaved Americans in Virginia, including the young woman Sally Hemings who would give birth to his children under bondage. After his death, 130 enslaved workers were sold to pay his debts.

Ever the critic, former Massachusetts Gov. Thomas Hutchinson called out this hypocrisy of the colonists' Declaration: "How far life, liberty, and the *pursuit of happiness* may be said to be unalienable," he wrote in his letter to the King, "only I could wish to ask the Delegates of Maryland, Virginia, and the Carolinas, how their Constituents justify the depriving more than a hundred thousand Africans of their rights to liberty."

Unlike the immortalized "founding fathers," Paine never owned a slave and belonged to a defiant anti-slavery movement, but he too failed to envision African Americans—and Native Americans—as part of his resistance. Nonetheless, in 1775, he published a poem by the celebrated poet Phillis Wheatly, who had been enslaved until a feted literary tour to London shamed her master into an act of manumission.

Having been "snatched from Africa's fancy'd happy seat," Wheatley had reminded her British and American readers in 1772 that her "love of Freedom" sprung from their own aversion to "tyrannic sway." The celebrated poet, whose work appeared in the *Pennsylvania Magazine* in Philadelphia, had already written in more lyrical terms of subversion to the British Earl of Dartmouth. She questioned "the strange Absurdity of their Conduct whose Words and Actions are so diametrically opposite. How well the Cry for Liberty, and the reverse Disposition for the exercise of oppressive power over others agree,—I humbly think it does not require the Penetration of a Philosopher to determine."

"How is it that we hear the loudest yelps for liberty," added British author Samuel Johnson, "among the drivers of Negros?"

A decade before the Declaration of Independence, Boston agitator James Otis had written "The Rights of the British Colonies Asserted and Proved," famously declaring that taxation without representation is tyranny. Tea Party Patriots would invoke his sentiment for decades— even two centuries later. But other excerpts in his work typically go unread: "The colonists are by law of nature freeborn, as indeed all men are, white or black." In 1764, Otis had asked in another pamphlet: "Are not women born as free as men?"

Struck by lightning, Otis died in 1783, though he had struggled with bouts of mental illness exacerbated by a head wound from a British tax collector.

His anti-slavery challenge and call for women's rights remained unanswered; at the same time, his sister, Mercy Otis Warren, would become a prominent writer and continue to raise similar questions. The Patriots, in an irony that would seem unthinkably tone-deaf, embraced the metaphor of slavery as a defining element of their rapport with England. The "oppressive taxes" on the backs of the American colonists, Alexander Hamilton wrote in 1774, consumed the "fruits of his daily toil." He warned his fellow Patriots to "beware of slavery." Paine was even more unrestrained. "People! the natural rights of man can never be attacked but by tyrants," he declared. To accept a monarchy with passive obedience rendered the American "the easy slave of tyrants." Ignorance, Paine added, was slavery's sister.

Limping with gout, the elder neighbor of George Washington, George Mason, turned that sentiment on its head. An intransigent founding father, and one of the most overlooked architects, Mason ended up leading the constitutional resistance.

An aristocratic slave-owning plantation owner, Mason was a member of the House of Burgesses in Virginia. His powerful pen had drafted the Fairfax Resolves of 1774, expressing solidarity with Boston over tax representation. As early as 1765, in challenging the Stamp Act, Mason had referred to slavery as "one of the first Signs of the Decay, and perhaps the primary Cause of the Destruction of the most flourishing Government that ever existed." He admonished the emerging colonies to remember the divisive role of slavery in the Roman Empire. Mason suggested Virginia's state motto against tyranny: *Sic semper tyrannis.*

Unlike Paine, and even Washington and Jefferson, Mason abhorred public attention and did his best to work behind the scenes as a delegate to the Virginia Revolutionary conventions, and then as a member of the Continental Congress. In 1773, Mason called slavery a "slow Poison, which is daily contaminating the Minds and Morals of our People." Its proponents, he wrote paradoxically as a slave-owner himself, were "petty tyrants."

In drafting the Virginia Declaration of Rights, which would be ratified a couple of weeks before the Declaration of Independence in 1776, Mason played a profound role in influencing Jefferson's own vision of American rebellion—and who would play a part in it.

> That all men are born equally free and independent, and have certain inherent natural Rights, of which they cannot by any Compact, deprive or divest their Posterity; among which are the Enjoyment of Life and Liberty, with the Means of acquiring and possessing Property, and pursuing and obtaining Happiness and Safety.

"All men are born equally free and independent" still did not include enslaved ones, regardless of Mason's beliefs. "When our liberties were at stake," lamented Luther Martin, a delegate from Maryland, "we warmly felt for the common rights of men." With the triumph of the American Revolution and danger gone, Martin accused his colleagues of being "more insensible to those rights."

That changed a decade later, when a constitutional convention brought together delegates from the thirteen states to draw up a constitution. While Paine had agitated for a new constitution back in 1776 in *Common Sense*, the duty of drafting the preamble ironically fell on the shoulders of his mortal enemy, Gouverneur Morris, who came from a wealthy family in New York. Morris's legacy, though, was entwined in Paine's fate. Years later, after Paine barely escaped the guillotine and languished on his deathbed in a Paris prison, and as the French Revolution descended into the madness of the "reign of terror," Morris would gleefully turn his back on Paine when he served as the American envoy in Paris. Paine never quite recovered. Saddled with a wooden foot, Morris became one of our founding fathers.

As the "Penman of the Constitution," Morris's invoking of "we the people" did not come from any deep well of inspiration. His initial draft was prosaic, not poetic: "We the People of the States of New-Hampshire, Massachusetts, Rhode Island and Providence Plantations, Connecticut, New-York, New-Jersey, Pennsylvania, Delaware, Maryland, Virginia, North-Carolina, South-Carolina, and Georgia, do ordain, declare and establish the following Constitution for the Government of Ourselves and Posterity."

Morris truncated the sentence out of fear that one of the states might not attend the Convention. By default, the preamble's shortened version, "We the people of the United States," suddenly reclaimed the essence of the natural rights of men.

"What right had they to say, *We, the people?*" demanded Patrick Henry, the Virginia governor, whose fiery speech in 1775 had left its immortal mark: "Give me liberty, or give me death!" Outraged that fifty-five men at the Convention claimed to speak on behalf of the nation, Henry disparaged the consecrated line. "We, the states, perhaps," would have been more fitting.

Held in secrecy in September 1787, in Philadelphia, a fierce debate ensued at the Convention on slavery's recognition in the Constitution. Representing Maryland, Luther Martin maintained that slavery was "inconsistent with the principles of the revolution" and dishonored the American character. The Southern delegates, such as Charles Pinkney from South Carolina, rejected that claim; slavery had been part of the natural order of every society in the world, he claimed, from "Greece, Rome and other ancient states" to France, England, Holland, and modern states. In the end, despite his opposition to slavery, calling it a "curse," Morris and other Northerners agreed to the concessions demanded by South Carolina and Georgia, to keep them in a less perfect union.

Slavery would be allowed for the next two decades. Enslaved African Americans would be counted as three-fifths of the number of white inhabitants in states with slavery.

Mason walked out. Along with two other delegates, he refused to sign the Constitution. His "Objections" were printed two months later in the *Virginia Journal*; the list was long, beginning with the absence of a Bill of Rights, and ending with his frustration that the Constitution would allow slavery.

The following summer of 1788, as Virginians convened to vote on the ratification of the Constitution, Mason continued to speak out:

> The augmentation of slaves weakens the states; and such a trade is diabolical in itself, and disgraceful to mankind. Yet by this constitution it is continued for twenty years. As much as I value an [sic] union of all the states, I would not admit the southern states into the union, unless they agreed to the discontinuance of this disgraceful trade, because it would bring weakness and not strength to the union. And though this infamous traffic be continued, we have no security for the property of that kind which we have already. There is no clause in this constitution to secure it; for they may lay such a tax as will amount to manumission. And should the government be amended, still this detestable kind of commerce cannot be discontinued till after the expiration of twenty years. For the fifth article [of the Constitution], which provides for amendments, expressly excepts this clause. I have ever looked upon this as a most disgraceful thing to America. I cannot express my de-

testation of it. Yet they have not secured us the property of the slaves we have already. So that "they have done what they ought not to have done, and left undone what they ought to have done."

Mason was overruled. Virginians joined the rest of the nation—the "we the people" of white male landowners that represented less than a quarter of the nation's population.

A comparable lack of electoral representation remains today—though for entirely different reasons. In 1981, singer and poet Gil Scott-Heron shared a similar mood in his song "B-Movie," about the electoral victory of President Ronald Reagan: "Well, the first thing I want to say is: Mandate my ass! Because it seems as though we've been convinced that 26 percent of the registered voters, not even 26 percent of the American people, but 26 percent of the registered voters form a mandate or a landslide." The Trump victory in 2016 presented a comparable dynamic of imbalanced representation: In the popular vote, Hillary Clinton won 28.43 percent (65,845,063) of eligible voters to Trump's 27.20 percent (62,980,160).

We the people—44.37 percent or 102,731,399 eligible voters—did not vote.

Later in his life, a British abolitionist confronted Paine on his inaction in the abolitionist movement. "The cause would have suffered in my hands," he demurred, disingenuous at best, deceitful in truth. "I could not have treated it with any chance of success; for I could never think of their condition but with feelings of indignation."

The truth, for the truth teller, was elsewhere.

Addressing a mixed audience at the Franklin Hall in Boston in 1833, African American writer and abolitionist Maria Stewart called out this back side of white supremacy in the resistance: "Like King Solomon, who put neither nail nor hammer to the temple, yet received the praise; so also have the white Americans gained themselves a name, like the names of the great men that are in the earth, while in reality we have been their principal foundation and support. We have pursued the shadow, they have obtained the substance; we have performed the labor, they have received the profits; we have planted the vines, they have eaten the fruits of them."

"THE GREATEST IN THE UNITED States Constitution is its first three beautiful words," Trump said in his first address to the United Nations General Assembly in September 2017. "They are 'We the people.' Generations of Americans have sacrificed to maintain the promise of those words, the promise of our country and of our great history."

Trump claimed the United States had the oldest constitution in the world.

Writers of resistance, as the flip-side of authoritarian aberration and historical inaccuracy, have dispelled the mythology that frequently trots out this cavalcade of American exceptionalism—and its procession of seemingly infallible leaders.

In his work on Paine and the American Revolution, historian Harvey Kaye took a counter view, offering a progressive version of an exceptional America. In an essay on Wisconsin Public Radio, he reproached liberals and radicals for allowing conservatives exclusive rights to "the democratic idea of American exceptionalism ... that We the People can govern—that we don't need kings and aristocrats—that we can govern ourselves."

Paine's experience in the French Revolution may have been a nightmare, but it never shifted his perspective as a global citizen—not as a nationalist. "My country is the world," he wrote, "and my religion is to do good." The "cause of America" might have been "the cause of all mankind" for Paine, but it wasn't the only one. "Where liberty is, there is my country," Benjamin Franklin once told Paine, who replied, "Where liberty is not, there is mine."

Of course, the concept of revolution—or the Revolution—had blanketed the dreams of American colonists like an heirloom quilt for a century before Paine. For some, their English grandparents had lived through the Glorious Revolution of 1688 in England, the Declaration of Rights in 1689, and might have cheered the ascension of William III in the town square. Back in the colonies, though, the Americans understood that the dominion of monarchy remained like a locked gate into the kingdom. The Act of Toleration in 1689 loosened the restrictions for Protestant worshippers and dissidents; in 1692, the "liberty of conscience" law passed for all Christians—except Catholics—bringing an end to Puritan control, and aided the eventual rise of Quakers, Anglicans, and Baptists in the rest of the forming colonies.

My own ancestors, as founders of New Sweden along the Delaware River in the 1640s, took part in an uprising in 1653, when Swedish colonists signed a petition against the repressive policies of the colonial governor. Some were executed for treason; my ancestor Olaf Stille was tried for mutiny. Others fled into Native communities. By 1664, in defiance of the Dutch and British, the remnants of the indigenous Lenapes—devastated by European-introduced diseases and encroachment—Swedes and Finns forged a new society from the Native identity, according to historian Jean Soderlund, "as a free people, subject to no one."

Five years later, a mysterious "Long Swede" organized a failed armed uprising against the new English overlords. The colonial governor of New York dismissed it as a "silly intention of an Insurrection amongst the Finns at the Delaware." The fear of rebellion remained, nonetheless.

In 1776, the American resistance movement for Independence recognized that it was not unique or exceptional. The cruel symbolism of the "massacre" of American Patriots in the fall of 1777 at the Paoli Tavern in the outskirts of Philadelphia was a reminder for Washington and his commanders, and the members of Congress who had fled from the city aggrandized for its revolutionary declaration. A surprise night attack by the British devastated holdover Patriot troops, who had remained nearby to slow the advancing forces.

The nearby tavern had been named after Pasquale Paoli, the Corsican resistance leader who had won independence for his island in the Mediterranean in 1755. Inspired by the Enlightenment movement in Europe, Paoli brought together the divided factions in Corsica through a democratically elected Diet, and drew up a constitution that rejected monarchy and declared the representative government to be "legitimately Master of itself." Two decades before the American Revolution, Corsica's constitution was hailed by Scottish author James Boswell as "the best model that hath ever existed in the democratical form."

In eschewing any claim to king, Paoli won worldwide acclaim, including the compliments of Voltaire, who commended the Corsican for "placing himself at the head of a democratic government." All adult males had the right to vote.

The Corsican constitution, according to historian Dorothy Carrington, "had a liberal character rare in a period when the rule of absolute monarchs, aristocracies and oligarchies, was general throughout Europe. The principle of egality inherent in the system is what makes it most remarkable. The law, emanating from the Diet, applied equally to all citizens, nobles and clergy included; taxation was moderate and equitable."

France invaded Corsica in 1769, ending the fifteen-year experiment in democracy, but Paoli's fight to defend his country's independence was covered closely in the American newspapers. Defeated, Paoli eventually fled to England. The *Memoirs of Pascal Paoli*, published in 1768, had already made him a household name in the American colonies. *The New York Journal* hailed Paoli as "the greatest man on earth." The radical Sons of Liberty in Boston toasted his feats, as one of the world's greatest patriots. Ebenezer Mackintosh, the "First Captain General of the liberty tree" in Boston, according to historian Alfred Young, named his son Paskal Paoli Mackintosh in honor of the Corsican. In 1775, Paine included a poem dedicated to the Corsican struggle in his *Pennsylvania Magazine*, which described Paoli's compatriots as "fellow freedom fighters."

Responding to the English criticism of the French takeover of Corsica, a letter in a Parisian newspaper made the link between the two colonial resistance movements: "The Corsicans are not so remote from us as the Americans are from you; they never enriched us with their labour of their commerce; they never engaged in our wars, and fought as brothers, side by side, with us, and for us, bleeding in the same cause; they never loved and honoured us; they are not our children. But all of this your American colonies have been and are to you."

Writing in London, Benjamin Franklin concurred: "Two great and powerful Nations are employing their Forces in the Destruction of Civil Liberty!"

IN 1780, PAUL AND JOHN Cuffe invoked the Boston Tea Party and its cry of "no taxation without representation," refusing to pay their taxes until they could vote as free citizens in Massachusetts. Of Wampanoag and African descent, the Cuffes petitioned the legislature for being "taxed both in our Polls and small pittance of estate" when they were denied the vote. In effect, the Cuffes demanded reparations: "By reason of Long Bondage and hard Slavery, we have been deprived of enjoying the profits of our labor or the advantage of inheriting estates from our Parents, as our neighbors, the white people do."

We the people resisted. Native Americans included.

"History is a prophet who looks back," Eduardo Galeano wrote in his masterful saga of the "other America," *Open Veins of Latin America*, "because of what was, and against what was, it announces what will be."

William Apess, one of the most prophetic writers of resistance, would never be accepted as part of "we the people" in his lifetime. Native Americans were dismissed as less than human in the Declaration of Independence; as ratified in the Constitution, Natives have since been considered alongside foreign nations in acts of commerce. Citizenship would take another 150 years.

On a cold January evening in 1836, Apess approached the podium on the stage of the Odeon Theatre in Boston. He walked in a slow gait of anticipation. His formal black attire suggested his former role as a Methodist preacher; he carried the confidence of a circuit rider who was used to performing to the unconverted. No backdrop or ornately painted scenes framed his shoulders; the curtain was drawn, the lights on. Apess nodded at the podium, opened a notebook, and then looked at the audience, which leaned closely on rickety chairs and with an air of expectation.

The crowd was not an antagonistic one. The illuminated Bostonians had made their way in the dark evening and purchased a ticket; they cherished orators in those days like celebrities—and refreshing ones, too, so far from the dour confines of their churches. More so, many in the audience had rallied on behalf of the aggrieved Cherokee Nation, and applauded their support as allies of *Cherokee Phoenix* newspaper editor Elias Boudinot, who beseeched their "assistance to become respectable as a nation." Even the Massachusetts member of Congress, Edward Everett, had spoken on a platform with Boudinot and Apess.

The Cherokee resistance had been crushed; the tribe's Constitution in 1827, written in their own syllabary and read by a population more literate in its language than its armed invaders, had been trampled into the red clay of Georgia. Relocated across the Mississippi River, the Cherokee would join the specious narrative of the "vanishing tribes," such as the Pequot, who had been devastated in their war with the first Massachusetts colonists nearly two centuries earlier, with many of the surviving children, women, and men sold into slavery in the Caribbean. Apess did not simply confront history, but historicide—the erasure of his people's existence in a narrative that accepted Andrew Jackson's requiem of "extinction of one generation to make room for another."

"I do not arise to spread before you the fame of a noted warrior, whose natural abilities shone like those of the great and mighty Philip of Greece, or of Alexander the Great, or like those of Washington— whose virtues and patriotism are engraven on the hearts of every white in America, never to be forgotten in time," Apess began, in a dramatic but subdued voice.

Apess announced that he spoke on behalf of the Pequot, his ancestors, and "those few remaining descendants who now remain as the monument of the cruelty of those who came to improve our race and correct our errors."

His lecture was entitled "Eulogy on King Philip," the Wampanoag leader Metacomet whose devastating alliance of resistance against English encroachment in New England in the late 1670s had solidified an anticolonial consciousness of occupation. Metacomet refused to submit to English rule a century before the American Revolution. His head remained fixed on a pike at Ft. Plymouth for years after he had been killed, beheaded, and quartered, a foreboding statue to anyone who would defy the colonial conquest.

King Philip, Apess declared, yet lives in our hearts. Behold "the greatest man that ever lived upon American shores."

Apess removed the head of Metacomet from the pike of memory and held up the image to his audience with a bold challenge: "So will every patriot, especially in this enlightened age, respect the rude yet all-accomplished son of the forest, that died a martyr to his cause, though unsuccessful, yet as glorious as the American Revolution."

The theatergoers conferred, their comfort with his presence clear, so Apess continued with a story—and a chilling one.

> Upon the banks of the Ohio, a party of two hundred white warriors, in 1757 or about that time, came across a settlement of Christian Indians and falsely accused them of being warriors, to which they denied, but all to no purpose; they were determined to massacre them all. They, the Indians, then asked liberty to prepare for the fatal hour. The white savages gave them one hour, as the historian said. They then prayed together; and in tears and cries, upon their knees, begged pardon of each other, of all they had done, after which they informed the white savages that they were now ready. One white man then begun with a mallet, and knocked them down and continued his work until he had killed fifteen, with his own hand; then, saying it ached, he gave his commission to another.

Asking his Boston crowd to set aside their sanitized family sagas, Apess brought out characters in search of another history to take the stage. His aim: "To melt the prejudice that exists in the hearts of those in possession of the soil, and only by the right of conquest."

"While the son of the forest drops a tear and groans over the fate of his murdered and departed fathers," Apess had written, "let it be forgotten in your celebration, in your speeches, and by the burying of the rock that your fathers first put their foot upon . . . We say, therefore, let every man of color wrap himself in mourning, for the 22nd of December and the 4th of July are days of mourning and not of joy."

Apess dispelled the notion of the intrinsic piety of religious pilgrims in the American Eden. The Christian goodness had been betrayed by subsequent aberrations. To the contrary, Apess lectured his audience, the theology of this "errand in the wilderness" had been morally corrupt and murderous from the start. Central to Apess's story is the reversal of the vocabulary of violence, the lexicon of memory for Metacomet's bloody war.

> How inhuman it was in those wretches, to come into a country where nature shone in beauty, spreading her wings over the vast continent,

sheltering beneath her shades those natural sons of an Almighty Being, that shone in grandeur and luster like the stars of the first mag-
nitude in the heavenly world; whose virtues far surpassed their more
enlightened foes, notwithstanding their pretended zeal for religion
and virtue. How they could go to work to enslave a free people and
call it religion is beyond the power of my imagination and outstrips the
revelation of God's word.

Two hundred years of conquest later, this history is a still presence,
not a tale of bygone days, in the culture of "white savages."

Assemble all nations together in your imagination, and then let the
whites be seated among them, and then let us look for the whites, and I
doubt not it would be hard finding them; for to the rest of the nations,
they are still but a handful. Now suppose the skins were put together,
and each skin had its national crimes written upon it—which skin do
you think would have the greatest? I will ask one question more. Can
you charge the Indians of robbing a nation almost of their whole continent, and murdering their women and children, and then depriving
the remainder of their lawful rights, that nature and God require them
to have? And to cap the climax, rob another nation to till their grounds
and welter out their days under the lash with hunger and fatigue under
the scorching rays of a burning sun?

The dark voice of President Andrew Jackson delivered a plaintive
reckoning in Apess's narrative with the paternalistic rendering of judgment: "You see, my red children, that our fathers carried on this scheme
of getting your lands for our use, and we have now become rich and powerful; and we have a right to do just as we please."

In Apess's words, Jackson's last line echoed a sentiment carried out
since the American Revolution: "But this has been the way our fathers
first brought us up, and it is hard to depart from it," Jackson reasoned, as
if exonerated by tradition itself.

"What, then, shall we do?" Apess turned the question over to the
audience in the theater. "Shall we cease crying and say it is all wrong,

or shall we bury the hatchet and those unjust laws and Plymouth Rock together and become friends? And will the sons of the Pilgrims aid in putting out the fire and destroying the canker that will ruin all that their fathers left behind them to destroy?"

The righteous or guilt-racked among the brethren would have applauded, but Apess didn't let them off the hook. This was not a rally for the faraway Cherokee, whose flourishing nation would be dismantled in the courts, and its citizens-turned-refugees removed by gunpoint.

Apess brought the unavoidable fate of Native Americans on stage. "I would ask you if you would like to be disenfranchised from all your rights, merely because your skin is white, and for no other crime."

> Look at the disgraceful laws, disenfranchising us as citizens. Look at the treaties made by Congress, all broken. Look at the deep-rooted plans laid, when a territory becomes a state, that after so many years the laws shall be extended over the Indians that live within their boundaries. Yea, every charter that has been given was given with the view of driving the Indians out of the states, or dooming them to become chained under desperate laws . . .

His sympathetic crowd recoiling, Apess backed off with a rhetorical question: "I know that many will say they are willing, perhaps the majority of the people, that we should enjoy our rights and privileges as they do. If so, I would ask, Why are we not protected in our persons and property throughout the Union?"

Apess's history of resistance ultimately brings out "we the people" on stage as a final exhibit. The silent audience must stare—at Apess, at the reality that Native Americans are not vanishing, at the resurrection of a bloody history that now gives voice to the core truth of the Constitution. "I say, then, that a different course must be pursued, and different laws must be enacted, and all men must operate under one general law."

Invoking Metacomet—King Philip, as named by the English—Apess grafted memory onto the reality of the times: "Give the Indian his rights, and you may be assured war will cease."

The war, of course, of the white savages. The resistance, of the people, had just begun.

ON THE THIRD DAY IN office, Trump signed an executive order that overruled an Army Corps of Engineers decision and fast-tracked the completion of the Dakota Access Pipeline. The first stretches of a pipeline that would eventually carry half a million barrels of crude oil had been rerouted away from North Dakota towns, due to concerns over water contamination, and snaked across the watersheds of indigenous communities—including a precarious attachment of pipeline under the Missouri River. A former stakeholder in Energy Transfers Partners, the Dallas-based company behind the nearly 1,200-mile pipeline, Trump disregarded legal procedures and land treaties that had ignited a historic resistance campaign on the Standing Rock Sioux nation.

Vogue magazine, too, had joined the resistance: "Congratulations, Donald Trump, You Just Reignited the DAPL Resistance," ran a headline.

Ladonna Brave Bull Allard, a member of the Standing Rock Sioux Tribe, reframed the "we the people" connotations of the executive order in an interview with *Vogue*: "We are expendable people. We always have been. But we have the answers on how to save the world. We have the answers on how to live with this earth. We have to stand up and share that knowledge."

"By granting the easement, Trump is risking our treaty rights and water supply to benefit his wealthy contributors and friends at DAPL," said Dave Archambault II, then chairman of the Standing Rock Sioux Tribe. "We are not opposed to energy independence. We are opposed to reckless and politically motivated development projects, like DAPL, that ignore our treaty rights and risk our water." Referring to the contaminated drinking water crisis in Michigan, he added, "creating a second Flint does not make America great again."

If the roots of the American Revolution were part of what Paine termed a "continental crisis," resistance movements beyond the original thirteen colonies were older than an elm tree on the Boston Common. That "continental" term, lugged over from Paine's Europe, may have been borrowed from John Donne's poem and its famous line, "no man is an island." On American soil, however, the Iroquois or Haudenosaunee origin story defined the continent as "Turtle Island," going beyond Donne's "piece of the continent, a part of the main." In a letter to the leaders of the Delaware and other tribes, Jefferson embraced this island narrative, however disingenuously: "Your blood will mix with ours, and will spread, with ours, over this great island."

But it also reminds us that resistance and revolutionary times were afoot elsewhere on the North American continent, and provided as much historical context as the eastern seaboard rebellion.

Within that historical framework, the Native resistance continues today.

"Tribal nations across Turtle Island have been emboldened by the resistance movement at Standing Rock, and are taking unprecedented actions to protect our lands, waters, sacred places, and treaty rights," wrote Winona LaDuke, from the White Earth reservation in northern Minnesota, in the days following Trump's order. "In the Great Lakes, Native communities have been fighting for years to shut down old oil pipelines that threaten our territories and to resist Canadian energy company Enbridge's plans to expand a massive network of pipelines through the region."

Fighting for years, centuries—dating back to 1492, Native observers would remind newly American inhabitants.

On July 4, 1776, on a mission to extend the Spanish Crown to California and the Pacific coast, Father Francisco Garcés was on his own "errand in the wilderness" in Arizona. The friar's imperial strategy, cloaked in evangelical furor, was no less ambitious than the market-driven pursuits of the English. Garcés rested among the Hopi in northern Arizona, updating his notes on the astonishing canyons and Grand Canyon, and the gardens of the Havasupai. In central Arizona, the plentitude of the Akimel O'odham along the Gila River impressed him: their grain, vegetables, beans. He disregarded their democratic councils and villages, which had formed in the ruins of another empire, the prehistoric Hohokam. History didn't interest Garcés.

The irony of an overstretched empire in the desert would have been lost on him. In 1781, he lost his life during the "Yuma Revolt" against Spanish encroachment on the Colorado River. The resistance from Native America effectively loosened the stranglehold of the Spanish Crown through a war of attrition, forty years before independence would come to Mexicans in California and the American Southwest.

"Five years after American colonists declared their independence from England, an Indian tribe on the lower Colorado River launched a rebellion to achieve their own independence from Spain," concluded sociologist Jack Ferrell. "The revolt by the Quechan Indians, while costly to both sides, was ultimately successful. It permanently closed Spain's land route to California, and left a legacy which continues to shape the society of the Southwest to this day. A tribe which had proven itself capable of resistance also retained the capacity to adapt to changing circumstances."

On the other side of the continent, William Apess captured those changing realities for Natives along the Massachusetts seaboard in 1833. As a writer of the resistance, he did not only add an indigenous chapter to the historical memory of the United States; he also played an extraordinary part in a Native community's own Declaration of Independence. Apess was the author of several books, including a somewhat sentimental memoir, *A Son of the Forest*, examining his Native roots and conversion to Christianity. Born to a family of mixed Pequot and European ethnicities on the border of Massachusetts and Vermont in 1798, Apess did not pull any punches about his abusive childhood, his indentured status as a youth, and his freedom through enlistment in the militia forces during the War of 1812.

His work *Indian Nullification of the Unconstitutional Laws of Massachusetts Relative to the Mashpee Tribe* dismissed the "savage" or "mob" context of outside writers with his subtitle, *The Pretended Riot Explained,* and rejected Paine's continental analysis of rebellion. Apess countered with the natural rights of an "island," an indigenous people ruled by themselves— in the ocean of the United States.

Indeed, no riot occurred on Cape Cod in Massachusetts in the Mashpee settlement, the remnants of an indigenous community formally organized in the 1660s. In 1833, the Wampanoag community in Mashpee
remained under the control of an outside board of overseers appointed by
the governor. Harvard College maintained a minister at its local church.
When Apess, then an itinerant Methodist minister, preached to a largely
white audience in the area, he was stunned to find a Native community
removed from its own sacred spaces, albeit Christian ones.

Joining forces, they set into motion a movement that forced the
self-righteous Northern establishment to reconsider the constitutional
belittlement of Natives and to confront the hypocrisy of its longtime
concessions to Southern slave states. As South Carolina pressed its articles of nullification against federal oversight, and the besieged Cherokee
in the South garnered support from the Boston abolitionist community
for their sovereign rights, Apess asked, "why should not the remaining
Indians in this Commonwealth be placed upon the same footing as to
rights of property, as to civil privileges and duties, as other men? Why
should they not *vote*, maintain schools (they have volunteered to do this
in some instances,) and use as they please that which is their own?"

Adopting the Pequot author Apess into their community, the Mashpee filed a petition with the Massachusetts government in June 1833, effectively declaring their independence:

> Resolved, That we, as a tribe, will rule ourselves, and have the Con-
> stitution; for all men are born free and equal, says the Constitution of
> the country. Resolved, That we will not permit any white man to come
> upon our plantation, to cut or carry off wood or hay, or any other arti-
> cle, without our permission, after the 1st of July next.
>
> Resolved, That we will put said resolutions in force after that date
> (July next,) with the penalty of binding and throwing them from the
> plantation, if they will not stay away without.

Famed abolitionist William Lloyd Garrison's newspaper in Boston,
The Liberator, immediately embraced Apess's challenge: "We are proud

to see this spontaneous, earnest, upward movement of our red brethren. It is not to be stigmatized as turbulent, but applauded as meritorious. It is sedition, it is true; but only the sedition of freedom against oppression; of justice against fraud; of humanity against cruelty."

The local press did not cheer. The nearby *Barnstable Patriot* editor accused Apess of being an outside agitator, "a talented, educated, wily, unprincipled Indian, professing with all, to be an apostle of Christianity," seeking to stir up "sedition, riot, treason!" The editor warned the government authorities back in Boston of impending violence, of "their independence of the laws of Massachusetts," and the Mashpee willingness "to arm themselves to defend it." Apess laughed at the exaggerated stories in the press: "They bellowed like mad bulls and spouted like whales mortally gored by the harpoon, I do not think the figure of speech would be too strong. There was a great deal of loose talk and a pretty considerable uproar."

In truth, the Wampanoag's revolt was not about taking up arms, but protecting natural resources—in this case, the forests. On July 2, Apess and a group of local men confronted outside loggers hauling away a load of timber from the Mashpee settlement—an important source of revenue. No weapons were raised; no violence tendered. The loggers hightailed it back to the authorities in Barnstable.

On July 4, Apess was arrested and hauled off to jail, charged with inciting a riot and trespassing. He disregarded the charges. "The laws ought to be altered without delay, that it was perfectly manifest they were unconstitutional," he replied.

"In my mind, it was no punishment at all," Apess wrote, "and I am yet to learn what punishment can dismay a man conscious of his own innocence. Lightning, tempest, and battle, wreck, pain, buffeting, and torture have small terror to a pure conscience."

In a dramatic act of nonviolent civil disobedience, Apess remained in jail for several days, gambling that the attention to the Mashpee revolt would gain broader support. Harvard students, including Henry David Thoreau, would take note of Apess's forewarning words of resistance; the controversial Harvard-appointed minister to Mashpee would eventually be replaced.

Indeed, one of Boston's leading attorneys and writers, former *Boston Daily Advertiser* editor Benjamin Hallett, took up Apess's case and rallied the abolitionist community behind him. Hallett not only got the charges dropped; he filed the grievances of the Wampanoag with the state authorities, asserting their sovereign rights as a nation outside the bounds of federal law and taxation. The Massachusetts legislature sided with Apess and the Mashpee in 1834, scrapped the board of overseers, and appointed a new commissioner to work directly with the Mashpee "selectmen" and town council.

Apess's personal life, like Paine's, did not fare well—a cautionary tale for contentious and messy disputes within resistance movements today. Infighting within the Mashpee community and its religious factions, disputes over compensation, along with the brutal attacks by the neighboring white newspapers, led to inevitable conflicts for Apess. He left the Methodist Church; his attempts to start his own congregation failed. He accumulated debts. His fame allowed him to stage his own oratory performances at the theater in Boston, but his success was short-lived. Within a couple of years, he quietly moved to New York City, where he died in 1839 from an aneurysm.

Among the thousands of monuments or statues to the "founding fathers" of the United States, you will not find any of Thomas Paine in Washington, DC, nor is there any historical tribute to Apess. Their living legacy, in the form of Native American and resistance movements today, remains their only tribute.

Our apparent lack of recognition of resistance leaders in American history might be one of our most telling misconceptions: Far from languishing in a roundabout of stone, figures like Apess and Paine and Maria Stewart, among others, carved out their own monuments in the form of stories that should remain as vital today as in their own times.

When the Mashpee town council wrote in defense of Apess in 1835, they ultimately addressed the subterfuge of "we the people" in the American experience. "The red children of the soil of America address themselves to the descendants of the pale men who came across the big waters to seek among them a refuge from tyranny and persecution," the Mashpee statement read. "We say to each and every one of you that the

Great Spirit who is the friend of the Indian as well as of the white man, has raised up among you a brother of our own and has sent him to us that he might show us all the secret contrivances of the pale faces to deceive and defraud us. For this, many of our white brethren hate him, and revile him, and say all manner of evil of him, falsely calling him an impostor."

Speaking at a roundtable discussion with *Democracy Now!* journalist Amy Goodman in the fall of 2017, Dallas Goldtooth with the Indigenous Environmental Network pointed to a similar duplicity in the prosecution of Native people who had stood up to outside contractors and private police forces that had rammed through the Dakota Access Pipeline. "We're seeing an unfair court system in place in North Dakota that is persecuting water protectors, whose only reason for being there is to protect water and to protect indigenous communities' right to self-determine what happens to their lands and communities and bodies," Goldtooth said, at a gathering in California, as oil now flowed across the Dakotas under a Trump order that disregarded a court-ordered environmental review. "And it's really absurd that we're in that position now. And it makes sense, because it's kind of this trickle down. If you have a tyrant in the White House who is blind, and who is willingly blind, to the effects of climate change and the effects that the fossil fuel industry has on the land, it's going to trickle down."

2

Let Your Motto Be Resistance

Let your motto be resistance! Resistance! Resistance! No oppressed people have ever secured their liberty without resistance. What kind of resistance you had better make, you must decide by the circumstances that surround you, and according to the suggestion of expediency. Brethren, adieu!
—Henry Highland Garnet, speech at the National Negro Convention, Buffalo, New York, 1843

NOT LONG AFTER DAYBREAK ON Saturday, June 27, 2015, Brittany "Bree" Newsome and James Ian Dyson climbed the stairs to the South Carolina statehouse in Columbia. They approached a flagpole, where the flag of the Confederate States of America was framed by the overcast sky. The Confederacy had seceded in 1861 from the United States, raising an army against American citizens, openly invoking a clause that allowed it to abandon the U.S. Constitution. The Confederacy kept four million African Americans in bondage; it enforced the underpinnings of a quasi-feudal system with whips and chains, family displacement, rape and murder. An estimated 600,000 Americans died in the ensuing Civil War.

With a helmet and climbing gear, Newsome hopped over a small black fence, and then slowly began to scale the thirty-foot flagpole. The flag had been fixed at half rest for the past days, after a twenty-one-year-old domestic terrorist intent on triggering a "race war" gunned down state senator Clementa Pinckney and eight other black Americans inside a church in Charleston, South Carolina.

Climbing to the top, Newsome, a thirty-year-old African American woman from North Carolina, unhooked the Confederate flag, as police officers encircled the base. "You come against me with hatred and oppression and violence," she shouted down. "I come against you in the name of God. This flag comes down today." Within hours of the police arresting Newsome and Tyson, videos of her act of civil disobedience went viral around the world.

With then Gov. Nikki Haley joining leading South Carolina Republicans, and national leaders including President Barack Obama, the calls to remove the Confederate flag from the statehouse finally moved the legislature to action. In less than two weeks after Newsome's dramatic action, police and state officials unhooked the Confederate flag from the pole and folded it as a relic for a museum.

"Truth is power, and it prevails," as Sojourner Truth often told her abolitionist audiences in the mid-nineteenth century.

Two years after Newsome's protest, a white supremacist march to honor the statue of Confederate General Robert E. Lee in Charlottesville, Virginia, turned deadly. The historical realities cast by Confederate statues came alive across the country. Gunning his car in a congested pedestrian area of counter-protesters, a domestic terrorist mowed down Heather Heyer, a thirty-two-year-old legal assistant and civil rights activist, among others. The march had been organized by self-proclaimed Nazi, Ku Klux Klan, and other alt-right extremist groups. Heavily armed militia members faced off against nonviolent clergy. A night-time parade of tiki-torch extremists had encircled and attacked students on the University of Virginia campus.

The White House response turned dark. Trump initially refused to condemn the violence or white supremacist hate groups, claiming he did not "know all the facts." Instead, Trump accused "many sides" for the racially motivated attacks.

Former Klan leader David Duke posted a tweet in support of Trump, blaming the Black Lives Matter movement and the alliance of "antifa" or anti-fascist groups: "Thank you President Trump for your honesty & courage to tell the truth about #Charlottesville & condemn the leftist terrorists in BLM/Antifa."

During his presidential campaign, Trump had often bristled at Black Lives Matter's message of justice, which had been founded by three women in 2013. "The first time I heard it I said, 'You have to be kidding,'" Trump told Fox News host Bill O'Reilly. "I think it's a very, very, very divisive term. There's no question about it."

Sojourner Truth had staved off the hostile naysayers that black lives matter in her times. Born into slavery among Dutch-speaking Americans in 1797 in New York—not the South—the famed orator escaped thirty years later, was forced to litigate the freedom of one son in court, and then liberated herself from her slave name in 1843, taking to the road as an itinerant resistance leader.

"Ain't I a woman?" she asked a women's convention in Akron, Ohio, in 1851.

In an extraordinary moment of unity and resistance, national and global condemnation of Trump's reluctance to denounce the violence of self-avowed white supremacists carrying Nazi and Confederate flags trended on Twitter, resounded in spontaneous street protests, and echoed in legislature chambers. Resignations of many major business, labor, and community leaders from presidential advisory councils forced the White House to dissolve long-held positions.

"Racism and murder are unequivocally reprehensible and are not morally equivalent to anything else that happened in Charlottesville," Campbell's Soup president and chief executive Denise Morrison wrote in her letter of resignation. Sen. Bernie Sanders added: "@realDonaldTrump, you are embarrassing our country and the millions of Americans who fought and died to defeat Nazism."

Bowing to political pressure, including most of the Republican leadership in Washington, Trump finally signed a Congressional resolution a month later "rejecting White nationalists, White supremacists, the Ku Klux Klan, neo-Nazis, and other hate groups."

In an interview on Air Force One that same day, however, Trump still proclaimed a moral equivalence between violent Nazis and anti-fascist counter-protesters.

"Many of those people were there to protest the taking down of the statue of Robert E. Lee," Trump told reporters. "So this week, it is Robert E. Lee. I noticed that Stonewall Jackson is coming down. I wonder, is it George Washington next week? And is it Thomas Jefferson the week after? You know, you really do have to ask yourself, where does it stop?"

In fact, towns and cities, including New Orleans and Lexington, Kentucky, had moved quickly to remove some of the estimated 700 Confederate statues in the nation, many of which had been erected in the last few decades. Borrowing a common Revolutionary War–era tactic, activists in Arizona tarred and feathered two of the six Confederate monuments constructed since World War II in a state (or territory) that did not even exist during the Civil War.

With the Charlottesville tragedy still fresh on the nation's conscience, Trump took the stage at a campaign rally in Phoenix, Arizona, defiantly defending the white nationalist protesters. He claimed they only sought to halt the removal of a "very, very important" statue—that of Confederate Gen. Robert E. Lee. According to the memoirs of one former plantation worker enslaved by Lee, the Confederate general had responded to a possible slave revolt by overseeing brutal whippings: "Not satisfied with simply lacerating our naked flesh, Gen. Lee then ordered the overseer to thoroughly wash our backs with brine, which was done."

"They're trying to take away our culture," Trump railed. "They're trying to take away our history."

Lee's history of treason notwithstanding, Trump's vindication of the Confederate hero offered a teachable moment for modern-day Patriots.

In an op-ed in the *Washington Post*, Newsome went beyond Civil War history to remind Trump of a deeper American tradition of resistance to the sway of tyrannical dominion:

On July 9, 1776, upon hearing the Declaration of Independence read for the first time, a mob of American colonists descended upon a statue of King George III in Bowling Green park in Lower Manhattan, tied

ropes around the sculpture and pulled it to the ground. The lead from
the statue was then turned into bullets and muskets in preparation for
the Revolutionary War.

ON APRIL 30, 1789, ONA Maria Judge did not appear in the background
of wigs, silk stockings, and pomp in New York City, as the federal Congress of men ushered in the first presidential inauguration. The "light
mulatto girl, much freckled, with very black eyes and bushy hair," as
she would be described in an advertisement seven years later, labored in
George Washington's household a few blocks away as the enslaved body
servant of Martha Washington. She would have assisted the First Lady
with her gown that morning, held the garment, and then stepped back
and watched its glorious elegance, a sliver of her face in the background
of the dressing room.

Ona Judge's role in the early American resistance has similarly been
placed in the background of her times. And yet, the recovery of her presence is part of the process of reversing the erasure of an important part
of history. Judge did not just liberate herself; she disrobed the duplicity
of a new nation founded on the principle of inalienable rights for all.

Judge's story, like others in the resistance, allows us to explore our
history beyond the appearance of things. To reconsider the historic scene
on the balcony of the Federal Hall in Lower Manhattan, for example,
where an oath was taken in our nation's first capital in 1789, set against a
monumental backdrop that celebrated the general, the forefathers, and
the victors of the American Revolution.

The irony of the "reverence for the characteristic rights of freemen,"
as George Washington declared on the balcony of the Federal Hall,
would not have been lost on Judge, who had been enslaved since her
birth at Mount Vernon.

Born in 1773, the year of the Boston Tea Party, she was the daughter
of a white indentured servant and an African American "dower slave,"
bequeathed to Martha Washington from her deceased first husband's
huge estate in Virginia.

Judge had never been considered freeborn. The dowry of slavery insured perpetuity, each generation linked in captivity like an heirloom chain. Writing in 1764, Boston attorney James Otis had already warned his fellow colonists that any demand of freedom to the British Crown reflected like a mirror on their own treatment of enslaved Americans: "Nothing better can be said in favor of a trade that is the most shocking violation of the law of nature, has a direct tendency to diminish the idea of the inestimable value of liberty, and makes every dealer in it a tyrant, from the director of an African company to the petty chapman in needles and pins on the unhappy coast."

Relegated to being a playmate for Martha's granddaughter in her childhood, Judge lived a youth tethered to Martha's command. As a teenager in Mount Vernon, she had numbered as one of hundreds of Americans enslaved by Washington and his wife on their plantation. Denied any schooling, Judge excelled as a seamstress, and then found herself loaded up into a wagon for New York City's historic occasion. The move separated the teen from her enslaved mother. It also removed her from the time warp of the Mount Vernon plantation in Virginia.

Freedom surrounded Judge on the streets of New York City. Thousands of African Americans had arrived in the city during the American Revolution, seeking sanctuary among British troops. Others had responded to Lord Dunmore's promise: "I do hereby further declare all indented servants, Negroes, or others (appertaining to Rebels,) free, that are able and willing to bear arms, they joining His Majesty's Troops." According to documents filed by Lund Washington, who had overseen his cousin's affairs at Mount Vernon, sixteen enslaved laborers owned by the Washington family had fled when a British sloop anchored off the Potomac River in the spring of 1781, as the Revolution raged in its final stretch. "There is not a man of them, but would leave us," Lund wrote, "if they believe'd they could make their escape ... Liberty is sweet."

While an estimated 3,000 blacks boarded defeated British ships for refuge in Canada in 1783, thousands had remained behind to face an uncertain fate in New York. An outraged Washington, accompanied by Thomas Paine, who happened to be visiting, rode his horse to the banks of the Hudson River and watched the departure of Black Loyalists who sought their freedom elsewhere. That included Harry Washington, an enslaved horse groomer who had escaped from Washington's Virginia plantation, and who would go on to attempt a rebellion against the colonial government in Sierra Leone.

Ona would not have been unaware of this fact; the stories of fugitives and freed slaves passed quickly along the coastal routes. Another young woman from Mount Vernon, the enslaved Deborah Squash, had escaped from Washington's plantation as a teenager and made her way to New York City. She and her husband had also boarded one of the British ships for Nova Scotia at the end of the American Revolution—in search of liberty for all.

The British insolence outraged Washington. He sent an underling to the docks to search for his own slaves. British commander Sir Guy Carleton defied a last-minute insertion in the treaty to return the liberated fugitives. "Delivering up Negroes to their former masters," he told Washington, "would be a dishonourable violation of the public faith." On the docks of the liberated city, as formerly enslaved Americans boarded the ship, the British filled a registry—the *Book of Negroes*—with the testimonies of their escapes, and the details of their bondage. Washington viewed that registry as stolen property; the British commander saw it as a rap sheet of crimes. The Treaty of Peace, Carleton declared, did not oblige the British to violate "their faith to the negroes who came into the British lines."

The incongruous status of a slave in a state of emancipation became even more evident when Washington transferred his family and entourage to the presidential residency in Philadelphia in 1790. The President's household grew to include ten enslaved Americans.

It also sat at the cross streets of abolitionist fervor in our nation's temporary capital.

Whether Paine had a hand in shaping the preamble of the Act for the Gradual Abolition of Slavery in Pennsylvania in 1780, as many debate—a decade before Judge's arrival—the law leaned heavily on the inalienable rights recognized by the American Revolution and embodied by Washington:

When we contemplate our abhorrence of that condition, to which the arms and tyranny of Great Britain were exerted to reduce us, when we look back on the variety of dangers to which we have been exposed, and how miraculously our wants in many instances have been supplied, and our deliverances wrought, when even hope and human fortitude have become unequal to the conflict, we are unavoidably led to a serious and grateful sense of the manifold blessings, which we have undeservedly received from the hand of that Being, from whom every good and perfect gift cometh. Impressed with these ideas, we conceive that it is our duty, and we rejoice that it is in our power, to extend a portion of that freedom to others, which hath been extended to us, and release them from the state of thralldom, to which we ourselves were tyrannically doomed, and from which we have now every prospect of being delivered.

Contrary to its abolitionist title, the Pennsylvania law did not "free" enslaved Americans. It prohibited the importation of slaves into the state and set up a more restrictive system of registration. It granted gradual emancipation for children of enslaved Pennsylvanians.

The Pennsylvania law, however, exempted members of Congress, and provided a loophole for slave owners like Washington and his wife, Martha. As warned by his attorney general, Washington understood that he needed to remove his enslaved laborers out of the state every six months to avoid a slaveholding restriction, even if that openly flouted an amendment to the law in 1788.

In fact, Washington's preoccupation with his escaped slaves underscored the passing of the federal Fugitive Slave Act of 1793. Overriding state laws, the Act empowered slave owners to cross state lines and "seize or arrest" any escaped slave. The agent or bounty hunter acting on behalf of the slave owners only needed to provide "oral testimony or affidavit." Anyone harboring or interfering with the arrest was liable for punishment; conversely, it provided virtually no protection for the rights of free blacks who might be fraudulently kidnapped. "The law made rendition essentially a private matter," historian Eric Foner wrote, "identifying little role for the state or federal governments."

Washington signed the Act into law on February 12, 1793. Ona Judge had just turned twenty.

With disquieting precision, Washington gave orders to circumvent the intention of the Pennsylvania law by exploiting the six-month rotation system. In a letter to his secretary Tobias Lear, he spelled out his motives:

> In case it shall be found that any of my Slaves may, or any for them shall attempt their freedom at the expiration of six months, it is my wish and desire that you would send the whole, or such part of them as Mrs. Washington may not chuse to keep, home—for although I do not think they would be benefitted by the change, yet the idea of freedom might be too great a temptation for them to resist. At any rate it might, if they conceived they had a right to it, make them insolent in a State of Slavery.

Washington understood the deceitful nature of his operations— and their implications for his public persona as the president. He wrote Lear of his plan to "deceive both them (the enslaved) and the Public," through a staged journey back to Mount Vernon for a family visit. He commanded his secretary to keep the plans secret, "known to none but yourself and Mrs. Washington."

Lear's response underscored the sentiment of most white Americans in this period; while against the idea of slavery, he deferred to Washington's authority, and therefore conjured an excuse that such duplicity was in the interest of the enslaved: "You will permit me now, Sir (and I am sure you will pardon me for doing it) to declare, that no consideration should induce me to take these steps to prolong the slavery of a human being, had I not the fullest confidence that they will at some future period be liberated, and the strongest conviction that their situation with you is far preferable to what they would probably obtain in a state of freedom."

The "sacred fire of liberty" that Washington summoned in his first inauguration, "arising out of the present crisis," also burned in Judge.

She had met many free African Americans and abolitionists in New York City and in Philadelphia, including visitors to the President's House. As Martha Washington's body servant, Judge had already navigated the social networks in Philadelphia, moving freely in the market place and attending social events.

In 1796, Judge learned of Martha Washington's plan to sign over her dower enslavement to the First Lady's granddaughter as a wedding present, ensuring her bondage back in Virginia. "I wasn't going to be her slave," she would tell a journalist nearly a half century later.

At the age of twenty-three, having spent her adulthood in the nation's revolutionary center, often a witness of the proceedings of state at the President's House, Judge quietly organized her plan of action.

"Whilst they were packing up to go to Virginia, I was packing to go, I didn't know where," she told the editor of the *Granite Freeman*, a newspaper in New Hampshire. "For I knew that if I went back to Virginia, I should never get my liberty. I had friends among the colored people of Philadelphia, had my things carried there beforehand, and left Washington's house while they were eating dinner."

A ship secretly awaited Judge at the port. Captain John Bowles commanded the *Nancy*, a sloop that made regular trips between Portsmouth, New Hampshire, and Philadelphia. His role remains mysterious, though Judge's refusal to name him until he died, "lest they should punish him for bringing me away," suggests he was aware of her fugitive status.

Dismissing Judge as too simple, Washington claimed her "escape has been planned by some one who knew what he was about, and had the means to defray the expence of it and to entice her off: for not the least suspicion was entertained of her going, or having formed a connexion with any one who could induce her to such an Act." Washington couldn't believe Judge's "ingratitude," claiming she had been "treated more like a child than a Servant."

Washington didn't hesitate to track down his "child" with "impunity." The President of the United States posted an ad with a $10 reward in the *Philadelphia Gazette & Universal Daily Advertiser* on May 24, 1796:

> She has many changes of good clothes, of all sorts, but they are not sufficiently recollected to be described—As there was no suspicion of her going off, nor no provocation to do so, it is not easy to conjecture whither she has gone, or fully, what her design is; but as she may at-

tempt to escape by water, all masters of vessels are cautioned against admitting her into them, although it is probable she will attempt to pass for a free woman ...

Judge didn't need to pass for a free woman; she liberated herself. And her shrewd defiance of Washington triggered an obsession with her capture. He learned of her residence in New Hampshire when the daughter of the New Hampshire senator recognized Judge on the streets of Portsmouth later that fall. Washington immediately invoked the Fugitive Slave Act to "seize her and put her on board a Vessel bound immediately to this place, or to Alexandria."

In an interview with the Portsmouth's Collector of Customs Joseph Whipple, Judge spoke of her "thirst for complete freedom," winning over the local officials. Whipple warned Washington of angering the town's fervent abolitionist community without going through the courts. Washington didn't relent; he proposed a careful plan of abduction, which would not "excite a mob or riot ... or even uneasy Sensations in the Minds of well disposed Citizens." Whipple's second reply, most likely orchestrated with Judge, placed the nation's commander in chief into a bind. Whipple contended that Judge would voluntarily return, but only if Washington agreed to grant manumission on Martha's death. The offer offended the President: "To enter into such a compromise ... is totally inadmissible."

The resistance continued in the President's House. Within a few months, Washington's enslaved chef Hercules, who had been highly feted for his culinary abilities, escaped from Mount Vernon, while the First Family was celebrating Washington's sixty-fifth birthday in Philadelphia. Again disparaging his enslaved laborer for a lack of gratitude—Martha had even given him a couple bottles of rum after his wife's death—Washington issued an order to apprehend Hercules. At the same time, Washington wrote a nearby plantation friend in Virginia of his decision to openly break his vow to never purchase another human being, and instead "break" this "resolution" and pursue another enslaved laborer as a chef.

Called a "celebrated dandy" by Washington's step-grandson, Hercules understood his act of resistance haunted Washington until his death. The chef disappeared into the "free" state of Pennsylvania. The Washington family still spoke of his "black silk shorts, ditto waistcoat, ditto stockings, shoes highly polished, with large buckles covering a considerable part of the foot, blue cloth coat with velvet collar and bright metal buttons, a long watch-chain dangling from his fob, a cocked-hat, and gold-headed cane." Hercules created a different history for himself.

So did Ona Judge. In the process, she committed to a life of daily resistance as one of the most famous fugitives in America—the former enslaved body servant of the First Lady. Even as he retired to his Mount Vernon plantation, Washington never gave up his pursuit; in 1799, his nephew Burwell Bassett, Jr., arrived in New Hampshire with the task of kidnapping Judge. Once again outwitting the slave owners, Judge managed to escape to the neighboring town of Greenland in the middle of the night. Now in her confidence, the New Hampshire governor hosting Bassett had tipped off the fugitive.

Judge married a seaman and raised three children, though she suffered hardship in the small New Hampshire town. With her newfound literacy, she became a deeply religious Christian. When her husband died in 1803, a year after Washington's own passing, Judge scrambled to make ends meet, eventually seeing her daughters hired out as indentured servants and her son depart as a sailor. In her later years, she relied largely on the charity of the town.

In a rare interview with the *Liberator* abolitionist newspaper in 1846, Judge was described as a "pauper" maintained by Rockingham County officials. She chastised Washington for his lack of Christian morals as much as his slavery. "Card-playing and wine-drinking were the business at his parties, and he had more of such company Sundays than on any other day."

"Great names bear more weight with the multitude, than the eternal principles of God's government," the *Liberator* declared. "So good a man as Washington is enough to sanctify war and slavery; but where is the evidence of his goodness?"

The abolitionist newspaper concluded with Judge's enduring status as a "dower" slave:

This woman is yet a slave. If Washington could have got her and her child, they were constitutionally his; and if Mrs. Washington's heirs were now to claim her, and take her before Judge Woodbury, and prove their title, he would be bound, upon his oath, to deliver her up to them. Again—Langdon was guilty of a moral violation of the Constitution, in giving this woman notice of the agent being after her. It was frustrating the design, the intent of the Constitution, and he was equally guilty, morally, as those who would overthrow it.

In an earlier interview, Judge countered the reporter's conclusion with her own declaration of resistance: "No, I am free, and have, I trust been made a child of God by the means."

John Adams once said that Washington had the "gift of silence." The nation's first commander in chief kept his comments private; but Washington's silence on slavery did not go unheard. Visitors made note of Washington's slaves, and the vast number of "dower" slaves at his Mount Vernon estate. In 1796, British abolitionist Edward Rushton confronted Washington's legacy directly. "Shame, shame," he wrote in a letter to Washington. "Ages to come will read with astonishment that the man who was foremost to wrench the rights of America from the tyrannical grasp of Britain was among the last to relinquish his own oppressive hold of poor unoffending negroes."

Rushton's final question to Washington remained unanswered: "In the name of justice what can induce you thus to tarnish your own well earned celebrity and to impair the fair features of American liberty with so foul and indelible a blot?"

Washington may have never answered Rushton's biting query, but a letter to the Customs director in New Hampshire, as he pursued his fugitive slave Judge, revealed Washington's enduring allegiance to the politics of slavery:

> I regret that the attempt you made to restore the Girl (Oney Judge as she called herself while with us, and who, without the least provocation absconded from her Mistress) should have been attended with so little Success. To enter into such a compromise with her, as she suggested to

you, is totally inadmissible, for reasons that must strike at first view: for however well disposed I might be to a gradual abolition, or even to an entire emancipation of that description of People (if the latter was in itself practicable at this moment) it would neither be politic or just to reward unfaithfulness with a premature preference [of freedom]; and thereby discontent before hand the minds of all her fellow-servants who by their steady attachments are far more deserving than herself of favor.

Once again, the resistance answered Rushton instead.

"WHAT IF I AM A woman?" Maria Stewart asked on the stage of Franklin Hall in Boston in 1833. The mixed crowd shifted in disapproval; the older men had already expressed their scorn at her reproach. Yet, the main objection might have come from the elite circle of other women who found this extraordinary African American woman stretched too far beyond the bounds of accepted true womanhood.

"Had experience more plainly shown me that it was the nature of man to crush his fellow, I should not have thought it so hard," she lamented. "Wherefore, my respected friends, let us no longer talk of prejudice, till prejudice becomes extinct at home. Let us no longer talk of opposition, till we cease to oppose our own."

The last two years had generated intense scrutiny of the African American speaker—a compelling writer of resistance in Boston. Self-educated, financially stable, Stewart was the widow of a shipping agent who had thrived on the entrepreneurial genius of black sailors on the seas. Everyone knew Paul Cuffe, the famous colonial tax resister and one of the richest black men in Massachusetts's ports, had built a fortune as a whaler before his departure for Sierra Leone's colonial experiment. He would even inspire the Ahab character in Melville's *Moby Dick*.

But Stewart was no fictional character. Abolitionist readers of the *Liberator* had turned to the "Ladies Department" for the past year for Stewart's essays. It had become the most radical page. The ease with which she had entered the hall, as if black women could determine their entrance and exit in a world controlled by white men, had brought her words beyond the page to the public in a way few other black women had dared.

"Is not the God of ancient times the God of these modern days?" Stewart continued. "Did he not raise up Deborah, to be a mother, and a judge in Israel? Did not Queen Ester save the lives of the Jews? And Mary Magdalene first declare the resurrection of Christ from the dead?"

Inspired by fellow Bostonian transplant David Walker, the son of enslaved parents from the Carolinas, Stewart shared the call for immediate abolition—at any costs. Walker's *Appeal*, a pamphlet in the tradition of Paine with its own preamble, had riveted the black community with its harbinger of insurrection; it blasted the rhetorical deceit of Thomas Jefferson, only three years dead; it mocked Jefferson's hypocritical paeans to Roman slaves—as damning the progress of African Americans for centuries, forever "removed beyond the reach of mixture."

Circulated among underground networks, including black sailors who subversively stacked it among the packages of contraband along the seaboard ports, the *Appeal* was "read and re-read until their words were stamped in letters of fire upon our soul," according to one black abolitionist leader in New England.

And while the *Appeal* thrust the *Liberator* into a more radical direction, shaming its white abolitionist editor's privilege of passive resistance, it cast the armed resistance into the hands of men only. Stewart, on the other hand, according to historian Christina Henderson, did not just envision women at the head of the anti-slavery vanguard—she stood there herself.

"Methinks I heard a spiritual interrogation," Stewart countered. "Who shall go forward, and take off the reproach that is cast upon the people of color? Shall it be a woman? And my heart made this reply—If it is thy will, be even so, Lord Jesus."

Deeply Christian, and a deeply Christian moralist, Stewart's lean into black self-improvement had cast aspersions as much as inspiration on her own free community; she shared Walker's disillusion with the "disunited, as the colored people are now," blaming internal conflicts and infighting as obstacles to any liberation. In an attack on the elite black Masons before her, she had called out the obstacles hindering so-cial progress as self-inflicted. Her words could be blunt, sharpening the edges of her detractors, especially among men. "Is it blindness of mind, or stupidity of soul, or the want of education, that has caused our men who are 60 to 70 years of age, never to let their voice be heard, nor their hands be raised in behalf of their color?"

At the same time, she held her white liberal women friends account-able for their low ceiling of aspirations for women of color. Why did their businesses not hire African American girls, beyond calls of domes-tic servitude?

> Let our girls possess what amiable qualities of soul they may; let their characters be fair and spotless as innocence itself; let their natural taste and ingenuity be what they may; it is impossible for scarce an individual of them to rise above the condition of servants.

A decade before nationally known Black nationalist Martin Delany or famous abolitionist Frederick Douglass would command the same stage, Stewart methodically embraced her role as a writer of the re-sistance, publishing essays—not sermons—and performing them in counterspaces that had been reserved for white versions of abolition. "The first Black feminist-abolitionist in America," historian William Andrews has hailed her.

"O woman, woman! upon you I call," Stewart appealed, "for upon your exertions almost depends whether the rising generation shall be anything more than we have or not. "

Still negotiating the limits of "true womanhood" of the period, she extolled women to first "possess the spirit of independence . . . the spirit of men, bold, enterprising, fearless and undaunted." In her footsteps, women had to take the next move as resisters of an unwarranted preju-dice: "Sue for your rights and privileges. Know the reason that you can-not attain them. Weary them with your importunities."

Violence was inevitable, as part of an unrelenting weariness, as if she couldn't share the privilege of nonviolence. Stewart declared she would be "a willing martyr" for the African American cause: "I can but die for expressing my sentiments: and I am as willing to die by the sword as the pestilence."

Not as apocalyptic as Walker, Stewart reframed the resistance against slavery as part of a historical tradition of triumph:

> Look at the suffering Greeks! Their proud souls revolted at the idea of serving a tyrannical nation, who were no better than themselves, and perhaps not so good. They made a mighty effort and arose: their souls were knit together in the holy bonds of love and union: they were united and came off victorious. Look at the French in the late revolution! no traitors amongst them, to expose their plans to the crowned heads of Europe! "Liberty or Death!" was their cry. And the Haytians, though they have not been acknowledged yet as a nation, yet their firmness of character and independence of spirit have been greatly admired, and highly applauded. Look at the Poles, a feeble people! They rose against three hundred thousand mighty men of Russia; and though they did not gain the conquest, yet they obtained name of gallant Poles.

Like Apess and Paine, Stewart succumbed to the pressures of her public persona. After 1833, she never took the stage again; her essays were sparse. She, too, moved to New York City, taking her resistance into schools as a teacher.

The resistance movement against slavery never looked back.

"I AM AMONG THE MILLIONS who have experienced the shock, grief, and fury of losing someone to racial violence," Fania Davis wrote in *Yes! Magazine* in the summer of 2016. A civil rights trial lawyer and executive director of the Restorative Justice for Oakland Youth organization, she addressed the national outcry over the killings of Michael Brown in Ferguson and Eric Garner in New York—part of an epidemic of killings of black men by police. According to a *Guardian* report, "Counted," black males aged 15–34 were "nine times more likely than other Americans to be killed by law enforcement officers" in 2016. "They were also killed at four times the rate of young white men."

"Many note that even if indictments had been handed down, that wouldn't have been enough to stop the carnage," Davis continued. "The problem goes far beyond the actions of any police officer or department. The problem is hundreds of years old, and it is one we must take on as a nation. Truth and reconciliation processes offer the greatest hope."

Davis referred to the restorative experiences of truth and reconciliation commissions in Canada, South Africa, and even Greensboro, North Carolina, which dealt with the murder of anti-racist activists by the Ku Klux Klan in 1979. The Truth and Reconciliation Commission in South Africa, in the aftermath of apartheid, according to Davis, "facilitated encounters between harmed and responsible parties, decided amnesty petitions, and ordered reparations, and it recommended official apologies, memorials, and institutional reform to prevent recurrence."

The process of creating public spaces to openly face a heritage of white supremacy and a legacy of indiscriminate killing of people of color would not come easily. "The whole history of the progress of human liberty shows that all concessions yet made to her august claims have been born of earnest struggle," Frederick Douglass reminded his audience at an anniversary celebration of "West Indie Emancipation" in 1857. "Power concedes nothing without a demand. It never did and it never will."

From Ona Judge to Bree Newsome, the history of resistance has thrust watershed moments out of the darkness of acquiescence and into the public commons as a de facto "truth and reconciliation" commission.

Resistance has not allowed the onlookers to look away, especially in an age of social media; it brings the story to those who have refused to read it. It forces everyone to take part in the discussion of "truth," and the still small possibility of "reconciliation" from their own vantage points—albeit determined by a more honest narrative; Bree Newsome handing the Confederate flag to its complicit overseers.

In this respect, the tradition of civil disobedience, nonviolent and violent, has played a key role in American history. Bringing to the surface the hidden tension that is already alive, as Martin Luther King, Jr., noted, it has sparked an unavoidable national discussion where silence has prevailed. The attention in the media and the chat rooms might focus on the tactics—taking a knee, blocking a road, sitting-in, or refusing to get up. Yet, when the shouting is over, the breaking of "unjust" laws serves as a warrant on history, served to every citizen as an accomplice in the national story, bringing the reality of justice into conversations where it had never existed.

The paradox of this national dialogue, however, is how unreconciled factions often remain in separate corners—frequently employing the same language. The fervent response of the "resistance," ranging from religious leaders to students to civil rights groups and antifa activists, held the line against the historical revision of white supremacy in Charlottesville; and yet, Charlottesville had been one of the epicenters of the "Massive Resistance" movement in the mid-1950s, when segregationist legislators in Virginia cut off state funding for any schools that attempted to integrate. A decade later, Gov. George Wallace in Alabama depicted segregationists as the real inheritors of the American Revolution. In a Fourth of July speech, he framed the Civil Rights Act of 1964 as an "assassin's knife and a blackjack in the hand of the Federal force-cult, where the left-wing liberals will try to force us back into bondage." Wallace, who had famously declared "segregation now, segregation tomorrow, segregation forever," did not even flinch at the cruel twist of his slavery metaphor: civil rights laws were "bondage to a tyranny more brutal than that imposed by the British monarchy which claimed power to rule over the lives of our forefathers under sanction of the Divine Right of kings."

This truth and reconciliation factor of resistance is even more compelling when the laws on the books undercut the morality of their law makers—such as the first Fugitive Slave Act aggressively defended by George Washington. Or when laws on the books have not been justly enforced: a decade before Rosa Parks's historic refusal to move from her seat on a public bus in Montgomery, twenty-six-year-old Irene Morgan had refused to move from her seat in a segregated section on a bus in Virginia, leading to her arrest as an African American. An eventual U.S. Supreme Court decision in 1946, *Morgan v. Virginia*, ruled that segregation on interstate buses was unconstitutional—not that any Southern state followed its decree.

To be sure, legions of nameless resisters had fought segregated car-
riages, streetcars, and boats for decades. In 1865, Sojourner Truth sought
to desegregate horse carts in Washington, DC; in challenging segregated
compartments on a train in Tennessee, after being wrestled from a car
and ejected, Ida B. Wells brought her case for integration to the state
Supreme Court in 1884.

In a similar way, untold stories remain buried in history of those who
challenged the segregated lunch counters and diners a generation or two
before the modern civil rights movement. In 1942, James Farmer led a
sit-in of African American students at the Jack Spratt Coffee House on
Chicago's South Side, after he had been refused service for breakfast.
Their occupation of the diner broke the color barrier, and after a policeman refused to arrest them, the restaurant owner relented and served
coffee. In his classic study *Speak Now Against the Day: The Generation Before the Civil Rights Movement in the South*, author John Egerton chronicled
a political initiative during the desperate economic crisis of 1932 that
brought "hope to a beleaguered populace mired in colonial dependency."
By the time of the historic Montgomery bus boycott, Egerton showed,
this multiracial movement against the entrenched white ruling class had
moved forward on two "hallowed American constitutional principles—
equal justice under the law and the right of citizens to petition their
government for a redress of grievances"—and broken the ground for a
movement toward freedom.

In 1958, in the aftermath of the successful Montgomery bus boycott,
which resulted in the U.S. Supreme Court decision striking down segregation on public transit as unconstitutional, King reclaimed the words
of Unitarian abolitionist Theodore Parker from the 1850s: "Yes, 'the arc
of the moral universe is long, but it bends toward justice.' There is something in the universe which justifies William Cullen Bryant in saying,
'Truth crushed to earth will rise again.'"

The cultivation of that earth and its rising, of course, would come
from the plow of resistance.

A handful of big moments in history tend to dominate our resistance
credo—the extraordinary Montgomery bus boycott launched by long-

time NAACP secretary Rosa Parks in 1955, which set off the civil rights movement and gave a platform to a twenty-six-year-old preacher named Martin Luther King, Jr. Yet, a plodding, tedious and no less inspiring culture of resistance and its nameless participants and organizers has always laid the groundwork for the rise of such "hinge" movements for social change.

"I set up the office of the Southern Christian Leadership Conference in 1958," civil rights organizer Ella Baker told an interviewer years later, referring to King's main organization, "but you didn't see me on television, you didn't see news stories about me." Wary of leader-centered resistance movements, Baker played an extraordinary behind-the-scenes role over decades that gave rise to a new generation of civil rights activists, including the formation of the Student Nonviolent Coordinating Committee in 1960, which served as the shock troops for sit-ins and direct action. "The kind of role that I tried to play was to pick up pieces or put together pieces out of which I hoped organization might come. My theory is, strong people don't need strong leaders."

By definition, these acts of resistance are rarely popular in their own times: upsetting the status quo, offending the public trust, engendering unrest, bringing the crisis to the doorstep of a sheltered nation. They become even more complex and controversial when an element of violence, intended or otherwise, comes into play.

In response to National Football League players in the fall of 2017, who had been kneeling during the national anthem for over a year to raise awareness of police brutality and racial discrimination, Trump characterized the protests as "disgraceful," and called on league owners to outlaw such an act of free expression. A trickle-down effect took place in public schools across the nation, where various districts attempted to forbid or punish similar acts of resistance, despite a 1943 Supreme Court ruling—*West Virginia State Board of Education v. Barnette*—that upheld a student's right to refuse to salute the flag or stand during the Pledge of Allegiance. "If there is any fixed star in our constitutional constellation," Justice Robert H. Jackson wrote, "it is that no official, high or petty, can prescribe what shall be orthodox in politics, nationalism, religion, or other matters of opinion or force citizens to confess by word or act their faith therein."

HISTORY REMINDS US THAT MOST acts of resistance require years to become accepted or even part of the national mythology of freedom; it was not until the 1850s, as fugitive black slaves were apprehended in Boston, that abolitionists recast the depiction of escaped slave Crispus Attucks as the first martyr of the American Revolution, murdered by British soldiers at the Boston Massacre in 1770. Outraged by the abuse of roving British troops among American citizens, dock workers had joined Attucks on a march to confront a contingent of callous soldiers. In front of a government building, soldiers opened fire on the crowd, killing Attucks and four others. Patriot leader and future president John Adams, in fact, had defended the British at their trial for murder, referring to the American resisters as "outlandish," and nothing more than a motley rabble.

Adams's characterization of Attucks, in fact, provides a compelling insight into the enduring white depiction of black males as inherently dangerous—thereby exonerating any official police or military force who shot them down. Adams charged Attucks with being a hero of the "myrmidons," a reference to ancient Greek hordes, whose very presence in the street was "an unlawful assembly." The "very looks" of this "molatto fellow," Adams justified, "was enough to terrify any person, what had not the soldiers then to fear?"

In reaction to the Fugitive Slave Act of 1850, according to historian Mitch Kachun, a groundswell of public acclaim arose after abolitionists used "virtually every form of media available" to revive the legacy of Attucks and African Americans in the Revolutionary struggle. As the first martyr of the American Revolution, Attucks became a household name by the 1870s, according to Kachun, and the namesake for organizations and militias across the country.

One century later, in his book *Why We Can't Wait*, Martin Luther King, Jr., recovered the history of Attucks as part of the continuum of civil rights. "A great-great-grandson of Crispus Attucks," he wrote, "might be ruled out of some restricted, all-white restaurant," notwithstanding the fact of his military uniform, and Attucks's legacy.

Journalist and author Amy Goodman, host of *Democracy Now!*, brought that legacy full circle in 2015, reporting on the failure of the Department of Justice to pursue criminal charges against a policeman in Ferguson, Missouri, for the murder of an unarmed African American teenager, Michael Brown. "It took the indiscriminate murder of a man of color, by armed agents of the state, to launch the revolution. Which brings us to Ferguson, Missouri," she noted. "From Crispus Attucks to Michael Brown 245 years later, two things remain clear: We never know what sparks a revolution. And black lives matter."

IN A VERITABLE SHOWDOWN OF resistance strategies in the abolitionist movement, two men took the stage at the National Convention of Colored Citizens (also referred to as the National Negro Convention) in Buffalo, New York, in 1843—Frederick Douglass and Henry Highland Garnet. They stood on opposite sides of the political spectrum, as well. Both had fled the slave state of Maryland; they were born around the same time , 1815 and 1818. A noted orator, writer, and leader of the abolitionist movement, Douglass cut a commanding figure that did not need any introduction. Garnet, on the other hand, an intense and dynamic preacher, hobbled to the stage with a wooden leg, though he did not lack for skills; a popular speaker at meetings throughout the New York region, Garnet's "thrilling eloquence" had drawn the attention of newspapers.

Garnet and an opposing faction wanted to take the anti-slavery fight to the battleground of Congress and local races, albeit under the banner of the radical Liberty Party. A complex split over the formation of the political party, among other matters, had divided black and white abolitionists alike, including Garnet and Douglass. Influenced by leading abolitionist William Lloyd Garrison, many spurned the American electoral process as a sham: "Nonresistance," Garrison wrote, "is the rejection of political action, disunion, and a proslavery interpretation of the Constitution."

Personal infighting aside, a larger issue remained unresolved between Douglass and Garnet. In 1837, Philadelphia businessman William Whipper had published an important address on "Non-Resistance to Offensive Aggression." A leading reformer, Whipper had willingly invested a lot of his wealth from his lumber and coal companies to assist underground railroad and abolitionist activities. Whipper advocated nonviolence as the only way for African Americans to end slavery. "I am aware that there are those who consider the non-resistance wholly impracticable. The resolution asserts that the practice of non-resistance to physical aggression is consistent with reason." Advising pity for their racist attackers, including mobs who would "beat a single individual probably in his 'teens,' whose heart's law is non-resistance," Whipper argued that black Americans would ultimately triumph with weapons of "reason and moral truth."

More than a decade before Thoreau's famous declaration of nonviolent resistance, Whipper's commitment to nonviolence was groundbreaking—and unacceptable to Garnet.

Taking the stage before Douglass at the convention in Buffalo, Garnet cut a bold figure among the crowd. Enslaved as a young child, he had hidden in a wagon during his parents' daring escape from Maryland. Educated in New York, Garnet had turned to the ministry after studying at a theological institute in Whitesboro, New York.

Addressed to the "slaves of the United States," Garnet's speech silenced the crowd. He described a devastating portrait of bondage for millions of Americans, dating back to the birth of the nation. And yet "with one voice" the Patriots had cried, "Liberty or Death." Garnet reclaimed the armed resistance of the American Revolution as his own. "Among the diversity of opinions that are entertained in regard to physical resistance," he charged, pointing around the hall, "there are but a few found to gainsay that stern declaration. We are among those who do not."

The heckling, including Douglass's own, commenced. Any hint of unity frayed. Not since Walker's *Appeal* had a call for insurrection been so powerfully made; the shadows of Denmark Vesey's and Nat Turner's crushed revolts in the earlier decades remained a presence.

"Brethren, arise, arise!" Garnet exclaimed. "Strike for your lives and liberties. Now is the day and the hour. Let every slave throughout the land do this, and the days of slavery are numbered. You cannot be more oppressed than you have been—you cannot suffer greater cruelties than you have already. Rather die freemen than live to be slaves."

Garnet's parting words riveted the crowd: "Let your motto be resistance."

Aligned with the nonviolence creed of Garrison, Douglass acted quickly in Buffalo to prevent the convention from publishing Garnet's incendiary address. He pushed through a resolution for "moral persuasion." It underscored a rift in the abolitionist movement over the leadership role of blacks—at the behest of powerful white leaders like Garrison. Influential abolitionists, such as Wendell Phillips, considered militants like Garnet to be "one of our most dangerous enemies."

The *Liberator* panned Garnet's speech, without printing it, as "inflammatory, treasonous, poisonous and a flight of fancy."

Their long-standing personal conflicts notwithstanding, Douglass may have distanced himself from Garnet's mercurial career as a preacher, organizer, and diplomat for the next several decades, but their differences over resistance strategies narrowed with the passing of the Fugitive Slave Act of 1850.

YEARS LATER, WHEN FREDERICK DOUGLASS stood at the dock in Rochester, New York, waiting to board the Toronto-bound steamer, two men clamored up the gangway in a hurry. A third man, William Parker, hesitated and then reached into his jacket, removed a pistol, and handed it to an astonished Douglass. Parker called it a "token of gratitude and a memento of the battle for liberty at Christiana."

If Douglass had any reservation about armed resistance to entrenched slavery in the Southern states, it vanished in 1850 with the passing of the Fugitive Slave Act. Rolled out by an equivocating Congress as a "compromise," the new law provided punitive measures for any officials—in free Northern states or the South—who did not actively pursue runaway slaves in their area. Aggrieved slave owners, in addition, simply had to obtain an affidavit from a federal marshal, based on personal testimony of their claim of ownership over an enslaved American, who did not have the right to defend him- or herself in a trial. The Act resulted in the kidnappings of large numbers of free African Americans, especially in the border states.

Writing from London, where he had been on a lecture tour, Garnet conjured the "spirit of his people," proclaiming the law would "never, never, be enforced." Garnet, of course, was a fugitive, as was Douglass, who called the compromise a blatant act to "hunt slaves," rendering it "a slander" on the memory of the country's founders.

That spirit of Garnet's people was already alive and organized in the Christiana settlement in Lancaster County, Pennsylvania, where William Parker, along with his wife, Eliza Ann Howard, had formed a secret black militia to "fight for freedom at a moment's notice." Both Parker and Howard had escaped enslavement; an abandoned son of a white father, Parker had been orphaned when his black mother died. He fled from Maryland at the age of seventeen.

Recognizing that the Fugitive Slave Act effectively overruled any rights in a free state, Parker declared that since the laws for personal protection "are not made for us, we are not bound to obey them."

On September 9, 1851, tipped off that Parker might be harboring four enslaved men he claimed had escaped from his plantation, Edward Gorsuch from Maryland crossed the state line into Pennsylvania. A staunch white supremacist, from one of the oldest families in the state, Gorsuch understood that his endeavor would test the bounds of the Fugitive Slave Act in a free state. Despite attempts to slip into the Quaker stronghold without notice, under the pretense of searching for horse thieves, Gorsuch and his posse fooled no one. Parker's network of informants immediately informed him of Gorsuch's approach. The Maryland slave owner and his son were joined by four other armed men.

Gorsuch's assault on the Parker household did not go as planned. Along with Eliza Ann and her sister, other militia men had joined Parker at his home on the hill. Gorsuch disregarded entreaties by a marshal to present the affidavits and wait out the fugitives trapped inside. After an exchange of threats, Parker and Eliza Ann made it clear they were prepared to fight the "slavocrats." Gorsuch and his men then charged the house, declaring his intent to "get my property." Eliza Ann blew a horn to signal a call for nearby support; her noise drew blasts of rifle shot through her window. In the meantime, scores of neighbors, black and white, converged on the outer reaches of Parker's land. Aware of their outmatched numbers, posse members suddenly started to retreat. Relentless in his pursuit, Gorsuch continued, though he was soon struck by a club, and then a shot. Another posse member fell in a hail of bullets.

Refusing to be arrested, Parker and his men immediately fled the area, hiding in the nearby fields and barns. Over the next days, they journeyed at night across the state line until they reached Douglass's crucial destination on the underground railroad in upstate New York. Eliza stayed behind with their children.

Within hours, however, the media of the day—the telegraph—had tapped out reports that more than eighty armed blacks had killed Gorsuch, a Maryland slave owner, and attacked a U.S. marshal. The headline of armed resistance riveted the nation. As U.S. Marines arrived to occupy the area, the Christiana Resistance (also known as the Riot or Revolt) provoked a national discussion over the Fugitive Slave Act, drawing an expected response of indignation in the Southern states; newspapers called for charges of treason.

Eventually, over thirty men would be tried—and acquitted—of treason charges, in one of the largest proceedings before the Civil War. But these efforts of suppression ultimately backfired and contributed to a shift in moderate Northern views, according to historian Gordon Barker. Newspapers such as the *Albany Journal* pointed out the absurdity of trying Christiana resisters, when treason consisted in "levying war" against the U.S. government "or adhering to their enemies." Boston abolitionist Garrison seized on the trial to show the hypocrisy of the Fugitive Slave Act compromise. "The perilous times, so often predicted, are upon us," he said, warning of the South's designs to "successive encroachments" of its "despotic ways." Famed *New York Tribune* editor Horace Greeley remarkably noted that the "blacks had opposed civil law, it was true," but a "divine law of Nature was on their side."

In an act of "redemptive violence," Parker later wrote from Canada, where he gained asylum and was eventually joined by Eliza and his family, he had won his rights as a freeman by his "own right arm."

"Parker and his noble band of fifteen at Christiana, who defended themselves from the kidnappers with prayers and pistols, are entitled to the honor of making the first successful resistance to the Fugitive Slave Bill," Douglass concurred, also making a comparison to the nation's revolutionary forefathers. "The right of Revolution belongs to every man, to black as well as white, that these men had as perfect a right to fight for their liberty as our revolutionary fathers did for theirs."

His newspaper printed an article in 1854, "Is It Right and Wise To Kill a Kidnapper?" that fully embraced the Christiana Resistance as the vanguard in ending slavery. "Nothing short of resistance on the part of colored men, can wipe it out."

As a residual of an entrenched American way, the Fugitive Slave Act was not repealed by Congress until the summer of 1864—more than a year after Lincoln's Emancipation Proclamation. Yet, the fallout over the Christiana Resistance and subsequent revolts essentially rendered enforcement impossible. Resistance, in all its forms, had insured freedom for enslaved Americans until the Act's final demise.

"If Washington and Attucks opened the Revolution of the past," Boston abolitionist Charles Lenox Remond declared, "Parker, Jackson and Freeman opened the Revolution of the present."

3

Enemy of the People

One of the first rights of a freeman is to speak or to publish his sentiments; if any government founded upon the will of the people passes any ordinance to abridge this right, it is as much a crime as if the people were, in an unconstitutional way, to curtail the government of one of the powers delegated to it. Were the people to do this, would it not be called anarchy? What name shall then be given to an unconstitutional exercise of power over the people? In Turkey the voice of government is the law, and there it is called despotism. Here the voice of government is likewise the law and here it is called liberty.
—Benjamin Franklin Bache, *Aurora*, 1798

LESS THAN TWO WEEKS AFTER the extraordinary election of 2016, Vice President–elect Michael Pence attended a performance of the hip-hop Broadway musical *Hamilton* in New York City. At the end of the curtain call, cast member Brandon Dixon, who performed the role of one-time vice president Aaron Burr, walked to the edge of the stage, withdrew a piece of paper from his pocket and addressed Pence in the audience.

First, though, Dixon had to quiet the restive crowd. "There is nothing to boo here, ladies and gentlemen, we are sharing a story of love," he said. Then Dixon read his statement:

Vice President–elect Pence, we welcome you and we truly thank you
for joining us here at *Hamilton: An American Musical*, we really do. We,
sir, we are the diverse America who are alarmed and anxious that your
new administration will not protect us—our planet, our children, our
parents—or defend us and uphold our inalienable rights, sir. But we truly
hope that this show has inspired you to uphold our American values and
to work on behalf of all of us. All of us. Again, we truly thank you for
sharing this show. This wonderful American story told by a diverse group
of men [and] women of different colors, creeds, and orientations.

In a theater review, hailing the Broadway production for "changing
the language of musicals," the *New York Times* called it "a show about
young rebels grabbing and shaping the future of an unformed country."
The incoming White House administration already felt threatened.

By the next morning, Donald Trump had seized on the incident as
an affront to his victory, and turned to Twitter to get in a final catcall:
"The cast of Hamilton was very rude last night to a very good man, Mike
Pence. Apologize!"

During the 2016 presidential campaign and throughout his first year
in office, Trump had often bristled at any criticism of his comments in
the media. He dismissed it as "fake news." He insulted reporters in public. Whether he was hypersensitive or seeking to deflect any disapproval,
he continued to raise questions about First Amendment rights whenever
he was offended. By definition, Trump misconstrued the First Amendment as an instrument to protect political figures and office holders like
himself; to the contrary, Amendment One in the Constitution prohibits
the making of any law by the government from "infringing on the freedom of the press." Twitter, as always, was his tool of revenge:

It is not "freedom of the press" when newspapers and others are allowed to say and write whatever they want even if it is completely false!

Three weeks into his administration, frustrated by media scrutiny
of the White House and campaign ties to Russian associates, Trump
ramped up the Twitter volume. Within minutes of landing at his Mar-a-

Lago resort in Florida for a weekend reprieve in February, Trump posted a declaration:

> The FAKE NEWS media (failing @nytimes, @CNN, @NBCNews and many more) is not my enemy, it is the enemy of the American People. SICK!

Astonished by the "escalation" in Trump's accusations, the *New York Times* noted Trump's language was vaguely reminiscent of that deployed against "hostile foreign governments or subversive organizations." In effect, the *Times* concluded, "it also echoed the language of autocrats who seek to minimize dissent."

Dating back to the Roman Empire, the "enemy of the people" axiom had been a staple during the "reign of terror" in the French Revolution, and under Nazi Germany and the Stalinist-era regimes in the Soviet Union. "Donald Trump is demonstrating an authoritarian attitude and inclination that shows no understanding of the role of the free press," added famed journalist Carl Bernstein, who had uncovered the Nixon Watergate scandal for the *Washington Post.*

The great battering of constitutional rights continued. The breathless pace of Twitter and social media added to the anxiety over the enduring protections of the Bill of Rights, as if they could be altered or deleted in an instant, in an age of Trump.

Alexander Hamilton, in fact, had warned of political leaders whose "object is to throw things into confusion that he may ride the storm and direct the whirlwind." Fending off charges of being an aristocratic power player himself, Hamilton pointed to the role of intentionally disrupting public order from above: "The truth unquestionably is, that the only path to a subversion of the republican system of the Country is, by flattering the prejudices of the people, and exciting their jealousies and apprehensions, to throw affairs into confusion, and bring on civil commotion."

In an apparent attempt at humor, Trump reposted a video in the summer of 2017 that showed him pummeling a character with a CNN logo superimposed over his face at a "wrestle mania" event. The Committee to Protect Journalists publicly rebuked Trump's action, saying it "creates a chilling effect and fosters an environment where further harassment or even physical attack is deemed acceptable."

"It's very disturbing," Bernstein told CNN, in his renewed role as a media watchdog. "There is nothing lighthearted about it whatsoever— it is an incitement, it is definitive, as I say, of the way this president views a free press and its exercise under the First Amendment to the Constitution." Earlier that summer, in fact, Montana candidate for Congress Greg Gianforte had body-slammed a *Guardian* newspaper reporter during a special election campaign, irritated by his questioning. Sentenced in court to do community service and anger management classes, Gianforte still won his election handily.

With his CNN takedown Twitter post going viral, Trump relished the outraged response from the media, as if competing on the ratings meter of World Wrestling Entertainment. "My use of social media is not Presidential," he tweeted, "it's MODERN DAY PRESIDENTIAL. Make America Great Again!"

Disregarding the political and social ramifications of his tweets, Trump appeared to delight in the reality-TV uncertainty of his actions. Whether they were modern-day presidential or not, they fell short of the precedent for "tranquility at home" established by George Washington in his farewell address: "The alternate domination of one faction over another, sharpened by the spirit of revenge," he warned future leaders, "is itself a frightful despotism."

A report published that July by the Senate Homeland Security and Governmental Affairs Committee reinforced Trump's sense of persecution. To be sure, it concurred with Trump's Twitter rants and concluded his administration had experienced "an unprecedented wave of potentially damaging leaks of information that threaten national security." Attorney General Jeff Sessions immediately let loose the hounds on the media, announcing a review of policies, including a possible use of media subpoenas, which would force journalists to reveal their sources—under the threat of imprisonment. "We respect the important role that the press plays and will give them respect, but it is not unlimited," Sessions said.

Concerned by the Trump administration's crackdown on the press, Oregon Sen. Ron Wyden wrote a letter in the fall of 2017 to the Justice Department, seeking information on the "use of surveillance powers to target journalists and news organizations as part of leak investigations." Wyden sought to verify the Justice Department's use of subpoenas, search warrants, and national security letters to gather information on and from journalists.

Somewhere between threats and retaliatory interrogations lay the Trump administration's communication rules. The dizzying spiral of social media attacks on the press, driven by the extraordinary reach of the president, was compounded by the backdoor investigations of journalists by Justice Department officials. A perfect storm on First Amendment rights brewed on the horizon.

In responding to such media storms, Trump-appointed Supreme Court justice Neil Gorsuch lectured his audience of conservatives on the limitations of First Amendment freedoms in the fall of 2017. Speaking at the Trump International Hotel in Washington, DC, he gave his newly minted judicial opinion: "We have to all adopt certain civil habits that enable others to enjoy them as well. When it comes to the First Amendment, that means tolerate those who don't agree with us or those whose ideas upset us, giving others the benefit of the doubt about their motives."

Gorsuch's appearance at the Trump-leased hotel drew judicial concerns itself. With multiple lawsuits in play, including one by 200 members of Congress in the federal courts, alleging the violation of the Foreign Emoluments Clause in the Constitution—which prohibits the President from receiving gifts or payments from foreign governments without the consent of Congress—critics raised questions of ethics and political partisanship by the justice's speech at the private event under Trump's awning. "Justice Gorsuch should have known better than to sign up as the headliner for an event that will line Donald Trump's pockets in a way that is at best ethically sketchy," Nan Aron, the president of the progressive Alliance for Justice, said in a statement.

The controversy of his speech notwithstanding, Gorsuch's call for civil habits remained far away from the White House doors. A week after the justice's Trump Hotel rendezvous, Trump unleashed a torrent on

Twitter, apparently annoyed by an NBC report that Secretary of State Rex Tillerson had called him a "moron" after a high-level meeting. A day later, in charging NBC News and "the networks" with inventing a story about plans to expand the U.S. nuclear arsenal, he declared "it is frankly disgusting the way the press is able to write whatever they want to write." Instead of investigating possible links between Russian operatives and his campaign officials, Trump called on the Senate Intelligence Committee to investigate "Fake News Networks."

"This is the kind of statement one expects to hear from a despot, not from an American president," Jameel Jaffer, the director of the Knight First Amendment Institute at Columbia University, told CNN. "The free press is a pillar of our democracy, not a threat to it. Calling on the intelligence committee to investigate the press is particularly absurd. That committee was established after the national-security abuses of the 1950s, '60s, and early '70s to help ensure that the government's national security policies don't compromise constitutional freedoms— including the freedom of the press."

As if seeking to brainstorm with his 40 million followers on Twitter, Trump shifted tactics and soon lit up his Twitter account with a legal question over his "fake news" obsession:

> With all of the Fake News coming out of NBC and the Networks, at what point is it appropriate to challenge their License? Bad for country!

In a direct reply through Twitter, FCC commissioner Jessica Rosenworcel gave Trump the short answer: "Not how it works." She included a link to an online FCC handbook on the rules. CNN anchor Jake Tapper held up a copy of the Constitution on his program, calling on the President to "look into it."

The response on the rest of Twitter was not as diplomatic. Michael Copps, a former FCC commissioner, criticized Trump's tweets as an act of intimidation against the press:

> This madcap threat, if pursued, would be blatant and unacceptable intervention in the decisions of an independent agency. The law does

not countenance such interference. President Trump might be happier as emperor, but I think the American people would strip him of his clothes on this issue. Additionally, it's not just NBC stations that will find this threat chilling, but also smaller independent stations around the country who might lack the resources to fight back.

Dissatisfied with the complexities of the rules, Trump abandoned any legal questions and cut straight to his intent; he called for an outright crackdown on television networks:

> Network news has become so partisan, distorted and fake that licenses must be challenged and, if appropriate, revoked. Not fair to public!

Republican Sen. Ben Sasse from Nebraska finally called Trump's bluff—of course, via Twitter:

> Are you recanting of the Oath you took on Jan. 20 to preserve, protect, and defend the 1st Amendment?

Sasse had appealed earlier that year: "Please just stop. This isn't normal and it's beneath the dignity of your office."

Trump rang in the New Year in 2018 with a torrent of Twitter posts on "Fake News" that jettisoned any attempt of White House normalcy, effectively institutionalizing his conflicts with the media in a reality TV format:

> I will be announcing THE MOST DISHONEST & CORRUPT MEDIA AWARDS OF THE YEAR on Monday at 5:00 o'clock. Subjects will cover Dishonesty & Bad Reporting in various categories from the Fake News Media. Stay tuned!

The Committee to Protect Journalists, an independent nonprofit that promotes press freedom worldwide, pre-empted Trump's award showcase with its own "Press Oppressor Awards" on January 8, 2018. Trump earned the top prize: "Overall Achievement in Undermining

Global Press Freedom." The United States, with its First Amendment protection for a free press, according to the group, "has long stood as a beacon for independent media around the world." Trump, by contrast, "has consistently undermined domestic news outlets and declined to publicly raise freedom of the press with repressive leaders."

The imbroglio over President Trump's unabashed attack on the media, however, was a reminder that our nation's struggle with the paradoxical role of a free press had changed little over the past two centuries. People had been "looking into" the First Amendment since George Mason's inclusion of the "freedom of the press as the greatest bulwark of liberty" in the Virginia Declaration of Rights in 1776.

Far more disconcerting was the default response by news media organizations that lent credence to Trump's casting of doubt over the profession itself. Only days after Trump's October Twitter surprises, the *New York Times* issued new rules for their journalists on Twitter etiquette, undercutting a fundamental premise in journalism—that journalists themselves can uphold the distinction between news reporting and editorial opinion.

When *Chattanooga Times* publisher Adolph Ochs took over the *Times* in 1896 and reset its course in journalism history, his commitment "to give the news impartially, without fear or favor, regardless of party, sect, or interests involved," did not also require his journalists to take a loyalty test. In one of the worst periods of yellow journalism, Ochs did not challenge the merits of a partisan press, but upheld the fundamental belief in the role of journalists as truth tellers.

A half century later, "the future of race relations," as former *New York Times* managing editor Gene Roberts and *Atlanta Journal-Constitution* editor Hank Klibanoff chronicled in *The Race Beat*, "rested largely in the hands of the American press." Their insider's account traced the role of the media in covering the civil rights movements. Frontline reporters at the time, the authors noted how "the black press was at the center of a developing Negro protest in the United States," and "the mainstream press—the white press—would have to discover racial discrimination and write about it so candidly and so repeatedly that white Americans outside the South could no longer look the other way. Then they would see segregation, white supremacy and black disfranchisement as being at odds with the American conscience ... and demand change."

As a rebuke to undefined "personal opinions," the *Times* guidelines in 2017 trod a dangerous line of self-censorship under the guise of internal review: "In social media posts, our journalists must not express partisan opinions, promote political views, endorse candidates, make offensive comments or do anything else that undercuts *The Times*'s journalistic reputation."

The *Times* was hardly alone. ESPN kicked off this aberrant policy when it suspended *SportsCenter* host Jemele Hill for her personal tweets on the National Football League protests. Hill had also drawn the wrath of the White House for labeling Trump a white supremacist in one of her tweets.

These self-imposed gag rules did not generate better journalism, but bent the Constitution one step closer toward the darkest period in American history—the passing of the Sedition Act of 1798. In fact, Trump's rattling of the media on Twitter recalled another Hamilton spectacle; though, this time, journalists played the protagonists and fought back against attacks on the free press.

While the infamous "Reynolds Pamphlet" in 1797 on Hamilton's disclosure of his affair with the married Maria Reynolds took center stage at one point in the Broadway musical, the assault on the free press and the First Amendment as part of its score might be the most chilling cautionary tale for our times.

As President George Washington's de facto prime minister, Hamilton's official role as Secretary of the Treasury carried broad powers; in 1798, he was appointed major general of the U.S. Army, as wartime threats emerged with Britain and France. With two political factions increasingly dividing the new nation, Hamilton played a key role with the Federalists, who preferred a strong national government and largely sided with Britain over its French rivals. The Democratic Republicans, led by Jefferson, stood on the opposite side of the stage.

Despite Hamilton's earlier sentiments that the United States should elect a president and senate for lifelong terms, his later concerns about the "dangerous ambition" of leaders that lurked behind the "mask of zeal for the rights of the people" carry a message for our own times. Writing in his *Federalist Papers*, Hamilton reminded Americans of the vagaries of history and its pretenders to the throne: "Of those men who have overturned the liberties of republics, the greatest number have begun their career by paying an obsequious court to the people; commencing demagogues, and ending tyrants."

Paine had warned of the same threat in *Common Sense* in 1776—the rise of a demagogic tyrant, exploiting the fears and "popular disquietudes," collecting the "desperate and discontented," who played by his own rules and disregarded the liberties guaranteed by a constitution.

Onto that stage came John Adams, who succeeded Washington as president in 1796. He once wrote about preferring the title of "His Highness, the President of the United States and Protector of the Rights of the Same."

As admirers of the British system of government, Adams and Hamilton both accepted a division in society between the "few and the many." An aristocracy was unavoidable; the United States would be ruled by the rich, the wellborn, and the able. Writing Jefferson in 1787, Adams proposed to showcase the all-embracing role of the elite with a sort of American version of the House of Lords, a senate for life. "You are afraid of the one—I of the few," he claimed, as if such a plan would limit any grab at power. "You are Apprehensive of Monarchy; I, of Aristocracy."

What neither Adams nor Hamilton could tolerate was dissent—especially from the many. Adams was a thin-skinned president, reminiscent of present-day office holders. He chafed at the giggles over his moniker "His Rotundity," and railed against what he considered deceptive and false characterizations of his administration by certain journalists. Like Trump's ranks of "fake news" purveyors, Adams singled out three contentious newspapers, including the *Argus* in New York City, that he planned to take down; Abigail Adams, his wife and confidante, directed her invective at the printing press of Benjamin Franklin Bache, who possessed "the malice and falsehood of Satan."

The grandson of the famed inventor and founding father, and muckraking editor of the Philadelphia *Aurora* newspaper, "Benny" Bache didn't cower under Adams's monarchical haughtiness. His grandfather, as an early American printer, had instilled more than printer's ink in the family tradition: "If all printers were determined not to print anything till they were sure it would offend nobody, there would be very little printed," Franklin had written in his "Apology for Printers" in 1731—a generation before the American Revolution. As a child, Bache had attended some of his grandfather's diplomatic tours in Paris and Geneva. Educated in Europe and at the University of Pennsylvania, he founded his newspaper at the age of twenty-one. Within a few years, he had already been banned from covering the proceedings of the House of Representatives on the floor with the rest of the journalists after his reports exposed some salty language from a brawl. "The right of the people of the United States to listen to the sentiments of their representatives," he declared in vain, "was acknowledged by the first agents whom they appointed to express their voice in that assembly."

Bache's role as one of the first journalists to hold the line on the freedom of the press has largely been forgotten in history—or dismissed. In his study of the early years of the American republic, historian Gordon Wood claims "no editor did more to politicize the press in the 1790s." Yet, thanks to a defiant and courageous resistance campaign led by journalists like Bache, an opposition movement was galvanized to challenge one of the most egregious infringements of constitutional rights—the infamous Sedition Act of 1798—and to hold the president accountable for a dubious collusion between American and foreign interests in U.S. elections, and an ominous overreach of federal powers.

The media did not just play a role in the resistance—they led it.

Beyond any cautionary tale, they wrote the operating instructions for writers, reporters, and chroniclers of this extraordinary moment of crisis in our nation to resist tyrannical grabs at power.

Politics were bitterly divided in 1798, too. In fact, the issue of "leaks" to the press aggravated the White House two centuries ago as much as it does today. Federalist Noah Webster, whose hallowed dictionary we all cherish now, employed a few choice words against the Democratic Republicans and journalists in opposition to his side of the aisle: "The refuse, the sweepings of the most depraved part of mankind from the most corrupt nations on earth."

As early as 1792, the *Federal Gazette* attacked oppositional newspapers "who willfully or ignorantly misrepresent the design of a law" and those who "are busily at work to kindle sedition." It launched a "newspaper war" against Democratic Republican newspapers such as the *Aurora* that went beyond the page; street fights, shattered windows, and an unremitting exchange of personal attacks ensued.

A line in the sand had been drawn over the Jay Treaty in 1795, a questionable pro-British trade and settlement agreement that had been engineered by Hamilton and hammered out by Justice John Jay, which exacerbated the Federalist-Republican divide. While the treaty negotiated the final withdrawal of British troops from the continent, it provided most-favored-nation status to Britain, and openly shifted the American alliance away from the French. "Jay was burned in effigy, guillotined in effigy, hanged in effigy, from Maine to Georgia," wrote nineteenth-century British historians George Walter Prothero and Ernest Alfred Benians. "The press teemed with pamphlets, coarse, spiteful, and serious; and for months the chief newspapers gave up whole columns of each issue to attacking or defending the work of Jay. The democratic societies, the people at public meetings, the State legislatures, denounced or praised the treaty."

As a French partisan, Bache declared "America realigned with a despotic rather than a republican state," and charged the treaty with serving the financial interests of a handful of wealthy merchants.

The pushback on the Jay Treaty, however, concerned Bache. An editorial in the *Aurora* spelled out the increasingly conflictual relationship between freedom of the press and the winnowing of democracy in the form of an aristocratic takeover of government:

Profession costs nothing and it will be remembered that the present administration has been an administration of profession only; the profession of republicanism, but the practice of monarchy and aristocracy; ... the profession of affection for the Constitution, but an enmity to it so great as to have rendered it a mere nose of wax; the profession

of an interest in the people's rights, but a refusal to let the people be
made acquainted with the transactions of a government emanating
from themselves, in a word, the profession of honor, justice, candor,
dignity and good faith, when dishonor, injustice, treachery, meanness
and perfidy have given hue to our public proceedings.

To compound Bache's muckraking dangers, he had published Paine's
incendiary attacks on George Washington, not long after the author of
Common Sense had been released from prison in Paris. Paine had been
tried and convicted in absentia for sedition in England for the publication of *Rights of Man*, whose concepts of the natural rights of all citizens
became one of the most-read works of all times.

In light of the French Revolution, Paine's call for reforms in England,
and the elimination of aristocratic titles, sent a shock wave through
the British government; Paine also resented what he perceived as Jay's
floundering concessions to the British. Convinced that Washington had
turned his back on Paine's desperate situation during the French Revolution's descent into the "reign of terror," which had nearly delivered
Paine to the guillotine and had left him seriously ill, the deeply troubled
patriot unleashed his rage and resentment onto the Republican pages
against the one symbol of national unity:

> The part I acted in the American revolution is well known; I shall not
> here repeat it. I know also that had it not been for the aid received
> from France in men, money and ships, that your cold and unmilitary
> conduct (as I shall shew in the course of this letter) would, in all prob-
> ability, have lost America; at least she would not have been the inde-
> pendent nation she now is. You slept away your time in the field till
> the finances of the country were completely exhausted, and you have
> but little share in the glory of the final event. It is time to speak the
> undisguised language of historical truth . . .
>
> If the inconsistent conduct of Morris exposed the interest of
> America to some hazard in France, the pusillanimous conduct of
> Mr. Jay in England has rendered the character of the American gov-
> ernment contemptible in Europe. Is it possible that any man who has

contributed to the independence of America, and to free her from the tyranny and injustice of the British government, can read, without shame and indignation, the note of Jay to Grenville. It is a satire upon the declaration of Independence, and an encouragement to the British government to treat America with contempt . . . the world will be puzzled to decide, whether you are an apostate or an impostor; whether you have abandoned good principles, or whether you ever had any.

Far from being completely partisan in the beginning, the *Aurora* had actually saluted President Adams's bitter victory over Jefferson, and welcomed his administration into office. The newspaper hailed its mission to "dispel the shades of ignorance, and gloom of error and thus tend to strengthen the fair fabric of freedom on its surest foundation, publicity and information." The honeymoon between the *Aurora* and Adams did not last long.

Abigail Adams was one of the first to size up the "scurrilous rants" of the administration's nemesis in the press. In her letters, she reminded friends that Bache had described her husband as an "old, querulous, Bald, blind, crippled, Toothless Adams." His *Aurora* newspaper also chastised Adams for turning a blind eye to Hamilton's infamous case of adultery, printing the allegations uncovered by muckraker James Thomson Callender.

The *Aurora* went on the attack. After publishing a leaked letter from the French foreign minister that demonstrated his nation had no war intentions against the United States, as pro-England Adams had suggested, Bache was arrested for sedition—before the Sedition Act had even been passed. His real crime was the embarrassment of Adams's bungling of diplomatic relations with France. Bache feared the ramifications of Adams's "war speech" to Congress in the early summer of 1798, in which the President had ramped up the American military arsenal for an apparent conflict with France. When the initial charges against Bache were dropped, a Federalist-appointed judge quickly issued another arrest warrant for the *Aurora* editor, who was hauled to the Philadelphia jail. He was charged with "tending to excite sedition, and opposition to the laws, by sundry publications."

Using the pretense of a threatened nation, invoking unholy French alliances among the American press and supposed spies, Congress passed the Sedition Act of 1798 with the intention of clamping down on the emerging free press hailed by Bache. "To write, print, utter or publish, or cause it to be done, or assist in it, any false, scandalous, and malicious writing against the government of the United States, or either House of Congress, or the President"—this was now a crime, warranting imprisonment for journalists and all others. Adams did not stop with the press: Congress passed an Alien Friends Act to grant the President the powers to deport anyone he deemed dangerous.

In another era, Trump's "enemy of the people," in other words, were not simply dismissed on Twitter—but jailed, in a harrowing reminder of political power gone awry.

According to Jefferson, the law had been designed specifically to suppress oppositional media—he noted "Bache's has been particularly named." Now in power, Adams seemingly abandoned the notion of a free press he had so ardently supported in the past; in 1780, Adams had called it "essential to the security of freedom in a state" in his authorship of the Constitution in Massachusetts.

Even as he suffered from yellow fever, awaiting trial, Bache openly mocked this denial of freedom of the press. He fended off attacks by mobs fueled by military parades; his home and office were repeatedly vandalized. Undeterred, Bache published the Sedition Act side-by-side with the Bill of Rights on the front page of his newspaper. The headline ran: "The Gag Rule." The opposite side ran the key words: "Congress shall make no law abridging the freedom of speech or of the press."

In the spirit of Paine, whose work he had published in his newspaper, Bache printed his own pamphlet on the Sedition Act debacle, with the irresistible title: "Truth will out!: the foul charges of the Tories against the editor of the Aurora, repelled by positive proof and plain truth, and his base calumniators put to shame."

A feisty member of Congress from Vermont, Matthew Lyon, became the first person jailed under the Act. An Irish immigrant, Lyon had already been involved in a notorious brawl on the floor of Congress. His disdain for the machinations of the aristocrats in power, especially over the levy of a direct tax on lands and properties—and slaves—to underwrite the first national "standing" army since the Revolution, had placed him in the corner of Congress as a dangerous official.

Resistance, in fact, to Adams's and Hamilton's Direct Tax had spread throughout the backcountry. In parts of rural Pennsylvania, for example, Revolutionary War veterans like John Fries had launched a "constitutional resistance," refusing to pay the tax, attacking tax collectors, and liberating fellow travelers who had been jailed. Invoking a continuum of resistance from the American Revolution, according to historian Paul Douglas Newman, "they spliced the Stamp Act and Direct Tax together as parts of a single program and protested against them in a manner similar to their protests against the British Stamp Act."

The organized resistance terrified Federalists like Adams and Hamilton, who feared the country teetered on the edge of a new insurrection. For the resisters, Newman noted in his study of "Fries's Rebellion," their actions broadened the idea of liberty, property, and participation in the democratic process; resistance served as a counterspace to the notion of an "ordered liberty." Fries, in fact, reasoned that they should not be punished, since they were simply protesting "unconstitutional" acts by the government. In the end, his conviction for treason would be pardoned by Adams.

Lyon's eventual crime was more pathetic—he published a letter in his newspaper that Adams displayed "a continual grasp for power [and] unbounded thirst for ridiculous pomp, foolish adulation and selfish avarice."

As the "first citizen who suffered in resisting tyranny," according to the *Aurora*, Lyon amazingly campaigned and then won reelection from his jail cell in Vermont during the election in the fall of 1798. In a landslide. His journal, *The Scourge of Aristocracy*, hailed his civil disobedience a success.

In a letter to a fellow Republican in Congress, Jefferson quietly cast Lyon's judges as "objects of national fear." The vice president, who would later hail the period as the "reign of witches," admitted his own alarm at the witch hunt. "I know not which mortifies me most," he wrote, "that I should fear to write what I think, or my country bear such a state of things."

Several newspapers pursued a similar track of resistance, despite the fact that a dozen or so editors were imprisoned or violently attacked in the streets, their newspapers run out of business, or their careers derailed. Ann Greenleaf, the editor of the New York *Argus*, suffering from yellow fever herself, defiantly reprinted articles against Adams, and was then hauled into court for writing that the "federal Government was corrupt and inimical to the preservation of liberty." After exposing Hamilton's secret plan to put together a group of investors to buy the unrepentant *Aurora* and shut it down, Greenleaf was charged with sedition and forced to sell her newspaper. Hamilton appealed to Adams's Secretary of State Timothy Pickering to do the dirty work, claiming Greenleaf's efforts were "audacious calumnies against the government."

Released from jail, Bache wouldn't back down. He disregarded the mobs that attacked his newspaper office repeatedly with rocks. "Like the British monarch, John Adams now has the Alien and Sedition Acts to silence his critics," he wrote to his readers. He defended the First Amendment in defiance. Legions of other newspapers and critics defied Adams and the Federalists.

Unfortunately, Bache would never have his day in court; he died a few months later from the scourge of yellow fever. The scourge of the Sedition Act witch hunts would continue against select journalists for another year, though not without consequence. Before his death, Bache had challenged other editors: Is there "any alternative between an abandonment of the constitution and resistance?"

Meanwhile, according to historian Douglas Bradburn, organized resistance to the Alien and Sedition Acts ensued simultaneously in Kentucky and Virginia. "The Lexington Kentucky *Gazette* summoned organized resistance before the laws were actually passed by calling on the Fourth of July for meetings, committees of correspondence, and general mobilization to oppose Federalist policy and the rush to war." The Federalist newspapers dismissed the efforts in Kentucky and Virginia as the ravings of "savages," a notch below the "wild Irish" among the Democratic Republicans in Philadelphia.

Galvanized by Jefferson and James Madison, the Kentucky and Virginia Resolutions were drawn up to challenge the constitutionality of the Alien and Sedition Acts as an infringement on state's rights; numerous petitions from towns and counties followed. The resolutions accused the Federalists of governing by a "rod of iron": "Let him say what the government is, if it be not a tyranny, which the men of our choice have conferred on our President," the eighth resolution noted, "that the men of our choice have more respected the bare suspicion of the President, than the solid right of innocence, the claims of justification, the sacred force of truth, and the forms and substance of law and justice."

The newspapers played a critical role, according to Bradburn, in turning "a diverse opposition into a coherent movement by tying the petitions and remonstrances to their circulation of the Virginia and Kentucky Resolutions."

Hamilton, of course, was outraged. In a letter to one of his fellow generals, Hamilton warned that the resolutions coming out of Virginia and Kentucky were in "direct resistance to certain laws of the Union" and should be considered as an attempt to "change the government." Hamilton charged "renegade aliens" with leading the "most incendiary press" to foster resentment for the Adams administration. Hamilton was specifically referring to the new editor of the *Aurora*, William Duane.

Born in the American colonies, prior to the American Revolution, and then raised in Ireland, Duane straddled the razor's edge as an alien enemy who had also been deported from colonial India for his newspaper reports against the British. Taking over the publishing reins from Bache's wife, whom he would eventually marry, Duane led *Aurora* on a systematic campaign to defy the Adams administration, and effectively bait them into more prosecutions—even violence—as a way of bringing down the unjust Act. The administration's first charges against Duane, in fact, were conjured from a "riot" he had supposedly incited in attempting to "obtain signatures to the petition against the Alien Act, with the intent to subvert the American government."

Quickly acquitted of the bogus charges, Duane launched an investigation into undue influence by a foreign country—England—in the American elections, claiming the Brits had funneled as much as $800,000 in secret payments. "These are facts," Duane declared, "which no perfidious artifices can evade, nor impudence deny. They are such facts as the American people must remember and act accordingly, or suffer their liberties to perish, and their posterity to be enslaved."

Even George Washington cringed at the accusations and gave his support for treason charges. As with the Fries Rebellion, Washington disapproved of any unrest that would "destroy all confidence" people had in their government, regardless of state corruption. Resistance, in Washington's mind, was no longer acceptable.

A Federalist-baited mob nearly murdered Duane when it dragged him into the streets and took turns brutally beating him in a circle. Crawling back into his printing office, Duane resolutely filed a story in the next day's issue of the *Aurora*, chronicling the entire incident. Questioning his American-born status, many Federalists called on Adams to simply deport the wild Irish nuisance.

As his attorney successfully delayed his trial over sedition charges, Duane continued his indefatigable reporting on the British influence in American affairs. His actions horrified the Federalists. As the election of 1800 drew closer, officials under Adams withdrew the prosecution to take the wind out of Duane's increasingly strong sails of dissent. He also attacked Adams for appointing family members and in-laws to government positions.

As fearless as Bache, Duane recognized each prosecution and trial of a newspaper editor disgraced the administration in front of the public. This included members of Congress, whose silence in the face of the treacherous act had become noticeable: "If they have a sense of honor left," Duane wrote, "their silence ... can only disgrace themselves."

Hauled before a Senate committee on charges of sedition, after he had published a leaked draft of a Federalist-backed bill to alter the electoral vote rules, Duane almost seemed to be seeking martyrdom. "No terror, no force, no menace, no fear," Duane countered, would shake him from "all freedom that the Constitutions secures to the press." In a cat and mouse game, Duane returned to his office and evaded arrest, as he awaited the countdown of the election.

By the election of 1800, according to Jefferson, the newspapers remained the "standard bearer for the political opposition." He framed the election as whether "republicanism or aristocracy would prevail."

Igniting a backlash against Adams and the Federalists, the resistance movement in Virginia and Kentucky against the repressive acts led to a near stalemate in the presidential election in 1800: Jefferson and Aaron Burr tied in electoral votes, Adams a distant third. Historian Jill Lepore referred to it as "possibly the least democratic election in American history." Summoning a special session of Congress, Jefferson managed to sway enough votes to become President.

"The changes in administration, which in every government and in every age have most generally been epochs of confusion, villainy and bloodshed," exclaimed Margaret Bayard Smith, the wife of a Republican newspaper editor, "in this our happy country take place without any species of distraction, or disorder."

Years later, Jefferson praised Duane and the *Aurora* for "rallying" the "whole Union," and providing "comfort in gloomiest days."

The Alien and Sedition Acts expired three days before Jefferson's inauguration. All those under prosecution, such as Duane, were pardoned. "The history of the monarchical forms of government have taught us," Duane wrote triumphantly in the *Aurora*, "never to trust power to any man" and to "preserve inviolate the freedom of the press."

THE CRACKDOWN ON FREE SPEECH commenced at the Trump inauguration on January 20, 2017. On the day before millions took the streets across the nation for the Women's March, a dragnet against antifascist protesters allied with the group DisruptJ20 resulted in the arrest of over 200 protesters, including a handful of journalists, charging them with felony rioting. Clashes with police took place in downtown Washington, DC; vandalism and property damage had occurred. The contentious actions of a small "black bloc" contingent, a loose association of black-clad self-proclaimed anarchists modeled on European counterparts, led to broader implications for the massive turnout of protesters in the following days.

In filing a federal lawsuit against excessive police force, including indiscriminate mass arrests of those not associated with the black bloc, ACLU lawyer Scott Michelman told *The New Yorker* of his concerns about the policing trend to force "a bunch of people into a mass detention whether or not they had any involvement in unlawful activities." The lawsuit sought to call out "guilt by association policing" and threats to First Amendment rights.

"When this sort of thing happens on Inauguration Day, it raises a special level of concern," Michelman said. "People in the future will start thinking, 'Well, do I want to go to this demonstration, or is there a chance somebody's going to break a window and I'm going to end up getting charged with multiple felonies that could put me away for more than ten years?'"

Three months later, as some charges were dismissed, the U.S. Attorney's Office expanded the others, issuing a superseding single indictment for 217 people with identical crimes, including felony rioting and attacks on police officers. Indicted on eight charges, including two violations of the Riot Act, journalist Aaron Cantú faced a possible sentence of decades in prison. A correspondent for the *Santa Fe Reporter*, and past contributor to *The Intercept, Al Jazeera, The Baffler*, and other publications, Cantú had been indicted after being corralled in a police crowd-control technique called the "kettle" and singled out for wearing black.

The politically motivated charges did not surprise the protesters. "It was a part of this riot," read the superseding indictment, that individuals participating in the black bloc, "cheered and celebrated the violence and destruction by participants in the Black Bloc," and also chanted anticapitalism slogans, as well as "Whose streets? Our streets."

On December 20, 2017, in the first trial of six of the defendants, including photojournalist Alexei Wood, a jury acquitted the protesters of all charges. "Today's verdict reaffirms two central constitutional principles of our democracy: first, that dissent is not a crime and second, that our justice system does not permit guilt by association," ACLU's Michelman said in a statement.

As a pamphleteer and preacher, Herman Husband had been charged with rioting in similar circumstances in the 1790s, when he helped to inspire rural communities in Pennsylvania to defy Hamilton's tax on whiskey to cover the national debt. Husband declared that such a tax placed an unfair burden on local farmers, many of whom relied on the spirits economy, and favored the wealthy elite in the eastern cities. A defiant leader of the North Carolina resistance movement prior to the American Revolution, Husband had written a pamphlet in 1769—"Shew Yourselves to be Freemen"—that underscored the "Regulators" movement against Tory colonial tax collectors considered corrupt. The Regulators' name came from efforts to "regulate" government policy in a more just and less arbitrary fashion.

Twenty-five years later, Husband became a focal point of a new regulator movement. When resistance turned violent against whiskey tax collectors in Pennsylvania in 1794, President Washington and Hamilton raised an army of nearly 13,000 soldiers. For years, according to historian Kurt Lash, Hamilton had pressed Washington to "take more aggressive action" and prosecute "delinquents and offenders" among dissenters in the region. The crackdown on dissent, Madison countered, would be the "greatest error" of Washington's political life. "In a republic, light will prevail over darkness, truth over error."

Washington led the troops into action himself, though the whiskey rebels dispersed long before any drum and fife corps came into sight. Washington's unruly soldiers, in fact, earned the reputation as the "Watermelon Army" for their looting of local farms. Husband, meanwhile, was tried for sedition, though eventually released. "In every revolution, the people at large are called on to assist and promised true liberty," he wrote, "but when the foreign oppressor is thrown off . . . then our own learned and designing men immediately aim to take their places."

While the whiskey tax would be repealed by Jefferson in 1801, the legacy of the American military being employed against domestic insurrections remained a cautionary tale.

Six months after the Trump inauguration in 2017, the Department of Justice still clung to the inaugural protests as a litmus test on the limits of freedom of speech and assembly. On July 17, the Justice Department issued a search warrant to a website-hosting company, DreamHost, demanding all available information related to the DisruptJ20 website used to organized the protests. The warrant was ambitious; it sought the IP addresses of 1.3 million visitors to the site, regardless of their connection to the indictment or protests.

"This specific case and this specific warrant are pure prosecutorial overreach by a highly politicized department of justice under [Attorney General Jeff] Sessions," said Chris Ghazarian, general counsel for DreamHost. "You should be concerned that anyone should be targeted simply for visiting a website."

Earlier in the spring, Twitter countered with its own lawsuit against the Trump administration, after it had been ordered by the Customs and Border Protection agency to disclose the contact information and IP addresses associated with the rogue Twitter accounts by government employees, such as @ALT_USCIS. Twitter argued such a precedent would have "a grave chilling effect on the speech of that account in particular and the many other 'alternative agency' accounts that have been created to voice dissent to government policies."

In the fall of 2017, *Foreign Policy* magazine published a leaked FBI file on ramped-up surveillance of wildly mislabeled "Black Identity Extremist (BIE)" movements. According to the internal memo, the FBI "assesses it is very likely some BIEs are influenced by a mix of anti-authoritarian, Moorish sovereign citizen ideology, and BIE ideology." The strange "Moorish" connotation carried its own blinkered categorization of dissent.

"Black identity extremism is the FBI's latest tactic to criminalize black activists and justify increased police presence in black communities," said social-justice educator and Black Lives Matter leader Janaya Khan in a recorded video response, reported on *The Root* website. "Right-wing extremism leads to far more police deaths than what the report cites."

The Trump clampdown on free speech had a ripple effect throughout the country—beyond federal policies. Analyzing the legislative agenda in twenty states, the ACLU found more than thirty anti-protest bills had been introduced in state legislatures in "an unprecedented level of hostility towards protesters in the 21st century."

According to the ACLU study, "many of these bills attack the right to speak out precisely where the Supreme Court has historically held it to be the most robust: in public parks, streets, and sidewalks."

———

RESISTANCE AS THE LAST BARRICADE to protect freedom of speech is not a metaphor, but a frontline reality of courageous Americans who have placed themselves between the First Amendment and a nation often cowed by fear, political persecution, and incarceration. In 1783, George Washington "dropped the curtain," in his words, to his military officers, who begrudged the anonymous attacks on his actions. "The freedom of Speech may be taken away," Washington forewarned, "and, dumb & silent we may be led, like sheep, to the Slaughter." This has always been true in wartime periods with unpopular presidents.

For more than two centuries, authoritarian power has solidified its tyrannizing ways in the form of emergency Sedition Acts or Espionage Acts or Riot Acts, revoking freedom of speech as a wartime precaution—until confronted by acts of resistance. Lest we forget: the forced removal of the Cherokee from their ancestral lands in Georgia and neighboring areas was preceded by the removal of the defiant and bilingual *Cherokee Phoenix* printing press in 1835, when the Georgia Guard broke into the newspaper offices in north Georgia, confiscated the press and type, and literally shut down dissent.

In 1916, Portland physician Marie Equi outmaneuvered the clutches of police and war-frenzied mobs when she put on lineman spurs and scaled a telephone pole—a twentieth-century replica of the liberty pole—and unfurled an anti-war banner, DOWN WITH THE IMPERIALIST WAR. The persecution of seemingly "other" voices, such as Equi's, an outspoken proponent of labor laws, birth control, and pacifism, reflects an anti-American strain in our historical experience—not the norm. The very definition of a witch hunt is often misleading, too; there are no witches, but there are resisters to a status quo bewitched by its own powers, yet unable to enforce an unpopular cause.

Like the seditious editors a century before her, and the anti-Trump protesters a century after her, Equi was no stranger to trumped up charges of felony rioting.

Declaring the American push into World War I as "nothing but capital against labor, a rich man's war," Equi was physically assaulted for driving her car alongside a Portland "War Preparedness" parade in 1916, defiantly unveiling an American flag framed by the banners, PREPARE TO DIE, WORKINGMAN—JP MORGAN & CO. WANT PREPAREDNESS FOR PROFIT—THOU SHALL NOT KILL. She had already been arrested for disseminating birth control publications and assisting abortions; as a well-known speaker, she drew the police at rallies in support of radical union strikes by the Industrial Workers of the World (IWW).

It was Equi's personal life that compounded the vicious attacks by federal agents and the attorney general's office. One report in 1918 referred to the openly lesbian doctor and her community of women as "perverts and degenerates." According to historian and biographer Michael Helquist, Equi seemed to "stir an inordinate amount of loathing and fear."

The American entry into World War I was not as popular as those "preparedness" marches would suggest. In his book on the war, *To Raise an Army*, John Whiteclay Chambers II studied the lack of popularity of the military draft, estimating that between 2.4 and 3.6 million men resisted service. This was particularly true in the South, according to historian Jeanette Keith, who concluded "the majority of southern draft resisters opposed conscription, not because the draft was federal, but because it forced them to support a cause they considered irrelevant at best, dubious at worst."

With radical labor groups leading widespread public opposition against the war, President Woodrow Wilson rammed through the Espionage Act of 1917 and the Sedition Act of 1918 largely to contain the growing dissent to an unpopular war. The Sedition Act, in fact, was passed in the last year of the war. Its language even borrowed from the historical debacle of Adams's Sedition Act of 1798: No American was allowed to "utter, print, write, or publish any disloyal, profane, scurrilous, or abusive language about the form of government of the United States, or the Constitution of the United States, or the military or naval forces of the United States."

In the hands of Attorney General A. Mitchell Palmer, the Acts were exploited to crack down on immigrants and political activists beyond the realm of any threat by wartime activists. Targeting labor organizations, Socialist Party members, and pacifists, the government rounded up, arrested, and imprisoned more than 2,000 Americans. In perhaps the most famous case, Socialist Party leader Eugene Debs, who had once served in the Indiana state legislature, was convicted on ten charges of sedition for speaking against the military draft. Unvanquished, Debs welcomed his prison sentence as a testimony to coming changes in American government. He spoke to the courtroom of his conviction of resistance:

> Your honor, I ask no mercy, I plead for no immunity. I realize that finally the right must prevail. I never more fully comprehended than now the great struggle between the powers of greed on the one hand and upon the other the rising hosts of freedom. I can see the dawn of a better day of humanity. The people are awakening. In due course of time they will come into their own.

As a prisoner, Debs won nearly a million votes as a Socialist Party candidate for president in the 1920 election. The ballot box became the portal of resistance, beyond the prison gates—much like the support of the imprisoned Matthew Lyon in 1798.

The Supreme Court, in fact, had ruled against the First Amendment rights of anti-draft advocates in the 1919 case *Schenck v. United States*. In issuing the majority opinion, Justice Oliver Wendell Holmes, Jr., introduced the enduring legal standard of "clear and present danger" when a nation is at war:

> The question in every case is whether the words used are used in such circumstances and are of such a nature as to create a clear and present danger that they will bring about the substantive evils that the United States Congress has a right to prevent. It is a question of proximity and degree. When a nation is at war, many things that might be said in time of peace are such a hindrance to its effort that their utterance will not be endured so long as men fight, and that no Court could regard them as protected by any constitutional right.

Although she had been warned, Equi's anti-war resistance persisted, nonetheless. In fact, she was arrested in Portland on the same day as

Debs. "Oh, it's very easy to attend a civic lunch, listen to a number of complimentary speeches from well-mannered and admiring people, while you wear your best clothes and play the part of a hero," she told an interviewer. "But to go out and mount a soapbox and declare war against the organized forces of capitalism is quite a different matter. The task of veering public opinion was never an easy one."

A month after the war came to an end in 1918, Equi was convicted for sedition in an Oregon court, by a judge who ruled she did not "keep quiet." Most observers saw the prosecutor's case as politically motivated. "For years I have been hounded in this town," Equi said when the guilty decision was announced. In appealing her case to the Ninth Circuit Court of Appeals and then the Supreme Court, Equi's defense team called out the attacks by the prosecution on her "private moral characters" as a lesbian.

On October 17, 1920—two months after women gained the right to vote with the ratification of the Nineteenth Amendment—Equi entered the San Quentin prison to serve a one-year term. "I'm going to prison smiling," the Portland newspapers reported Equi stating. "But I am not through. I shall keep on fighting until I die."

In many respects, Supreme Court Justice Holmes had vindicated Equi's resistance in a subsequent case. Writing a surprise opinion of dissent on the *Abrams v. United States* decision in 1919, which convicted two men for distributing anti-war material in violation of the Espionage and Sedition Acts, he had abruptly shifted course in light of the broad crackdown on dissent and freedom of speech. Joined by Justice Louis Brandeis, Holmes wrote:

> That, at any rate, is the theory of our Constitution. It is an experiment, as all life is an experiment. Every year, if not every day, we have to wager our salvation upon some prophecy based upon imperfect knowledge. While that experiment is part of our system, I think that we should be eternally vigilant against attempts to check the expression of opinions that we loathe and believe to be fraught with death, unless they so imminently threaten immediate interference with the lawful

and pressing purposes of the law that an immediate check is required to save the country.

Holmes's dissent "caused a sensation," according to author Thomas Healy, a former federal appeals court law clerk and reporter, and author of a history of the Supreme Court case. "Conservatives denounced it as dangerous and extreme. Progressives hailed it as a monument to liberty. And the future of free speech was forever changed."

Author and magazine publisher H. L. Mencken concurred with Holmes's opinion, berating the dismissal of First Amendment rights "by any jury that has been sufficiently inflamed by a district attorney itching for higher office."

Equi, who remained a fixture of resistance until her death in 1952, put it best: "I'm going to speak when and where I wish," she had said at one of her rallies in Portland. "No man will stop me."

4

To Undo Mistakes

O ye that love mankind! Ye that dare oppose, not only the tyranny, but the ty-rant, stand forth! Every spot of the old world is overrun with oppression. Free-dom hath been hunted round the globe. Asia, and Africa, have long expelled her. Europe regards her like a stranger, and England hath given her warning to depart. O! receive the fugitive, and prepare in time an asylum for mankind.
—Thomas Paine, *Common Sense*, 1776

ON A WINTER DAY IN 1801, Thomas Jefferson walked to the United States Capitol, accompanied by the district marshals, and addressed Congress in the Senate chambers with the "first annual message." Earlier that year he had given the first inaugural address in Washington, DC, where he reminded legislators that the nation had "banished from our land that religious intolerance under which mankind so long bled and suffered." Jefferson continued: "We have yet gained little if we countenance a political intolerance, as despotic, as wicked, and capable of as bitter and bloody persecutions."

Jefferson's speech was relatively brief. He touched on national security, agriculture, and the judicial system. As a final issue, Jefferson sought to correct a mistake in the naturalization law. He referred to it as a "revisal" to residency terms for immigrants, though in the aftermath of a tide of xenophobia (against the French and Irish, among others), Jefferson had sought to renew the American vision of the nation as a place of sanctuary:

And shall we refuse the unhappy fugitives from distress that hospitality which the savages of the wilderness extended to our fathers arriving in this land? Shall oppressed humanity find no asylum on this globe?

The hypocrisy in Jefferson's comments, of course, would have been lost on most observers in his period; the "savages of the wilderness" were now categorized as "domestic foreigners" in their own land, and Native Americans would be cut out completely from American citizenship for another 125 years; African Americans had arrived on this land in distress and in chains, kidnapped and enslaved, and would not be granted voting rights (for males) until the Fifteenth Amendment in 1870.

Yet, in borrowing from Paine, who had in *Common Sense* envisioned the United States as the "asylum for mankind," Jefferson cleared the overgrowth of xenophobia to give light to a basic American Revolutionary principle.

Immigration rights had been one of the main grievances in the Declaration of Independence in 1776; it charged the British crown with refusing "to encourage their migrations hither" under immigration laws. In 1783, George Washington had already embraced this sanctuary concept of the emerging country, "open to receive not only the Opulent and respectable Stranger, but the oppressed and persecuted of all Nations and Religions." The Constitution, as Revolutionary War veteran Jonas Phillips had added to Washington in a letter, needed to ensure that "all men have a natural and inalienable Right to worship almighty God according to the dictates of their own Conscience and understanding." As part of the growing Jewish community in Philadelphia, Phillips had been prevented by the Pennsylvania state constitution to hold office; the federal Constitution guaranteed that no religious test shall ever be required as a qualification to any office or public trust under the United States. Nonetheless, several states, such as North Carolina, kept Protestant loyalty oaths on their books for years.

Jefferson's nudge to correct the errors of residency requirements prior to citizenship came on the heels of his repeal of the Alien Friends Act, which had given the president the right to deport any resident immigrant considered dangerous to the peace of the United States.

As one of the most dangerous immigrants in our nation's history, Paine had no idea that he, too, would be swept up in a discriminatory twist of the laws.

In his critique of *Common Sense* in 1776, a covetous John Adams wrote his wife, Abigail, that Paine was "better at tearing down than building up." An admirer of elements of the British constitution, Adams feared Paine's demands for "representation more equal," jettisoning an English system of a king, lords, and the commons.

But Adams was wrong. As an immigrant from England, Paine's literary act of resistance debunked an already accepted trope of the American colonies as an "English Only" channel of immigration. Paine built a bridge to inclusion in the American experience that had never been constructed by the English; he did not "tear down" the English system so much as he relegated it to one strand in the American migration story. "This new world hath been the asylum for the persecuted lovers of civil and religious liberty," he wrote, "from every part of Europe."

KEY WORD: EUROPE. ONCE AGAIN, Paine committed his own colossal oversight of the one in five Americans in his times who traced their roots to Africa, and the majority indigenous communities inhabiting the frontier west of the Appalachians; his inclusion to the "asylum of mankind" was expressly European, even as he lyrically described every spot in the world as being "over-run in oppression." In an often overlooked passage of *Common Sense*, however, Paine noted the minority status of the English, the larger ethnic diversity of the colonies, and the shaping of an "English Only" mythology that would be utilized repeatedly for the next two hundred years:

> Not one third of the inhabitants, even of this province, are of English descent. Wherefore I reprobate the phrase of parent or mother coun-

try applied to England only, as being false, selfish, narrow and ungen-
erous. But admitting, that we were all of English descent, what does it
amount to? Nothing.

Paine's rhetorical question, of course, underscored the criteria for
much of the American immigration policy for the next century: the 1790
Alien Naturalization Act limited citizenship to a "free white person"
with "good moral character." To undo the mistake of white supremacy
as a litmus test of migration would require nearly two more centuries of
debate and iterations of the Naturalization Act.

In the meantime, even Paine found himself caught up in the machinations of immigration policy. In 1806, a still feisty but enfeebled Paine
went to vote at the local polling place in New Rochelle, New York, down
the road from a house and farm he had been gifted for his service in the
American Revolution. The 277-acre farm, in fact, had fixed Paine's citizenship in New York since 1784. He had divided his time between New
Rochelle and a house in New York City since 1802. While his sojourns
in England and France for fifteen years had taken him away from the
daily travails in the United States, Paine had kept up his prolific literary
production, publishing letters and pamphlets on various American subjects; his books *Rights of Man* and *The Age of Reason* had been phenomenal
bestsellers in the United States. Paine had dedicated his polemic on "all
national institutions of churches, whether Jewish, Christian or Turkish"
to his "Fellow Citizens of the United States of America."

Unlike England, which he had famously "disowned" as his place of
birth in one poem, he had never renounced his American citizenship;
but Paine had been granted honorary citizenship in France, like George
Washington and Benjamin Franklin, in order to serve in their National
Convention. While Washington and Franklin had passed on to the
pantheon of founding fathers, Paine soon learned his own controversial
views on religious freedom had broken some sort of covenant among the
political elite.

"You are not an American," election inspector Elisha Ward told
Paine, when he attempted to vote in 1806. "Our Minister at Paris,
Gouverneur Morris, would not reclaim you when you were imprisoned

in the Luxembourg prison at Paris, and General Washington refused to do it."

Dismissing Ward as an old Tory who had sided with the British and who resented his anti-Federalist role, Paine claimed his right to vote. James Monroe, as the Ambassador to France in the 1790s, had actually invoked Paine's American citizenship in assisting his release from prison during the tail end of the French Revolution. When Ward threatened to call the constable and imprison Paine, the forefather of the American Revolution relented and promised to take Ward to court.

"Our citizenship in the United States is our national character," he had written in his *Crisis* series.

Ward's politically motivated rejection of Paine's citizenship would seem absurd to any observer. But it exposes the arbitrary definition of our national character, even for the individual who first gave our country its name as the United States—an arbitrary judgment that still remains unresolved in the twenty-first century.

WHILE RESISTANCE OFTEN SHOWCASES ITS power in the streets, its key venue for change is often in the courts. That was true, to a certain extent, in the response by various resistance movements to one of the Trump administration's first executive orders—a temporary but effective travel and immigrant ban based on religion.

"The restrictions either previously or now were never, ever, ever based on race, religion, or creed," a White House official denied at a news conference after the first executive order on January 29, 2017, which had targeted and blocked the entry of anyone from seven Muslim-majority countries into the United States, including a suspension of travel visas and entry rights of green card holders. Issued a week into Trump's presidency, the ban included refugees from Iraq, Iran, Syria, Somalia, Libya, Yemen, and Sudan. Few had doubts the order carried out one of Trump's most repeated campaign promises: "A total and complete shutdown of Muslims entering the United States until our country's representatives can figure out what is going on."

Within hours of the announced order, while thousands of protesters filled the airport terminals, attorneys with the American Civil Liberties Union and the International Refugee Assistance Project had appeared in front of the federal district court in New York City on behalf of two Iraqis, including Hameed Khalid Darweesh, who had worked for the American government as an interpreter for the past decade. Nearly fifty other cases had been filed in courts across the country. "What I do for this country? They put the cuffs on," Mr. Darweesh told the *New York Times*. "You know how many soldiers I touch by this hand?"

Declaring that the removal of visa holders "violates their rights to Due Process and Equal Protection guaranteed by the United States Constitution," U.S. District Judge Ann M. Donnelly ruled "there is imminent danger that, absent the stay of removal, there will be substantial and irreparable injury to refugees, visa-holders, and other individuals from nations subject" to the order. A court of appeals upheld the decision, declaring that the order "in text speaks with vague words of national security, but in context drips with religious intolerance, animus, and discrimination."

A subsequent ruling in Seattle by U.S. District Judge James Robart, who had been appointed by President George W. Bush, resulted in the first nationwide injunction. In responding to a federal complaint filed by state officials in Washington and Minnesota, the judge agreed with the states that the federal order undermined "Washington's sovereign interest in remaining a welcoming place for immigrants and refugees."

"The Constitution prevailed today," Washington Attorney General Bob Ferguson said in a statement after the ruling. "No one is above the law—not even the President."

Determined to make good on his campaign slogans, Trump did not agree, turning to Twitter again in the summer of 2017: "That's right, we need a TRAVEL BAN for certain DANGEROUS countries, not some politically correct term that won't help us protect our people!"

Seemingly unaware of the legal dynamics, Trump's torrent of tweets had been used against him in the Fourth Circuit Court, which ruled that Trump's statements suggested the real purpose of his executive order was "to effectuate the promised Muslim ban, and that its changes from [the first executive order] reflect an effort to help it survive judicial scrutiny, rather than to avoid targeting Muslims for exclusion from the United States."

Resistance in the court derailed a third attempt by the White House to repackage its efforts to block Muslim travelers Trump had labeled as "bad people" with "bad intentions." U.S. District Judge Derrick K. Watson in Hawaii ruled the third incarnation of the order, which had been altered to include citizens from Chad, Iran, Libya, North Korea, Somalia, Syria, and Yemeni and Venezuelan government officials, "plainly discriminates based on nationality" in violation of "the founding principles of this Nation."

In a 7–2 ruling on December 4, 2017, the Supreme Court ruled that Trump's final travel ban on six Muslim-majority countries, as well as North Korea and Venezuela, could take effect while subsequent challenges in lower courts continued. The high court ruling did not recognize the ban as constitutional, but simply rejected an emergency injunction against the ban as necessary. "In the first month of its enforcement," *The Guardian* reported, "the president's order has largely faded from the news even as families are being denied entry to the US, separated from loved ones with no end in sight."

The courts played an "essential role," according to an amicus brief filed by the children of three Japanese Americans who had been interned in camps during World War II, in protecting "our fundamental values," and as a "check on abuses of government power, especially during times of national and international stress."

The experiences of their fathers—Gordon Hirabayashi, Minoru Yasui, and Fred Korematsu, all of whom lost Supreme Court challenges to the constitutionality of the internment orders in 1942—offered a powerful reminder to not make a similar mistake today. "Rather than repeat the failures of the past, this Court should repudiate them and affirm the greater legacy of those cases," the amicus brief continued. "Blind deference to the Executive Branch, even in areas in which decision-makers must wield wide discretion, is incompatible with the protection of fundamental freedoms."

"The court has a chance to make sure that one, it doesn't repeat the mistake that they made earlier, but also really to ensure that our system of constitutional democracy, with its checks and balances, operates the way that it was supposed to," Robert Chang, executive director of the Fred T. Korematsu Center for Law and Equality at the Seattle University School of Law, told NBC News.

This was the resistance's imperative "to undo the mistakes," as First Lady Eleanor Roosevelt had famously declared during her visit to the Japanese American internment camp on the Gila River Indian Community reservation in 1943. Breaking with President Franklin D. Roosevelt, the First Lady had already begun the process of publicly discussing the closure of the internment camps. Right before her trip to the Arizona desert camp in 1943, Roosevelt had read the dissenting opinion of her friend Judge William Denman on the U.S. Circuit Court of Appeals regarding the cases of Fred Korematsu and Gordon Hirabayashi. In an extraordinary opinion, Denman agreed with fellow Justice Frank Murphy, who called the treatment of 70,000 American citizens, including children, "torn from their homes, farms and places of business to be imprisoned together in large groups," which he found was "not unlike that of Hitler in so confining the Jews in his stockades" in Nazi Germany. In his dissenting opinion, Murphy likened the Court's upholding of the military order as the "legalization of racism," and as an example of "the abhorrent and despicable treatment of minority groups by the dictatorial tyrannies which this nation is now pledged to destroy."

The unthinkable mistakes behind the Japanese American internment camps now provided the "foresight" that Roosevelt rued in her own times. "We have no common race in this country," Roosevelt said in Arizona, also recognizing the internment of Germans and German Americans, as well as Italians and Italian American citizens, "but we have an ideal to which all of us are loyal: we cannot progress if we look down upon any group of people amongst us because of race or religion."

As an opening salvo to the Supreme Court and its own consideration of the Trump travel ban, the amicus brief by the children of Hirabayashi, Yasui, and Korematsu reminded both the justices and the nation that the resistance of their parents was as vital today as it was in the 1940s.

———

RETURNING FROM A SWING DANCE with his girlfriend Ida Boitano, a daughter of Italian immigrants in the nearby town of San Leandro, Fred Korematsu never questioned whether he was a loyal American or not in the Bay Area in the late 1930s.

Born in California in 1919, Fred attended the local schools, competed on the tennis and swim teams, went to a Holiness church on Sundays, and by the time he turned twenty-one Fred and Ida were engaged—though, without the possibility of getting married, since anti-miscegenation laws precluding ethnically mixed marriages would not be repealed for another decade in California. Toyosaburo "Fred" Korematsu was the third son of Japanese immigrants, who ran a nursery and florist shop in Oakland.

Unable to make ends meet as a chemistry student at the Los Angeles City College, Fred returned to the Bay Area and soon found a welding job in the shipyards in 1940. Though he had registered for the draft, an ulcer resulted in a 4F classification, rendering him physically unfit for service. But no health problem kept him from work. Within months, a union official delivered the bad news: "I'm sorry, this is wrong," he told Fred, but the union refused to allow Japanese American workers to remain on the job.

Korematsu, who did not speak Japanese and had always considered himself an American, was at a loss at what to do; several other shipyards turned him down, as well. "I'm an American," he would later recall, "and so it's sort of an insult to me." He returned to help his parents.

The day after the bombing of Pearl Harbor on December 7, 1941, President Roosevelt announced on national radio that the United States was at war with Japan. He also set in motion a series of orders for random house searches, confiscation of property, and police sweeps of potential saboteurs—and the eventual internment of Japanese Americans and Japanese residents. Despite the fact that there was not a single incident of domestic sabotage committed by Japanese Americans during the war, according to Lorraine Bannai in her study of the court case, *Enduring*

Conviction, a general sense of hysteria swept through communities in California and other states with large Asian communities.

Within two months, unable to justify actual threats of domestic violence or terrorism, federal officials released a report underlining the "racial affinities" connected to immigration, and claimed "Americanized" third-generation Japanese Americans still represented "undiluted strains" of Japanese belligerence, therefore meriting a threat as potential enemies. Roosevelt agreed and signed an executive order granting authority to the War Department for military control over certain western regions, including California, Washington, Oregon, and parts of Arizona. On May 3, 1942, the Civilian Exclusion Order No. 34 ordered the removal of all persons of Japanese ancestry from these deemed military areas.

In the first week of May 1942, the Korematsu family left behind their nursery, shop, and life possessions, reported to City Plaza in Hayward, California, with other Japanese Americans and immigrants, were issued a registration number, and then boarded buses for an unknown destination of internment. More than 110,000 Japanese Americans and family members would eventually be incarcerated in camps.

Fred Korematsu resisted. He changed his name to Clyde Sarah, spent his last $100 on a botched effort at plastic surgery to remove the folds around his eyes, and then found another job in Berkeley. But his stint of freedom with Ida only lasted a few weeks. According to the Oakland newspaper, Fred's identity had been divulged by a couple of police officers, who arrested him on the street. OAKLAND JAP HELD FOR FBI, ran the headline in the *Oakland Post-Enquirer*.

Supported by the local Northern California chapter of the ACLU, Korematsu took his case through the federal court system, filing appeals until a U.S. Supreme Court decision on December 8, 1944, upheld his conviction as justified due to the "military dangers" and "military urgency" of potential sabotage by Japanese sympathizers.

In his dissenting opinion, Justice Murphy found the "exclusion goes over 'the very brink of constitutional power,' and falls into the ugly abyss of racism." He countered that the singling out of all persons of Japanese ancestry did not meet the test as a public danger that is so "immediate, imminent, and impending" as "not to admit of delay and not to permit the intervention of ordinary constitutional processes to alleviate the danger."

As a citizen of the United States, Korematsu had attempted to appeal to his first federal judge with his patriotism: "I am ready, willing, and able to bear arms for this country. I am willing to enlist. As a citizen of the United States I am ready to render any service that I may be called upon to render our Government in our war against the Axis nations, including the Empire of Japan. I do not owe any allegiance to any country or nation other than the United States of America."

Detained at one point in a holding pen at a racetrack, Korematsu's family was forced to live inside a horse stall, with straw mattresses and a single naked light bulb. "These people should have been given a fair trial in order that they may defend their loyalty at court in a democratic way," Korematsu wrote to his lawyer. On April 11, 1943, James Wakasa, a sixty-three-year-old former World War I civilian cook for the U.S. Army, was gunned down by military police at the internment camp in Topaz, Utah, while walking his dog too close to the barbed-wire fence.

Throughout his legal battles, Korematsu maintained his resistance against the unconstitutional removal orders of Americans. And while his actions left him largely alone in the internment camp, ostracized by various factions of other Japanese Americans intent on demonstrating their loyalty to the American government, a study by the UCLA Asian American Studies Center found resistance to be more common than previously thought among interned Japanese Americans, "shattering the myth of the 'quiet Americans' who silently accepted their fate without question."

"There were riots, sit-down strikes, work stoppages and other episodes of unrest at the camps, much of it to protest deplorable living conditions there," according to the report. "The strikes early on in Poston and Tule Lake were major acts of resistance," UCLA professor Lane Ryo Hirabayashi noted. "The military was called in to restore order, and people were shot."

In one sense, according to David Yoo, professor and director of the UCLA Asian American Studies Center, "those who resisted were demonstrating a form of loyalty to America. It's not always popular to resist, but in many ways it's also exercising a very important part of what it means to be an American."

Korematsu returned to the Bay Area after the war, eventually married and raised a family, and returned to civilian life. But the underpinnings of his resistance never diminished; a movement for "redress" began to take shape in the late 1960s, led by the Japanese American Citizens League. One of the first campaigns brought the repeal of Title II of the Internal Security Act of 1950, which had granted authorization for mass detention without trial; President Richard Nixon signed it into law in 1971. Five years later, President Gerald Ford formally rescinded Executive Order 9066, which had led to the mass removal and incarceration of Japanese Americans and residents—thirty-four years after the fact—and declared that "this kind of action shall never again be repeated."

Korematsu's legacy of resistance came full circle in 1983. Through a Freedom of Information Act request, a legal team uncovered an internal government memo that had presented false evidence of a "military necessity" justifying approval of the evacuation order. A legal team representing various organizations filed a petition for writ of error coram nobis in federal court on behalf of Korematsu, Hirabayashi, and Yasui—the same three families who filed an amicus brief against the Trump administration's travel ban. In a request to reopen the landmark Supreme Court cases, the petition argued that "recently discovered evidence" indicated that "high government officials suppressed, altered and destroyed evidence in order to influence the outcomes of these cases at trial."

Offered a pardon by the U.S. government, in response to the petition, Korematsu refused: "I think I should be the one pardoning the government. They were wrong."

By the fall of 1983, the U.S. District Attorney's office in San Francisco filed its response to the petition, agreeing that it is "singularly appropriate to vacate this conviction for non-violent civil disobedience." While the U.S. government had not admitted its guilt—or deceit—its decision vindicated the resistance of these three men, among others. In her ruling on the petition, federal District Judge Marilyn H. Patel called the government's response "tantamount to a confession of error," and overturned Korematsu's conviction.

With its warning that Korematsu's case served as "caution that in times of international hostility and antagonisms our institutions, legislative, executive and judicial, must be prepared to exercise their authority to protect all citizens from the petty fears and prejudices that are so easily aroused," Patel's ruling remains profoundly timeless.

"Mr. Korematsu's name will always be familiar to legal scholars and historians, teachers and government officials, for his civil disobedience focused attention on the injustice of internment and the suffering of many fellow citizens," wrote the *Washington Post*. "He will be honored, as Martin Luther King is honored, for his nonviolent resistance to unjust law."

In 1988, President Ronald Reagan signed the Civil Liberties Act, which apologized for the internment of Japanese Americans and resident aliens, and agreed to "provide for a public education fund to finance efforts to inform the public about the internment of such individuals to prevent the recurrence of any similar event."

FOUR YEARS BEFORE REAGAN RECOGNIZED the mistake of internment based on ethnic discrimination, Rev. William Sloane Coffin took the pulpit at Riverside Church in New York City on Palm Sunday, and recalled the history of ethnic and religious persecution in the United States—and the undaunted resistance against it. "Civil disobedience has also been a time-honored community occupation, as a quick reading of American history will show," Coffin preached. "Said the great Quaker Mary Dyer as she went to her death in Boston, 'Truth is my authority, not some authority my truth.'"

From Dyer's seventeenth-century defiance of Puritan laws, to the underground railroad, to protests against the slaughter of Native Americans, to anti-war dissent dating back to the Spanish-American War, to those who marched with civil rights advocates in Selma, Alabama, in 1965 and burned draft cards with Vietnam War resisters in the 1960s and 1970s, Coffin framed resistance as a "human imperative to the divine indicative."

In calling on his congregation to join hundreds of other religious institutions in resistance against Reagan's policies to arrest and deport an estimated 250,000 refugees who had fled U.S.-backed and -funded civil wars in El Salvador and Guatemala, Coffin invoked the early American concept of "sanctuary." With more than 600 refugees being deported daily back to "likely torture and death," Coffin charged that the Reagan administration "so patently misapplies a law which intends an opposite result" that he did not even view the act of granting sanctuary as an act of civil disobedience. "It seems rather like common sense," Coffin said, "like a normal human reaction to an intolerable situation." In keeping with the spirit of the Statue of Liberty, Coffin said, the Refugee Act of 1980 required the U.S. to grant asylum or temporary refugee status to people unable to return to their country because of persecution. Fleeing an escalating war, Salvadorans and Guatemalans had earned such a status according to the UN High Commissioner for Refugees.

In 1981, goat herder and Quaker Jim Corbett shared a similar sentiment when he encountered Central American refugees along the Arizona-Mexico border. "Because the US Government takes the position that aiding undocumented Salvadoran and Guatemalan refugees in this country is a felony," Corbett wrote to the Southside Presbyterian Church in Tucson, "we have no middle ground between collaboration and resistance." Welcoming refugees into their places of worship as sacred spaces, the Sanctuary Movement was soon launched, as Thoreau once wrote, "to uphold a law when the government breaks it."

Hailing the Sanctuary Movement as the "best of our American heritage," Coffin recalled his own participation in World War II, when he had served as an intelligence officer across enemy lines. "It behooves us North American Christians to realize now what the German churches learned too late some forty years ago; that it is not enough to resist with confessions; we must confess with resistance."

More than three decades later, a coordinated effort by religious congregations to resist Trump's deportation forces emerged across the country after decades of failure by Congress to pass comprehensive immigration reform. Refusing ICE (U.S. Immigration and Customs Enforcement) orders to "self-deport," undocumented resident Leonor

Garcia from Mexico took sanctuary in the Forest Hill Presbyterian Church in Akron in the fall of 2017. "Welcoming Leonor into our space and really inviting her to make this her home for a while is very much at the root and core of our understanding of what Christian faith calls us to be and to do," Rev. John Lentz told the *Akron Beacon Journal*. At the Columbus Mennonite Church in Akron, Ohio, the congregation had also provided sanctuary that fall to Edith Espinal, a fifteen-year resident of the area. Having originally entered the country on "advanced parole" from Mexico, which granted her the opportunity to apply for asylum, Espinal's failed efforts at achieving residency had placed her legal status in jeopardy. The mother of two American children, Espinal's twenty-one-year-old son had sought to sponsor her residency.

Espinal's sanctuary moment in an age of Trump had its own precedent. "Families were kept apart because a husband or a wife or a child had been born in the wrong place," President Lyndon Johnson had said in 1965, signing the Immigration Act on Liberty Island. "It has been un-American in the highest sense, because it has been untrue to the faith that brought thousands to these shores even before we were a country. We can now believe that it will never again shadow the gate to the American Nation with the twin barriers of prejudice and privilege." In abolishing the quota system from each country, which President John F. Kennedy had called "intolerable," the Act shifted the demographics from European to larger Asian, Latin American, and African immigration.

While Johnson's landmark decision corrected "a cruel and enduring wrong in the conduct of the American nation," as he claimed, it underscores the disregard of the Trump administration for an emphasis on family migration a half century later.

"When Mexico sends its people, they're not sending their best," Trump had said at his presidential campaign kickoff. "They're not sending you. They're not sending you. They're sending people that have lots of problems, and they're bringing those problems with us. They're bringing drugs. They're bringing crime. They're rapists."

Four days into his administration, Trump signed an executive order "to ensure the public safety of the American people in communities across the United States as well as to ensure that our Nation's immigration laws are faithfully executed," that chillingly echoed the debunked threat charges behind the Japanese American internment order. Without legally defining "sanctuary cities," the order made any noncompliant entity, such as cities or states, ineligible for federal funds.

A new Sanctuary Movement, in effect, like the inspiring struggle by undocumented youth in the "Dreamers" movement for a permanent status of residency and pathway to citizenship, had forced cities and states to take their own side of resistance. Since the "Dream Act" had been introduced in 2001, and throughout the Obama administration, Dreamers and their family members had defiantly led campaigns as "undocumented, unafraid and unapologetic." Referring to Espinal's case, Columbus, Ohio, Mayor Andrew Ginther reminded the local media that while his city might not be a "sanctuary city," it had passed an executive order that instructed the local police force to "not arrest, detain or investigate anyone for immigration violations unless a warrant or criminal violation was observed." Nonetheless, as Ruben Castilla Herrera, director of the Central Ohio Worker Center, pointed out, "We need policy and legislation, but ultimately, sanctuary comes from the people."

Over 400 towns, cities, and counties—including some of the nation's largest population centers, such as New York City, Los Angeles, Chicago, Philadelphia, New Orleans, and San Francisco—had issued some sort of sanctuary or noncooperation order by the spring of 2017, including the small town of Clarkston, Georgia. Passing a city order that law enforcement officials in the southern town "shall not arrest, detain, extend the detention of, transfer custody of, or transport anyone solely on the basis of an ICE 'detainer request,'" the town openly celebrated its role as the "Ellis Island of the South." Clarkston's City Council took the vote after ICE conducted raids at homes and workplaces, specifically targeting Somali immigrants. In a town of 7,000 residents, nearly half were immigrants or refugees.

Within three months, a federal court struck down the executive order's proposed cut of federal funds for sanctuary cities that resisted cooperation, citing constitutional directives over Congressional spending powers. Once again ramping up unfounded hysteria over safety, the White House called the court ruling a "gift to the criminal gang and cartel element in our country, empowering the worst kind of human trafficking and sex trafficking, and putting thousands of innocent lives at risk."

A "slew of studies," NBC News reported, found immigrants—both legal and undocumented—committed fewer crimes than Americans born in the United States. A University of California analysis in 2017, in fact, found "crime rates are lower when localities stay out of the business of federal immigration enforcement." More specifically, the study noted 35.5 fewer crimes committed per 10,000 people in sanctuary counties compared to non-sanctuary counties.

Not only were sanctuary cities safer, Los Angeles Mayor Eric Garcetti argued, "splitting up families and cutting funding to any city— especially Los Angeles, where 40 percent of the nation's goods enter the U.S. at our port, and more than 80 million passengers traveled through our airport last year—puts the personal safety and economic health of our entire nation at risk."

Attorney General Jeff Sessions unleashed a specific attack on Chicago in the summer of 2017, speaking at a conference in Miami. He declared the city's sanctuary status reflected the breakdown in the rule of law. "Every year, too many Americans' lives are victimized as a result of sanctuary city policies, whether it be theft, robbery, drugs, assault, battery and even murder," Sessions said, without offering specific data linking such crimes to undocumented immigrants.

Mayor Rahm Emanuel countered that Chicago would "not cave to the Trump administration's pressure because they are wrong morally, wrong factually and wrong legally." U.S. Conference of Mayors Executive Director Tom Cochran also held Sessions accountable, claiming the Attorney General did not "understand what it means to run a city that welcomes immigrants" or "the Constitutional protections afforded to all people in our country and their impact on local policies."

For activists like Tania Unzueta, with the Organized Communities Against Deportation and Mijente groups, sanctuary in Chicago meant more than a symbolical measure to defy Trump, "but to actually transform our city's policies to stop targeting us for imprisonment, risk of removal and state violence at the hands of police and aggressive immigration agents."

Among numerous lawsuits in play, U.S. District Court Judge William Orrick III ruled in a summary judgment in the fall of 2017 that Trump's order "violates a fundamental constitutional principle of separation of powers—spending powers that belong to Congress—in a manner that is overbroad and coercive." Orrick's ruling came from a lawsuit filed by the city of San Francisco and the state of California, both entities which had declared themselves "sanctuaries" for undocumented residents.

With an estimated one-fifth of the national undocumented immigrant population in its state, California's open defiance of the Trump administration not only barred cities and counties from assisting ICE authorities, but also issued instructions to not provide release dates of any undocumented prisoners from city or council jails. Newspapers, such as the *Press-Telegram* in Long Beach, hailed "California's anti-Trump resistance bills." The *Washington Post* referred to the state's efforts as the founding charter of the California resistance. "California versus Trump becomes an instant rallying cry," added the *LA Times*.

Speaking at a church in Fred Korematsu's hometown of Oakland, California, on Sunday, October 22, 2017, state Senate President Pro Tempore Kevin de León, who authored the state's sanctuary law—the California Values Act—addressed the "nationalistic xenophobic tendencies" of Trump and his officials. Admitting it could not stop ICE agents from patrolling the streets, de León said the state law would "put a kink—a large kink—in Trump's perverse and inhumane deportation machine." At the signing of the bill, de León called it California's wall, "a wall of justice—against President Trump's xenophobic, racist and ignorant immigration policies."

Raised by a single immigrant mother from Guatemala in Los Angeles, de León had cut his political teeth as an activist against Proposition 187, leading protests against the anti-immigrant initiative that had passed during a wave of Republican-led xenophobia in 1994. While the federal court eventually struck down the California proposition to deny publicly funded education, health care, and welfare benefits to undocumented residents, de León called it one of "the most mean-spirited and un-American" measures in California history. In 2014, de León had pushed through a bill repealing the measure, even if it had not been enacted, as an effort to close a "dark chapter in our state's history," and bring "dignity and respect to the national immigration debate."

In many respects, the resistance had returned to confront the mistakes on immigrant rights since Jefferson's call in 1801 to revise undue restrictions, albeit within the context of limited enfranchisement in his age. Extending Paine's call for a "continental" view of the American Revolution to the West Coast, immigrant rights now defined the "national character" in its fullest.

"California was not part of this nation when its history began," de León had declared earlier in the year. "But we are clearly now the keeper of its future."

5

Cities of Resistance

To The States, or any one of them, or any city of The States,
Resist much, obey little.
> —Walt Whitman, *Leaves of Grass*, 1860

Resistance alone will not deliver us. I believe that we need to
birth a new future.
> —Valarie Kaur, *Revolutionary Love*, 2018

THE RESISTERS GATHERED NEAR THE Boston Common, just a block away from where the Liberty Tree had once stood. Hundreds of people lined the streets, some dressed in eighteenth-century garb, marching toward the waterfront with the same gusto of the British-occupied era, chanting "Down with King George," and then, "Down with King Richard."

On a wintry day in December 1973 the marchers then spilled along the edges of the Boston dockyards, aiming their rage at President Richard Nixon and the "profiteering" oil companies—and the environmental uncertainty of the age. In response to a groundswell of activism over widespread pollution and environmental ruin, Nixon had signed the Environmental Protection Agency (EPA) into existence in 1970, hailing it "a historic period when, by conscious choice, [we] transform our land into what we want it to become." In his State of the Union address that year, Nixon declared that "through our years of past carelessness we incurred a debt to nature, and now that debt is being called."

> The great question of the seventies is, shall we surrender to our surroundings, or shall we make our peace with nature and begin to make reparations for the damage we have done to our air, to our land, and to our water? Restoring nature to its natural state is a cause beyond party and beyond factions. It has become a common cause of all the people of this country. It is a cause of particular concern to young Americans, because they more than we will reap the grim consequences of our failure to act on programs which are needed now if we are to prevent disaster later.

And yet, Congress soon had to override Nixon's veto of the Clean Water Act, which proved to be one of the most indispensable laws of protection in our nation's history. Nixon's rhetoric aside, the legacy of the first Earth Day in 1970, and the rise of an environmental movement "left a permanent impact on the politics of America," Sen. Gaylord Nelson recalled. "It forcibly thrust the issue of environmental quality and resources conservation into the political dialogue of the Nation."

In 1972, a case arrived before the U.S. Supreme Court that also asked a fundamental question: Do trees have legal standing? The *Sierra Club v. Morton* case dealt with an attempt to halt a ski resort in the Sierra Nevada Mountains due to resulting "irreparable harm to the public interest." The Court ruled against the plaintiffs—and the trees—since Sierra Club itself could not claim injury. The law of nature, alas, was on its own.

But in his remarkable dissenting opinion, Justice William Douglass agreed that trees should be granted legal rights or personhood, noting that the "suit would therefore be more properly labeled as *Mineral King v. Morton*." His dissent resonated like a requiem in the clearing of the Liberty Tree at the Boston Common—and across the nation:

> Contemporary public concern for protecting nature's ecological equilibrium should lead to the conferral of standing upon environmental objects to sue for their own preservation . . .

The voice of the inanimate object, therefore, should not be stilled. That does not mean that the judiciary takes over the managerial functions from the federal agency. It merely means that, before these priceless bits of Americana (such as a valley, an alpine meadow, a river, or a lake) are forever lost or are so transformed as to be reduced to the eventual rubble of our urban environment, the voice of the existing beneficiaries of these environmental wonders should be heard.

Those inarticulate members of the ecological group cannot speak. But those people who have so frequented the place as to know its values and wonders will be able to speak for the entire ecological community.

Ecology reflects the land ethic; and Aldo Leopold wrote in *A Sand County Almanac* 204 (1949), "The land ethic simply enlarges the boundaries of the community to include soils, waters, plants, and animals, or collectively: the land."

The environmental resistance marched on. *Time* magazine had already hailed scientist Barry Commoner as the "Paul Revere of ecology" in 1970, invoking the tradition of the Revolutionary agitator from Boston who had alerted the Americans about the historic British assault at Lexington and Concord in 1775. As an artist, Revere had also done an engraving of the Liberty Tree protests in 1765, declaring "America in distress apprehending the total loss of Liberty."

Commoner's bestselling book in 1971, *The Closing Circle*, provided the context of a similar America in distress from the economic and environmental fallout of pollutants in the water, soil, and air, as well as problems from nuclear tests. At its root, Commoner's thesis was as revolutionary as *Common Sense* or any liberty campaign in the eighteenth century: Commoner challenged Americans to confront the systemic framework of capitalism that had undercut the nation's inherent connection to its resources and disregarded the economic costs of "environmental externalities." For Commoner, privately owned modern technology "cannot long survive if it destroys the social good on which it depends—the ecosphere." He declared, the "system is therefore in need of change." In an interview with Claude Lévi-Strauss in 1972, Commoner clarified his analysis:

We are suffering from a disordered and lawless form of humanism ... I refer to the conviction ... that man, lord and master of nature, exists on one side, and, on the other side there is nature, entirely exterior to him. That makes nature no more than a thing, an object, an instrument ... Perhaps it has never been more necessary than now, to say what the myths say: that a well ordered humanism does not begin with itself, but puts things back in their place. It puts the world before life, life before man, and the respect of others before love of self.

Such a lawless disconnect from nature was called out at the Boston Tea Party reenactment in 1973. Hailing it as "the first protest against the oil companies," Jeremy Rifkin, one of the People's Bicentennial Commission organizers back in Boston, criticized Nixon's failure to keep his environmental promises. "The Oil Party will be covered by the national media, and for this reason, we urge everyone to turn out, no matter what the weather is like. We need winter soldiers, not just sunshine patriots."

The lifting of Paine's Revolutionary phrases was intentional. The protest was dramatic, even risky. A party of protesters rowed out to a ship in the bay, a reproduction of the eighteenth-century *Beaver*. They dropped banners aside the vessel—Texaco, Exxon, Gulf, and Shell. And then they tossed empty oil drums into the harbor.

On the two-hundredth anniversary of the Boston Tea Party, they sought "to revive the revolutionary principles of 1776 and apply those to promote radical political change."

The reenactment of Boston's early American resistance was not simply a piece of street theater; it served as an act of historical recovery, a mooring of a vessel of time that had drifted from the American memory. Instead of partitioning the "environment" into a separate cause, it also served as a "truth and reconciliation" commission of the "environmental degradation" by government-regulated corporations and the "crucial, potentially fatal, hidden factor in the operation of the economic system." Commoner argued that "the true account books are not in balance" and the "deficit is being paid by the lives of the present population and the safety of future generations."

The protest in the Boston harbor in 1973, just like its predecessor in 1773, served another role: the dramatic act of resistance brought citizens to the waterfront on their own terms, in a historic moment for the environmental movement.

John Adams vilified the anti-British protesters that gathered at the Liberty Tree in 1770, and even served as the prosecuting attorney against the American colonists who were shot down in the Boston "massacre" the same year. Three years later, Adams embraced the radicalism of the "Sons of Liberty" and called the vandalism and acts of violence against private property at the Boston Tea Party "the most magnificent Movement of all." The resistance changed him, too.

More importantly, Adams had not joined the resistance on official terms—but on the terms set by a radical group of resisters who defied an unjust law. "The People should never rise, without doing something to be remembered—something notable," Adams wrote in a letter. "And striking. This Destruction of the Tea is so bold, so daring, so firm, intrepid and inflexible, and it must have so important Consequences, and so lasting, that I can't but consider it as an Epocha in History."

That epoch signaled the beginning of a struggle over history itself for the next two centuries.

ON OCTOBER 20, 2017, THE EPA under Donald Trump deleted dozens of online links on its government website that had addressed climate change. Trump-appointed EPA administrator Scott Pruitt had told multiple media venues over the year that human activity was not "a primary contributor to the global warming that we see."

A few days after the EPA censored "climate change" from its website, the Government Accountability Office released a report that the U.S. government "has spent more than $350 billion over the past decade in response to extreme weather and fire events." The report was based on interviews with twenty-six scientific and economic experts and thirty studies, as well as research from the EPA. In the hands of Pruitt's EPA, that research almost disappeared with a click.

A former attorney general for Oklahoma, Pruitt had spent years in a veritable war against the EPA during the Obama administration, filing fourteen lawsuits against environmental rules, often in tandem with fossil fuel companies. According to a *New York Times* report, Pruitt "closely coordinated with major oil and gas producers, electric utilities and political groups with ties to the libertarian billionaire brothers Charles G. and David H. Koch to roll back environmental regulations."

Under the veil of secrecy, including the construction of a $25,000 sound-proof office, gutting 3,000 employees from the agency, and cutting off funding for enforcement mechanisms under his control, such as the Justice Department's Environment and Natural Resources Division, Pruitt effectively worked to dismantle the nearly half-century legacy of the EPA. While Trump had openly called for shutting down the EPA during the 2016 presidential campaign, Pruitt quietly worked behind the scenes to disable what Nixon envisioned as the agency's founding mandate: "Clean air, clean water, open spaces—these should once again be the birthright of every American."

"I like what Donald Trump has done here as president," Alabama talk radio cohost Andrea Lindenberg told Pruitt in the summer of 2017. "He took a guy who wanted to get rid of the EPA—dismantle it—and put him in charge of it." Pruitt responded: "Ha. That's right," and then he provided an overview of "over twenty-two significant regulatory actions" to reverse Obama-era regulations on protecting clean water, clean air, and taking action on climate change.

As our nation's top official sworn into office to ensure "national efforts to reduce environmental risk based on the best available scientific information," Pruitt's statements denying climate change raised some troubling questions on his ability to carry out his agency's mandate—or even provide a forthright characterization of his agency's scientific work.

"I think that measuring with precision human activity on the climate is something very challenging to do and there's tremendous disagreement about the degree of impact," Pruitt told a CNBC news program in March, "so no, I would not agree that it's a primary contributor to the global warming that we see."

There was no "tremendous disagreement" according to Pruitt's own EPA scientists and the agency's long-standing website on climate change: "Humans are largely responsible for recent climate change." Prior to being deleted, the unequivocal EPA website continued:

Over the past century, human activities have released large amounts of carbon dioxide and other greenhouse gases into the atmosphere. The majority of greenhouse gases come from burning fossil fuels to produce energy, although deforestation, industrial processes, and some agricultural practices also emit gases into the atmosphere.

Greenhouse gases act like a blanket around Earth, trapping energy in the atmosphere and causing it to warm. This phenomenon is called the greenhouse effect and is natural and necessary to support life on Earth. However, the buildup of greenhouse gases can change Earth's climate and result in dangerous effects to human health and welfare and to ecosystems.

According to the National Oceanic and Atmospheric Administration, the last three years—2014, 2015, 2016—set a new global record for warming each year. Without the short-term warming impact of an El Niño, according to NASA, 2017 was the second-hottest year on record.

The erasure of federal studies on climate change by Pruitt and Trump revealed the true motives behind climate change skeptics or "climate denial." The truth was elsewhere: This was a climate cover-up.

Despite his one-time support of a letter that he signed with other business leaders in 2009, calling for "meaningful and effective measures to control climate change," Trump had "tweeted climate change skepticism 115 times," according to an assessment by the online *Vox* news site. Some typical tweets:

In the 1920's people were worried about global cooling—it never happened. Now it's global warming. Give me a break!

They changed the name from "global warming" to "climate change" after the term global warming just wasn't working (it was too cold)!

In the last days of December 2017, Trump tweeted another round of mocking comments during a week of arctic temperatures across the Great Plains to the East Coast, including "bomb cyclone" blizzards of snow, while record high temperatures took place in Australia and Alaska. "Very recent research does suggest that persistent winter cold spells (as well as the western drought, heatwaves, prolonged storminess) are related to rapid Arctic warming, which is, in turn, caused mainly by human-caused climate change," Jennifer Francis, a climate scientist at Rutgers University, told NBC News, based on her recent peer-reviewed study.

Francis and her team of scientists found that 50 percent of the summer ice extent and 60 percent of the volume in the Arctic have disappeared within a generation, and "the ice cover is now the smallest it has been in at least 1400 years," resulting in a "disproportionate and multifaceted role in the climate system." Trump came to a different conclusion on Twitter:

In the East, it could be the COLDEST New Year's Eve on record. Perhaps we could use a little bit of that good old Global Warming that our Country, but not other countries, was going to pay TRILLIONS OF DOLLARS to protect against. Bundle up!

According to the NASA Global Climate Change website, "multiple studies published in peer-reviewed scientific journals show that 97 percent or more of actively publishing climate scientists agree: Climate-warming trends over the past century are extremely likely due to human activities." Among the hundreds of scientific organizations that "hold the position that climate change has been caused by human action," NASA featured the statements of every major scientific organization, including the American Association for the Advancement of Science, the American Chemical Society, the American Geophysical Union, the American Medical Association, the American Meteorological Society, the Geological Society of America, the American Physical Society, and the U.S. National Academy of Sciences, the U.S. Global Change Research Program, and the Intergovernmental Panel on Climate Change, which concluded: "Scientific evidence for warming of the climate system is unequivocal."

Even Exxon's own research team understood its impact on climate as early as 1977. An *InsideClimate News* exposé in 2015 uncovered a memo to Exxon's Management Committee that found "there is general scientific agreement that the most likely manner in which mankind is influencing the global climate is through carbon dioxide release from the burning of fossil fuels."

In *The Closing Circle*, in 1971, Commoner had already carried the lamp of warning on climate change, noting that carbon dioxide emissions create a "greenhouse" effect.

Like Pruitt's own entanglement with oil and gas producers, this new administration of climate denial follows a long tradition of bankrolled public relations firms and bogus fronts, as James Hoggan and Richard Littlemore had documented in *Climate Cover-Up: The Crusade to Deny Global Warming* in 2009, which had deliberately sought to manipulate the media, mangle the language of real science, and derail any public policy or action to halt the spiraling climate crisis.

Longtime climate change activist and journalist Bill McKibben, who had first covered climate change politics in *The New York Review of Books* in 1988, nailed the unfolding realities in the Trump White House: "The level of complete corruption from the fossil fuel industry that marks this administration is like nothing we've ever seen," he declared on *Real Time with Bill Maher* in the spring of 2017.

In an extraordinary flurry of rollbacks of environmental protection rules within the first six months of the Trump administration, Pruitt had managed to end or halt more than a dozen regulations, including Clean Water Act protections over the dumping of toxic heavy metals from coal mining into valleys and waterways, the disposal of coal ash, fuel-efficiency standards, and mandated reviews of asbestos and pesticide use.

A career EPA official who resigned in March after twenty-four years,

Mustafa Ali told *Time* magazine, "They're trying to deconstruct and dismantle the basic protections. They're creating situations where more folks are going to get sick, some folks are going to die, more folks are going to be put in harm's way."

In the fall of 2017, Pruitt took EPA officials out of climate change's way; his agency canceled the keynote address and participation by three EPA scientists at a climate change conference in Rhode Island. "Removing climate change resources from the EPA website is offensive and dangerous," the Union of Concerned Scientists said in a statement. "At a time when Americans have lost their loved ones and their homes to floods and fires, are living without fresh water or electricity, and are experiencing multi-billion-dollar disasters exacerbated by climate change, this is not the time to impede public access to critical climate change information."

The purge of EPA history had come full circle.

With the alacrity of Revere, Commoner had forewarned of this corporate takeover of environmental governmental policy back in 1971, "that the world is being carried to the brink of ecological disaster not by a singular fault, which some clever scheme can correct, but by the phalanx of powerful economic, political, and social forces that constitute the march of history." Only the resistance to the current economic and environmental structure could "change the course of history," he concluded.

In the fall of 2017, over 15,000 scientists from 184 countries, including the majority of Nobel laureates, released a second "warning to humanity," as a follow-up to a historic warning from the world scientific community in 1992. "We have unleashed a mass extinction event, the sixth in roughly 540 million years, wherein many current life forms could be annihilated or at least committed to extinction by the end of this century," the scientists wrote in their open letter. "As most political leaders respond to pressure, scientists, media influencers, and lay citizens must insist that their governments take immediate action as a moral imperative to current and future generations of human and other life. With a groundswell of organized grassroots efforts, dogged opposition can be overcome and political leaders compelled to do the right thing."

THE FIRST LINE OF THE Declaration of Independence in 1776 called for the dissolution of the British control over the American colonies; the next phrase, less often remembered, invoked "among the powers of the earth, the separate and equal station to which the laws of nature and of nature's God entitle them."

In *Common Sense*, Thomas Paine referred to the "touchstone of nature" and "equal rights of nature" over thirty times. The king of England "hath wickedly broken through every moral and human obligation," he wrote, and "trampled nature." In his poetic framing of the American Revolution, Paine preferred the image of a tree—the Liberty Tree, the theme of the poem he wrote in 1775, referring to the ancient elm tree on the Boston Common that had served as the mustering ground of the early American resistance. It had been planted in the mid-seventeenth century. The symbolism of the tree, in the minds of colonists, was anything but comforting; the Liberty Tree provided the cover for raucous meetings, speeches, and notices posted to the trunk. The Tories and loyalists considered the Liberty Tree as a dark canopy of mob violence.

For Paine, the canopy of the tree created the public commons of democracy; nature itself, as he wrote in his notes "among the Indians," did not have "those spectacles of misery that poverty and want present to our eyes in the towns and streets of Europe." Such material poverty "exists not in the natural state."

Not everyone agreed with Paine. In fact, this vast continent of dense trees, stretching nearly a billion acres of forests, "was one dismal wilderness," John Adams wrote. His vision of America was the great clearing, the building of cities. "Now the forests are removed, the land covered with fields of corn, orchards bending with fruit, and the magnificent habitations of rational and civilized people."

Paradoxically, Jefferson, among others, saw the clear-cutting of the great forests as a way to lessen the harsh winters. "A change in our climate . . . is taking place very sensibly," Jefferson wrote in his *Notes on the State of Virginia* in 1787. "The elderly inform me, the earth used to be covered with snow about three months in every year. The rivers, which then seldom failed to freeze over in the course of the winter, scarcely ever do now."

Climate change was a good thing back then, at least in the eyes of colonists and then Americans who declared that "a country, in a state of nature, covered with trees, must be much colder than the same country when cleared." These nonscientific anecdotes went far to define the American deforestation policy of the day. It set in motion a ripple of seemingly irreversible onslaught of timber clear-cutting across the continent.

Yet, as a symbol of freedom the tree had always been the most important inspiration for the colonists, and then the resistance—arguably more so than the American bald eagle. As early as 1652, the Bay Colony in Massachusetts chose trees as the images on minted silver coins—willow, pine, and oak. By the 1760s, Liberty Trees as the burning grounds of resistance sprung up in all thirteen colonies, from Providence, Rhode Island to Charleston, South Carolina. Battle flags during the Revolution hoisted Liberty Trees; according to David Hackett Fischer, by 1775 American vessels flew Liberty Tree flags to identity each other.

To call the early Americans tree-huggers, of course, would stretch truth and boggle our imaginations today; to separate the early American experience from the fate of our natural heritage of forests, on the other hand, would erase a fundamental element of our national identity.

"And their temple was Liberty Tree," Paine wrote in his poem. "How all the tyrannical powers / Kings, Commons, and Lords, are uniting amain / To cut down this guardian of ours."

Within months of the publication of that poem, British soldiers stormed Boston Common and slashed and burned down the elm tree, turning the Common into a clearing of smoldering ruin—a powerful image of environmental devastation in our times. The Brits stacked fourteen cords of wood from the great elm. They assumed the era of protests, tar and feathering, and resistance—all that dissent rooted in nature and natural rights—was over.

In fact, the image of the Liberty Tree—eventually a stump, and then a plaque in the mid-1800s—and its symbolism of resistance waned with the passing of the American Revolution. First, it was quickly forgotten with the rush to build new communities, the immediate expansion of the frontier, and the religious dogma of "man's dominion" over nature. With the bloody French Revolution embracing the Liberty Tree as its own symbol a decade later, a backlash also rippled across the American states. To compound the fear for the elite, Jefferson's famous line of dissent addressing the backcountry rebellions in the late 1780s—"the tree of liberty must be refreshed from time to time with the blood of patriots and tyrants"—added to a further distancing of the Liberty Tree and its resistance origins among those in power.

The Liberty Tree disappeared in the annals of official history; its role had been deracinated from the continuing American story. "The old process of selective remembering and willful forgetting of the history of the Revolution," according to historians Alfred Young and Harvey Kaye, rendered the Liberty Tree even more illusory to the elite who sought to establish their "cultural domination" over an authoritative version of history.

"The Revolution has a different meaning if you start here," Nathaniel Sheidley, director of public history at the Bostonian Society, told *The Boston Globe* in 2015 at the site of the Liberty Tree. "It wasn't all about guys in white wigs."

In 1825, as he made his valedictory tour through the country, the French Marquis de Lafayette, who had commanded the forces beside Washington in the American Revolution, reminded the Americans that "the world should never forget the spot where once stood Liberty Tree, so famous in your annals."

Indeed, over the next two centuries, frontier Americans would unleash an assault on the virgin forests, clear-cutting three-quarters of the nation's natural carbon sink, and reducing the remaining forests area to 286 million acres. Once the Industrial Revolution ramped up in the early 1800s, railroads and steam-generated power made lumber a large-scale industrial commodity, and the great plunder from Appalachia to the Great Lakes and across the Western mountains roared with the saws. "Timber production soared from one billion board feet in 1840 to 46 billion board feet in 1904, enough to fill more than 10,000,000 modern logging trucks," according to Whit Bronaugh, a forest historian and scientist. "By 1880, lumber had overtaken agriculture as the most important driver of deforestation."

As deforestation swept across the Mississippi River and the prairies to the Rocky Mountains, naturalist and University of Iowa president Thomas Macbride warned his Midwesterners in the 1890s to hold the line at the edge of the forest: "I contend that the narrow measure of Iowa's woodland should as such be religiously preserved and in a thousand places extended . . . Every rocky bank, every steep hillside, every overhanging bluff, every sandhill, every clay-covered ridge, every rain-washed gully should be kept sacredly covered with trees. The people would act today if the situation were clearly understood. The question is whether we do the right thing now or wait until the expense shall have increased a hundredfold."

Macbride's admonition was not heeded; Iowa became the most altered state in the nation, eliminating 99 percent of its native prairie and forest. An estimated one to two acres were lost for every new inhabitant on the continent.

By the 1930s, the roots of the Liberty Tree had nearly been destroyed; Dutch elm disease wiped out virtually 90 percent of the elm population in the United States. One hundred million elm trees did not only lack legal standing; uprooted, they cleared the way for the depletion of carbon stocks in the soil.

Paine's Liberty Tree in our modern times, a "tale most profane," had become a casualty of "the tyrannical powers" of "Kings, Commons, and Lords" and our own government policies against our own interests. "A war against nature is inevitably a war against himself," pioneering scientist Rachel Carson forewarned readers in 1962 in her landmark book, *Silent Spring*.

"NOWADAYS ALMOST ALL MAN'S IMPROVEMENTS," Henry David Thoreau wrote in his essay "Walking," and the "building of houses and the cutting down of the forest and of all large trees, simply deform the landscape, and make it more and more tame and cheap."

Thoreau's answer to our human encroachment on nature was an audacious call for resistance: "A people who would begin by burning the fences and let the forest stand!"

According to biographer Laura Dassow Walls, Thoreau's "social activism and his defense of nature sprang from the same roots; he found society in nature, and nature he found everywhere, including the town center and the human heart." Living in Concord, where the first salvos of the American Revolution took place, and active in the abolitionist movement, including his secret efforts to help refugees from John Brown's armed resistance, Thoreau sought to "live the American Revolution not as dead history but as a living experience that could overturn, and keep overturning, hidebound convention and comfortable habits."

"The greater part of what my neighbors call good I believe in my soul to be bad, and if I repent of anything, it is likely to be my good behavior," Thoreau noted, and he questioned his readers, "What demon possessed me, that I behaved so well?"

Resistance was the art of misbehaving. The defense of nature, for Thoreau, was its intersection with other struggles: "Under a government which imprisons any unjustly, the true place for a just man is also a prison," he wrote in his classic text *Resistance to Civil Government*. "It is there that the fugitive slave, and the Mexican prisoner on parole, and the Indian come to plead the wrongs of his race, should find them."

This intersection of resistance emerged for climate justice advocates, as well—what Bill McKibben foretold as "an onslaught of daily emergencies" during the Trump years. "This winter may find climate activists spending as much time trying to block deportations as pipelines," McKibben wrote in the days following the election in 2016, "we may have to live in a hot world, but we don't have to live in a jackbooted one, and the more community we can preserve, the more resilient our communities will be."

One of Trump's first executive orders in late January 2017, and one which he touted repeatedly on Twitter as a sign of his success, in fact, targeted a diverse and fierce resistance:

Signing orders to move forward with the construction of the Keystone XL and Dakota Access pipelines in the Oval Office.

Months after Trump's executive order to greenlight the controversial Dakota Access Pipeline, a nearly 1,200-mile channel that would deliver a half million barrels of crude oil a day across Native lands and waterways from North Dakota to refinery terminals in southern Illinois, U.S. District Judge James Boasberg in Washington, DC, ruled that the Army Corps did not completely comply with the National Environmental Policy Act—the very law Nixon signed in 1970. He found that the government agency did not "adequately consider the impacts of an oil spill on fishing rights, hunting rights, or environmental justice."

And yet, the pipeline was allowed to run, as litigation continued in the courts.

The historic resistance launched by Native Americans on the Standing Rock Sioux nation against the Dakota Access Pipeline in the spring of 2016 brought the blatant display of historicide into full view of American audiences, and underscored the abdication of the "law of nature" from policy measures in Washington, DC. To be sure, Trump was a former stakeholder in the Energy Transfer Partners (ETP) company behind the $3.8 billion pipeline; Rick Perry, who led Trump's Department of Energy, had served on the board of ETP.

"We have named the site of our resistance on my family's land the Sacred Stone Camp," Lakota historian and water protector Ladonna Brave Bull Allard said in an interview in 2016, explaining the background of the first camp to host thousands of Native Americans and clean water advocates in a year-long campaign of sustained civil disobedience. "The stones are not created anymore, ever since the U.S. Army Corps of Engineers dredged the mouth of the Cannonball River and flooded the area in the late 1950s as they finished the Oahe dam. They killed a portion of our sacred river. I was a young girl when the floods came and desecrated our burial sites and Sundance grounds. Our people are in that water. This river holds the story of my entire life."

Just as the pipeline threatened water quality as it crossed the Missouri River at Lake Oahe upstream from the Standing Rock Indian Reservation, Brave Bull Allard saw the resistance as reflecting an unending struggle over the erasure of Lakota and indigenous history. She noted that over 380 identified archaeological sites stood in the pathway of the pipeline bulldozers. Writing in *Yes! Magazine*, she cited the precedent of the U.S. Army massacre of hundreds of indigenous people on a traditional hunting party, including children, at the Inyan Ska or Whitestone Hill in 1863. Army commander Henry Sibley had praised the attack as "one of the most severe punishments that the Indians have ever received."

Three weeks after the presidential election in November 2016, the U.S. Commission on Civil Rights had issued a public rebuke of federal, state, and local law enforcement officials on the "use of military-style equipment and excessive force" on DAPL water protectors. "The issue of the pipeline is not just about the pipeline alone," Commission Chair Martin R. Castro stated, "but rather it is about the entire relationship between the United States and sovereign Indian Nations, their rights, traditions and religious beliefs."

The resistance against the Dakota Access pipeline for Brave Bull Allard revived "our stories of survival":

> The U.S. government is wiping out our most important cultural and spiritual areas. And as it erases our footprint from the world, it erases us as a people. These sites must be protected, or our world will end, it is that simple. Our young people have a right to know who they are. They have a right to language, to culture, to tradition. The way they learn these things is through connection to our lands and our history.

On the night of Trump's election, in the tradition of the Boston Tea Party destruction of private property, two Catholic Worker activists based in Des Moines set fire to heavy machinery along the route of the DAPL pipeline. It was part of an eight-month-long property destruction campaign to delay construction. At a press conference in the summer of 2017, in front of the Iowa Utilities Board sign— symbolically calling out the state board's decision to reject a lawsuit by environmental groups to revoke a pipeline permit—Ruby Montoya, a schoolteacher from Colorado, and Jessica Reznicek, a longtime Iowa activist, described how they taught themselves to use oxy-acetylene cutting torches to pierce through exposed, empty steel valves and set back pipeline construction for weeks.

"We are speaking publicly to empower others to act boldly, with purity of heart, to dismantle the infrastructures which deny us our rights to water, land and liberty," Reznicek read in a statement. "We, as civilians, have seen the repeated failures of the government, and it is our duty to act with responsibility and integrity, risking our own liberty for the sovereignty of us all."

In a statement that echoed the actions by American colonists at the Liberty Tree, Montoya added: "Some may view these actions as violent, but be not mistaken. We acted from our hearts and never threatened human life nor personal property. What we did do was fight a private corporation that has run rampantly across our country seizing land and polluting our nation's water supply."

As a member of the 100 Grannies activist group in Iowa City, Miriam Kashia had been so inspired by the Standing Rock resistance that she and a group of Iowan elders launched their own civil disobedience campaign on the tail end of the pipeline in southern Iowa. Kashia was not a recent convert to the resistance; in 2014, at the age of seventy-one, she had joined a small but dedicated band of walkers, traversing the United States from Los Angeles to Washington, DC, in a 3,000-mile march to raise awareness about climate change. Near the Mississippi River in Lee County, Kashia and a group of "grannie" protesters walked through a wooded area and crop field, and then hopped over a chain-link fence at a pipeline construction area. Crews were drilling with boring equipment, aiming for the river. Security guards stood all around. Kashia and her friends recognized it was the private land of a farmer who had lost her rights to eminent domain. Lee County, historically, had been set aside in 1836 for Native Americans relocated from east of the Mississippi River.

"This is something people have got to understand," said fellow Grannie Ann Christenson, an eighty-year-old from Iowa City. "The motto of the 100 Grannies is 'educate, advocate and agitate.' We'd rather educate, but if we have to, we're going to agitate and go to jail. It is serious and time is very short. People don't seem to understand that this is urgent."

The cadre of radical grannies crawled under the fence onto the site. Then they hid behind the machinery—machinery that would allow barrels of oil to flow across sovereign indigenous lands, farms, prairies and forests and rivers with probable spills and bursts; to be burned with millions of tons of CO_2 every year.

"I was arrested," Kashia wrote, "along with about 30 other water protectors, in my peaceful attempt to prevent such a disaster on the Mississippi River. Boring under our farmland and our rivers in order to pump oil for private profit when the nations of the world agree that we must focus now on transitioning to sustainable energy is unthinkable and unconscionable. I cannot be complicit by ignoring this reality."

On May 23, 2017, the same day the Trump administration announced its intentions to cut the EPA budget by 31 percent, gutting regional programs for water protection, lead risk–reduction programs, and Superfund clean-up sites, Lee County Judge Gary Noneman dismissed the trespassing charges against the "grannies." Calling attention to the "lawlessness" of the pipeline permits, Christenson and Kashia did not celebrate their victory. "This isn't over. They may be pumping, but we're not done."

The next phases of resistance for Standing Rock and the pipeline would take numerous forms, through numerous entities and people.

"We will be developing not a camp, but a village, to show people how to live on the earth, to do organic farming, green energy, thermal, wind, and solar," Brave Bull Allard told *Teen Vogue* magazine in the spring of 2017. "We have amazing people from all over the world who have that technology, who want to share it. If the whole United States went into green energy, we could provide more jobs than fossil fuel. We can provide a way of living that causes people to live good with the earth."

This enduring meaning of resistance for Paine, like the Liberty Tree, was regenerative, full of flourishing "branches of liberty"—especially after the American Revolution. Resistance was fertile.

"FROM THIS DAY FORWARD, A new vision will govern our land," Trump had declared at his inauguration on January 20, 2017, speaking from the steps of the U.S. Capitol. "From this day forward, it's going to be only America first, America first."

Proclaiming the America First slogan as a fundamental principle for his relinquishment of American leadership in global agreements, Trump doubled down on his refusal to attend a high-level meeting of global leaders on climate change hosted by UN Secretary-General António Guterres at the UN General Assembly in the fall of 2017.

Indeed, "America First" had its own unique costs of denial: according to a National Oceanic and Atmospheric Administration analysis released on January 8, 2018, "the US experienced a historic year of weather and climate disasters," resulting in "16 separate billion-dollar disaster events tying 2011 for the record number of billion-dollar disasters for an entire calendar year." The cost from devastating hurricanes and record-breaking wildfires: $306 billion in damages.

"I was elected to represent the citizens of Pittsburgh, not Paris," Trump had claimed in his announcement. In response, Pittsburgh Mayor Bill Peduto captured the sentiment of an emerging climate resistance, redoubling his city's efforts for clean energy: "I can assure you that we will follow the guidelines of the Paris Agreement for our people, our economy and future."

Speaking to participants at the Global Citizen Festival in Hamburg, Germany, in the same days of the UN General Assembly, California Governor Jerry Brown announced his plan to host a global climate summit in San Francisco in September 2018. "I know President Trump is trying to get out of the Paris Agreement, but he doesn't speak for the rest of America," Brown said. "We in California and in states all across America believe it's time to act, it's time to join together and that's why at this Climate Action Summit we're going to get it done."

In shaping a new narrative for resistance, cities and states would also embrace Paine's vision of resistance as an agency of renewal and an act of global solidarity. "The cause of America is in a great measure the cause of all mankind," Paine wrote in *Common Sense* in 1776. "We have it in our power to begin the world over again."

Never has Paine's call for independence over compromise been so compelling in recent American history. Cities and states have become the new frontlines of climate resistance.

The wind turbines that rose out of the cornfields in the heartland reminded observers of one postelection truth, even in the red state of Iowa. Regardless of Trump's breaking of the U.S. commitment to the

Paris climate accord, the rise of clean energy across the heartland was already too well entrenched to be reversed.

By 2020, thanks to MidAmerican Energy's planned $3.6 billion addition to its enormous wind turbine operations, an astonishing 85 percent of its Iowa customers would be electrified by clean energy. Meanwhile, Moxie Solar, named the fastest-growing local business by Iowa's *Corridor Business Journal*, took part in a solar industry that now employed more than 260,000 people nationwide.

Far from surrendering to Trump's federal jettison of the Clean Power Plan, an Obama-era plan to reduce greenhouse gas emissions from power plants in a federal-state process, the cities and states of resistance took up the responsibility for effectively reining in carbon emissions. Those were the true battlegrounds. Worldwide, cities produced as much as 70 percent of greenhouse gas emissions.

The historic barrage of hurricanes in the fall of 2017—wiping out Puerto Rico's and the U.S. Virgin Islands' infrastructure, grinding the city of Houston to a stop, and placing Miami's downtown streets under water—served as a brutal and costly reminder that many of the planet's major cities lie along the coasts and are threatened by slowly rising seas. Seventy percent of those cities were already dealing with extreme weather like drought and flooding. Add aging infrastructure and waves of displacement and it was clear that city planners, mayors, and governors had to reenvision how their cities generate energy and provide food and transportation.

As part of the hashtag #AJustHarveyRecovery, Houston-based environmentalist and journalist Bryan Parras categorized these "catastrophes and disasters" as "not just environmental disasters—they're housing disasters. They're access to services. They're immigration issues of injustice." For Parras, among an alliance of groups in the region, "another Gulf" is possible. "We need a just transition for the sake of the life and livelihoods of our communities, our cultures and our ecosystems. We will no longer stand to be a sacrifice zone for this country, we demand justice and equity."

Climate adaptation was not enough; adaptation to a failed system, as Commoner had warned a half century earlier, was failure.

Instead, building on Commoner's four laws of ecology, urban theorist and author Herbert Giradet envisioned "regenerative cities" as a natural sequence in planning in an age of climate change. "The urban metabolism currently operates as an inefficient and wasteful linear input-output system," Girardet posited in his groundbreaking work in cities in Europe, Australia, and around the globe. "It needs to be transformed into a resource-efficient circular system instead. The only way to overcome notions of ever-greater scarcity is for cities to continually regenerate the living systems on which they rely for their sustenance."

"The concept of a regenerative city could indeed become a new vision for cities," the Germany-based World Future Council reported in 2017. "It stands for cities that not only minimize negative impact but can actually have a positive, beneficial role to play within the natural ecosystem from which they depend. Cities have to constantly regenerate the resources they absorb."

This concept had won broad support at a 2016 gathering of city leaders from around the world in Quito, Ecuador, hosted by the United Nations. The Habitat III conference approved a "new urban agenda" that urged cities to adapt to climate change but minimize their harm to the environment and move to sustainable economies.

Following this regenerative approach, the Australian city of Adelaide reduced its carbon emissions by 20 percent from 2007 to 2013, even as the population grew by 27 percent and the economy increased by 28 percent. The city experienced a boom in green jobs, the development of walkable neighborhoods powered by solar energy, the conversion of urban waste to compost, and a revamped local food industry. The city also planted three million trees to absorb carbon dioxide.

American cities now needed to begin the world over again, in the words of Paine; regenerative cities, in effect, were cities of resistance. On January 2, 2018, the Fayetteville City Council in Arkansas became the fifty-fourth city to commit to a 100 percent renewable energy plan by 2030.

Announced on the day of Trump's inauguration in 2017, California's move to reduce its carbon emissions to 40 percent below 1990 levels by 2030 marked a hopeful shift that other cities and states needed to emulate. This would involve setting high benchmarks for developing green enterprise zones, renewable energy, cultivating food locally, restoring biodiversity, planting more trees, and emphasizing walkability, low-carbon transportation, and zero waste.

California was not alone. "It only took two nanoseconds," Washington Governor Jay Inslee said in an interview with *YaleEnvironment360*, in explaining his own state's agreement with the U.S. Climate Alliance, an independent alliance of cities and fifteen states. "We heard the president wanted to run up the white flag of surrender. We wanted to send a strong message to the world: We're not going to surrender."

With or without significant federal support, reducing greenhouse gas emissions required major private investment, and ambitious private-public initiatives from mayors and governors. Representing $6.2 trillion of the U.S. economy and more than 130 million Americans, or 40 percent of the U.S. population, the "We Are Still In" coalition of cities, states, campuses, faith communities, and businesses effectively served as American delegates—instead of the coal-peddling Trump administration representatives—at the UN climate talks (COP23) in Bonn, Germany, in the fall of 2017.

Over 10,000 climate initiatives were underway in cities worldwide, according to the C40 Cities Climate Leadership Group, which represented 100 major cities. In Des Moines, Iowa, for instance, Mayor Frank Cownie committed his city to reducing its energy consumption 50 percent by 2030 and becoming "carbon neutral" by 2050. In declaring New York City's intent to become a carbon neutral city by 2050, Mayor Bill de Blasio called for "big solutions" to big problems. "In the Trump era, cities have to lead the way when it comes to fighting climate change. Hotter summers and powerful storms made worse by climate change are an existential threat to a coastal city like ours, which is why we need to act now." By 2016, New York City had already planted its one-millionth tree as part of a reforestation campaign. In a dramatic challenge to other cities, de Blasio announced New York City's intent to divest $5 billion from fossil fuel investments in its city pension funds portfolio, and join California cities in suing five major oil companies who had knowingly hidden their own scientific conclusions on fossil fuel links to climate change. "This city is standing up," the mayor said, on January 10, 2018. "We're going to take our own actions to protect our own people."

Initiatives like these have become a "fill the potholes" reality for many mayors, regardless of political games in Washington. In San Diego, the Republican mayor, Kevin Faulconer, helped to push through a climate action plan that commits the city to 100 percent renewable energy by 2035. Other cities following his lead included St. Louis, headquarters of the world's largest coal company, Peabody Energy, and dependent on coal-fired plants for 75 percent of its electricity; in October of 2017, the St. Louis Board of Aldermen unanimously voted to adopt a goal of obtaining 100 percent of its electricity from renewable sources by 2035.

Rural areas, in fact, may be even further ahead in the climate resistance.

Negotiators en route to the United Nations conference on climate change in Paris could have taken a detour on rural roads in my adopted home here in Johnson County, Iowa. A new climate narrative was emerging among farmers in the American heartland that transcended a lot of the old story lines of denial and cynicism, and offered an updated tale of climate hope.

Even before the 2016 presidential election, polls showed that 60 percent of Iowans, now facing flooding and erosion, believed global warming needed to be addressed. From Winneshiek County to Washington County, you could count more solar panels on barns than on urban roofs or in suburban parking lots. The state's first major solar farm was not in an urban area like Des Moines or Iowa City, but in rural Frytown, initiated by the Farmers Electric Cooperative.

In the meantime, any lingering traces of cynicism vanished in the town of Crawfordsville, Iowa, which claimed itself as the birthplace of the Republican Party in 1854. Children in the nearby Waco school district turned on computers and studied under lights powered 90 percent by solar energy. Inspired by local pig farmers, who used solar energy to help power some of their operations, the district's move to solar energy not only cut carbon emissions but also resulted in enough savings to keep open the town's once financially threatened schools' doors.

But here was the catch—and a reminder of the relevant symbolism of the Liberty Tree: Even if every coal-fired plant shut down in the United States, land misuse still accounted for an estimated 30 percent of the world's carbon emissions. The soils in the United States, like those of nations around the world, had lost calamitous amounts of carbon.

This was where Iowa's new climate narrative emerged as a great story for the resistance and other countries who had signed the climate accord in Paris. Despite the fact that the United Nations General Assembly had declared 2015 to be "the international year of soils," a global soil carbon sequestration campaign—one that recognizes direct links between climate mitigation, regenerative agriculture, and food security—rarely ranked at the top of any high level accords, or even conversations.

The 4 Per 1000 Initiative, sponsored by France's Ministry of Agriculture, Agrifood, and Forestry, called for a voluntary action plan to improve organic matter content and promote carbon sequestration in soil through a transition to agroecology, agroforestry, conservation agriculture, and landscape management. According to France's estimates, a "4 percent annual growth rate of the soil carbon stock would make it possible to stop the present increase in atmospheric CO_2."

Releasing a study in 2017 on the impact of "regreening the planet," an international team of researchers determined that "better stewardship of the land could have a bigger role in fighting climate change than previously thought." According to the findings in the *Proceedings of the National Academy of Sciences* journal, natural climate solutions, such as massive reforestation campaigns and better management of soils and grasslands, could account for 37 percent of all actions needed by 2030 under the Paris climate accord.

To see the wisdom of such a proposal, one only needed to visit the Versaland agroforestry farm in Johnson County, Iowa. In less than three years, a young farmer named Grant Schultz had planted more than 40,000 trees, introduced cover crops, composting, and multispecies grazing, and transformed a once degraded industrial corn farm into a vibrant carbon capturing and storing ecosystem.

In effect, Mr. Schultz and Versaland had completely shifted the climate change narrative in the heartland. Today's farmers and tree planters could play a key role in the climate resistance.

According to a white paper released in 2016 by the pioneering Rodale Institute, which studies and promotes organic farming, if management of all current cropland worldwide shifted to a regenerative model similar to that of Versaland and other organic farming sites, more than 40 percent of annual carbon emissions could potentially be captured. What Mr. Schultz and other Iowan farmers were doing was not only groundbreaking; it was also giving the heartland a new future.

From the Boston Tea Party to the Boston Oil Party, perhaps the time had come for the resistance to throw a Liberty Tree Party, and reclaim our American forests and launch a national reforestation campaign for climate mitigation. On July 4, 2017, India planted 66 million trees in a twelve-hour stretch as part of that nation's carbon sequestration plan.

"Dull, inert cities, it is true, do contain the seeds of their own destruction and little else," the urban visionary Jane Jacobs wrote. "But lively, diverse, intense cities contain the seeds of their own regeneration, with energy enough to carry over for problems and needs outside themselves."

In an age of climate change, and a shift in the federal government's priority on climate action, such a vision has become an essential framework for a new climate resistance.

IN THE FALL OF 2009, I filed a news story on the battle over mountaintop removal mining in Appalachia, and as always, I went to spend some time with one of my mentors in West Virginia. His name was Ken Hechler; a former U.S. Congressman, Hechler was in his mid-90s. As one of our nation's liberal titans, Hechler understood the vexing relationship with Big Coal and 150 years of denial of the true cost of mining. While black lung was first diagnosed in 1831, it took Hechler's congressional leadership as the U.S. representative from West Virginia to pass federal legislation to deal with its ravages in 1969. Still today, three coal miners die daily—and needlessly—from black lung disease. Though scientists recognized the deleterious impact of sulfur dioxide emissions as early as the 1860s, it took an aggressive grassroots movement to pass the Clean Air Act of 1990 to overcome the denial of acid rain, which had scorched the forests from the Appalachians to Canada.

In 1971, Hechler organized the first Congressional hearings on mountaintop removal and introduced the first federal bill to abolish strip-mining. As Hechler testified in a House committee in 1971: "Representing the largest coal-producing state in the nation, I can testify that strip-mining has ripped the guts out of our mountains, polluted our streams with acid and silt, uprooted trees and forests, devastated the land, seriously destroyed wildlife habitat, left miles of ugly highwalls, ruined the water supply in many areas, and left a trail of utter despair for many honest and hard-working people."

By the time the Trump administration came to power, an area the size of the state of Delaware—over 500 mountains and millions of acres of deciduous forest that had served as the carbon sink of the South—had been eliminated by clear-cutting and radical strip-mining operations called mountaintop removal. From Appalachia to Illinois to Black Mesa on the Dine (Navajo) Nation in Arizona to Montana and twenty coal-mined states, a health and humanitarian crisis from the lethal fallout of decades of mining continues to rage under the auspices of flawed regulatory measures, blatant disregard for civil rights, and media indifference.

Speaking at an event in eastern Kentucky to announce the Trump administration's intent to repeal an Obama-era greenhouse gas emissions rule for existing power plants, EPA chief Pruitt declared "the war against coal is over." The true war by the coal industry, of course, was ignored. Pruitt, like Trump, would never mention the huge reckoning coal-mined communities have paid with their health, lives, and livelihoods: that high rates of lung cancer and heart and respiratory problems will plague mining communities for generations. Huge toxic coal slurry impoundments, where the deadly refuge of coal processing hovers like time bombs, will poison watersheds and threaten entire communities for years. Black lung disease will still whittle away at the lives of workers for generations. Underground fires will burn unabated for decades. Streams and creeks contaminated by strip-mine discharges will remain without aquatic life. Coal companies and barons who have openly flaunted workplace safety and environmental laws will walk away free. The cumulative effect of CO_2 emissions from coal has forever altered our future.

With virtually no support from mainstream environmental groups, impacted residents—including farmers and grannies and retired coal miners and students—had courageously led a resistance for decades against violation-ridden mining, deadly coal slurry, and bankrupt coal companies that dominated a boom-bust economy.

The more time I spent with Hechler and former coal miners like Chuck Nelson in West Virginia and Stanley Sturgill in Kentucky, and veteran activists like Goldman Prize recipient Maria Gunnoe in West Virginia and longtime activist Kathy Selvage in southwest Virginia coal country—the children and grandchildren of union miners who have led movements for over a century for workplace safety measures, water and environmental protection, and basic civil rights—the more I realized this kind of climate resistance has been the bedrock of climate hope.

As the grandson of a black lung–afflicted coal miner in southern Illinois who lost his family's ancestral homestead and farm to strip-mining, and as a longtime chronicler of the coal industry, I deeply appreciated Hechler's century of hellraising in coal country—and across the nation.

Hechler was no stranger to history and its crises. As a military officer in World War II, he interrogated Nazi war criminals; as a history professor and bestselling author, he assisted Franklin D. Roosevelt with his thirteen-volume public papers. While his congressional colleagues attended a baseball game in Florida, Hechler drove to Selma, Alabama, in 1965, defied Klan threats, and marched as the only member of Congress willing to join the "aroused conscience of the nation" in the historic civil rights event.

On February 18, 1965, Jimmie Lee Jackson, an African American deacon of the Marion, Alabama, Baptist church, was brutally beaten by Alabama state troopers, and then followed into a café, where he was gunned down for protecting his mother and eighty-two-year-old grandfather from the police attack.

Days later, Hechler stood with Unitarian minister James Reeb, among forty Unitarian ministers who had responded to King's call to come to Selma. Reeb was a rural boy from Wyoming who was serving a church in Boston. On the night of the Selma march, he was attacked and clubbed outside a restaurant, and died two days later.

"Naturally, we are compelled to ask the question, Who killed James Reeb?" King asked in his eulogy at the funeral. "When we move from the who to the what, the blame is wide and the responsibility grows." King's words were harsh: James Reeb was murdered, he wrote, "by the indifference of every minister of the gospel who has remained silent behind the safe security of stained-glass windows. He was murdered by the irrelevancy of a church that will stand amid social evil and serve as a taillight rather than a headlight, an echo rather than a voice."

A few days later, the nation would be shocked again by the murder of another Unitarian—Viola Liuzzo, a mother of three in Detroit, who was so horrified by the TV images of the bloody marches in Selma that she drove down to Selma to help the marchers. She was gunned down on March 25, 1965, as she drove a marcher to his home. Unlike Reeb, though, Liuzzo went through a second round of battering, as her reputation yielded to the sexism of the day, rendering her a reckless woman in the era; a single woman in a car with a black man, who had left behind her family to join the struggle for civil rights. It would take years before Liuzzo was properly recognized for her bravery and commitment to her generation's resistance.

These are always the times that try women's souls.

"I used to be an agitator, then an activist," Hechler told me one day as he rested under a huge tree near a protest against the EPA's reckless oversight of a 2.8 billion-gallon lake of toxic coal sludge, as federally sanctioned mountaintop removal blasting took place nearby. "Now I am a hellraiser. There's not enough time left."

In her eighties, labor leader Mary "Mother" Jones had said the same thing in 1911, addressing a crowd at a rally. "Get it right, I'm not a humanitarian. I'm a hellraiser."

In the summer of 2009, at the age of ninety-four, Hechler had taken to the streets to stand up to the bankrolled wrath of union-busting Big

Coal thugs and joined a protest at Marsh Fork Elementary in the Coal
River Valley of West Virginia, where schoolchildren played amid toxic
coal dust and sat under the horrific reality of a massive coal slurry im-
poundment in the mountains. The nonagenarian Hechler was arrested,
along with former NASA climate scientist James Hansen, actress Daryl
Hannah, Goldman Prize recipients Judy Bonds and Maria Gunnoe, and
scores of Appalachian resisters.

"I don't mind being poor," Bonds, a coal miner's daughter and director of the Coal River Mountain Watch organization, told the crowd.
"And I don't mind being made fun of. But I draw the line at being blasted
and poisoned." She invoked Frederick Douglass's charge that "change
requires thunder and lightning." Judy reminded the crowd: "And you are
the thunder. You are the lightning."

One month after the presidential election of 2016, Ken Hechler died at
the age of 102. On behalf of the Earth Justice organization, Hechler once
made a tribute that captured the long haul of the resistance movements:
"There is a light at the end of the tunnel, but the tougher it gets, the more
exciting it gets when you can see victory. I'm still hoping that before I leave
this world I get to see that victory, which I'm sure is going to come."

In a landmark lawsuit in federal court, *Juliana v. United States*,
twenty-one children and youth gave new energy to Hechler's torch at
the end of the tunnel, suing the federal government for inaction on climate change, claiming it had violated "the youngest generation's constitutional rights to life, liberty, and property." Arguing in front of the
Ninth Circuit Court of Appeals in San Francisco on December 11, 2017,
which ruled that Trump and his administration must attend to a trial
set for the spring of 2018, Our Children's Trust director and co-counsel
Julia Olson posited that "children are disproportionately experiencing
the impacts of climate change, and will going forward." As a plaintiff on
behalf of his granddaughter, climatologist Hansen added, "We should be
on the offensive. We are seeing injustice against the young. The present
generation has a responsibility to future generations."

In the last years, I have held my son's hand on the banks of the Mississippi River as we watched his native state of Illinois teeter on the extreme edges of climate change from a prolonged drought that brought

the nation's greatest river to record low depths to an emergency state for spring flooding. We have stood in the ruins of our 150-year-old homestead in the devastated historic community of Eagle Creek, in the Shawnee Forest of southern Illinois; then, turning to guerilla reclamation, my billie boys, the ninth generation of Eagle Creek ancestry, planted the first native plum trees on the unmanaged grassland reclamation mining site as an act of resistance, in what was once one of the most diverse forests in the nation.

"To me young people come first, they have the courage where we fail," the music group Sweet Honey in the Rock often sang in the 1980s, recalling the inspiring words of civil rights organizer Ella Baker.

This sentiment might be best understood with the breakthrough March for Our Lives movement launched by Florida high school students, which has mobilized rallies in all fifty states to address gun violence issues. Or perhaps it might be found in a downtown Las Vegas elementary school, where educator Juliana Urtubey gathered bilingual Latinx students around caterpillar seats and an outdoor whiteboard in the spring of 2018, as they tended to a "Regenerative Edge-ucation" program and thriving outdoor garden. "My work as an educator has taken many turns through bilingual education, social justice education, adult education, and special education within low-income community settings," Urtubey once told me about her teachers' collective, based on a pedagogical approach of creating a nourishing space within community to engage in the patterns of nature to design and build healthy regenerative systems. "Knowledge, praxis, and action as resistance for maintaining language, culture, for closing achievement gaps, for community health, for building educational spaces that are determined by community."

"It has always been about seeds of resistance," Urtubey said.

"Youth is the seed time of good habits, as well in nations as in individuals," Paine reminded the emerging Americans in his pamphlet *Common Sense* in 1776. "It is not in numbers, but in unity, that our great strength lies."

The resistance is now in the hands of a new generation.

Acknowledgments

IT's AN HONOR TO BE back with editor and publisher Jack Shoemaker, whose incredible (and legendary) commitment to writers and writing continually reminds us, in these troubling days, that books matter. Thanks to Jack's decades of work, Counterpoint Press is a dream house for authors; his list of poets, novelists, and essayists has filled my shelves for years. Jack graciously published my first book, *The United States of Appalachia*, trusted my vision with an inspiring prod, and has challenged my writing over the years with wit and wisdom. I'm truly grateful.

Thanks, as well, to the Counterpoint Press team, which has worked wonders to place this book on the fast track to publishing: Olenka Burgess, Jennifer Alton, Megan Fishmann, Alisha Gorder, Jennifer Kovitz, Sarah Baline, and Dustin Kurtz; and to the superb production crew: Jordan Koluch, copyeditor Dan O'Connor, Kelli Trapnell, and Wah-Ming Chang.

My folks, as always, are my first readers, Mam and Paps, Jean and John, and their guidance on this book has been as important as the enduring stories of their own life work, in the classroom, in the courtroom, on the picket lines—from coal country to the high country of the Southwest to New Zealand. Frankly, I never rebelled against my parents; I rebelled with my parents.

Several other readers gave me some important feedback on first drafts and subsequent conversations: thank you so much Doug Biggers, Bob

Kincaid, Kristina Castañeda, Corey Hagelberg and Kate Land and the Calumet Artist Residency, Erik Bitsui, Alessandro Portelli, Chris Rundle, Glenn Alessi, and Guy Lydster. Deep gratitude for the advance praise and support from Sandra Steingraber, Jeff Chang, Bill McKibben, and Naomi Benaron. And thanks to Miriam Kashia and the Unitarian Universalist Society of Iowa City, Coralville, Iowa, for their inspiring works.

Written in a passion of patriotism, as Paine might say, *Resistance* draws on decades of research, work, and writing; my eighth book, it's a culmination of years of reporting and activism, untold days in the archives, and untold nights of writing. It also draws on the work and theories of some of my exemplars, including Studs Terkel, who encouraged me with his ninety-three-year-old wisdom to collect my stories on the frontlines, and many professors and writers who shaped my early studies in various schools many years ago: my dear friend Carlos Muñoz, Jr., at the University of California, Berkeley; Stanford historian Clayborne Carson (who guest taught an unforgettable course on the civil rights movement at UC Berkeley); Eric Foner at Columbia University; and Nell Painter and Barbara Welter at Hunter College. That was me in the corner, dear professors, taking notes, reading your books, and I thank you for your insights and towering legacies as social historians.

To my billie boys, Diego and Massimo, this book is a result of your wonderful questions and thoughts, our conversations, and the long haul ahead.

And finally, and most importantly, Carla, *mi compañera de lucha, mi inspiración, mi amor,* who has made every book possible, especially in this last year in Sardinia, thank you is not enough. *Sempre di piu.*

Bibliographic Notes

Author's Note

xi Fannie Lou Hamer quotation, "Sick and Tired of Being Sick and Tired," *The Speeches of Fannie Lou Hamer: To Tell It Like It Is* (University Press of Mississippi, 2010), p. 81.

xii take our children in our hand, and fix our station a few years farther into life, Thomas Paine, *Common Sense*, reprinted in *Thomas Paine: Collected Writings: Common Sense / The Crisis / Rights of Man / The Age of Reason / Pamphlets, Articles, and Letters* (Library of America, 1995), p. 25.

xii The sun shines today also, Ralph Waldo Emerson, *The Selected Writings of Ralph Waldo Emerson* (Modern Library, 1992), p. 15.

xii Pray for the dead and fight like hell for the living, Mary "Mother" Jones, *Autobiography of Mother Jones* (Charles H. Kerr and Company, 1925), p. 21.

xiii bring out to the light all that has been under the cover all these years, quoted in David L. Chappell, *A Stone of Hope: Prophetic Religion and the Death of Jim Crow* (University of North Carolina Press, 2004), p. 73.

xiii To sin by silence, when we should protest / Makes cowards out of men, Ella Wheeler Wilcox, quoted in Sandra Steingraber, "Lessons for Our Time from Rachel Carson," keynote address to the Rachel Carson 75th Anniversary Jubilee Celebration and Colloquium in Washington, DC, Nov. 30, 2016.

xiii Today's announcement is an opportunity, "'Silence Breakers' of Color Among Those Named *Time* 'Person of the Year'," Sameer Rao, *Colorlines*, December 6, 2017.

xiii Today, the majority of South Africans, black and white, recognize that apartheid has no future, Nelson Mandela, *New York Times*, February 12, 1990.

Introduction

3 Let them call me rebel and welcome, I feel no concern from it, Thomas Paine, "American Crisis I," reprinted in Paine, *Collected Writings*, p. 97.

3 It left to the Americans no other modes of redress, Thomas Paine, "Dissertations on Government," Feb. 18, 1786, reprinted in Philip Foner, *The Complete Writings of Thomas Paine, Volume 2* (Citadel Press, 1945), p. 370.

4 The whole country cringes in indignation at these heartless barbarians, Dolores Ibárruri, "Fascism shall not pass," August 23, 1936, Brian MacArthur, *Penguin Book of Historic Speeches* (Viking, 1995), p. 607.

4 Resistance is an organized effort by some portion of the civil population, *Department of Defense Dictionary of Military and Associated Terms*, Washington, DC, Joint Chiefs of Staff (G.P.O., 1994).

5 History is to ascribe the American Revolution to Thomas Paine, John Adams, quoted in Jill Lepore, *The Story of America: Essays on Origins* (Princeton University Press, 2012), p. 63.

5 Even those who are jealous of, and envy him, quoted in Craig Nelson, *Thomas Paine: Enlightenment, Revolution, and the Birth of Modern Nations* (Penguin, 2007), p. 163.

5 As I was with the troops at Fort Lee, Thomas Paine, "American Crisis I," reprinted in Paine, *Collected Writings*, p. 92.

5 Our style and manner of thinking have undergone a revolution, Thomas Paine, "Letter to the Abbé Raynal," reprinted in Foner, *The Complete Writings of Thomas Paine, Volume 2*, p. 243.

6 committed an error for the interests of his country, "France's Macron says U.S. interests to be harmed by climate deal withdrawal," *Reuters*, June 2, 2017.

6 The time in which we could fully rely on others is a bit in the past, "Angela Merkel and the Insult of Trump's Paris Climate-Accord Withdrawal," *New Yorker*, June 1, 2017.

6 Our withdrawal from the agreement represents a reassertion of America's sovereignty, "Trump Will Withdraw U.S. From Paris Climate Agreement," *New York Times*, June 1, 2017.

8 Watched protests yesterday but was under the impression that we just had an election! Donald J. Trump, Twitter, January 22, 2017. twitter.com /realdonaldtrump/status/823150055418920960.

8 Thy ev'ry action let the goddess guide, Phillis Wheatley, *The Poems of Phillis Wheatley* (University of North Carolina Press, 1988). p. 167.

9 made as free as any inhabitant, Frank Grizzard and D. Boyd Smith, *Jamestown Colony: A Political, Social, and Cultural History* (ABC-CLIO, 2007), p. 171.

10 its attempt to enrich the few at the expense of the many, Leonard Richards, *Shay's Rebellion: The American Revolution's Final Battle* (University of Pennsylvania Press, 2003), p. 63.

10 Therefore whenever any incroachments are making either upon the liberties, quoted in Robert Martin, *Government by Dissent: Protest, Resistance, and Radical Democratic Thought in the Early American Republic* (NYU Press, 2013), p. 31.

11 This government will set out a moderate aristocracy, George Mason, "George Mason's Objections September 1787," retrieved at edu.lva.virginia .gov/docs/MasonsObjections.pdf.

11 a historic level of wealth that's at least fifty times greater than the Cabinet that George W. Bush led, "President-elect Trump's $14 billion Cabinet," CBS News, December 14, 2016, retrieved at www.cbsnews.com/pictures /donald-trumps-14-billion-cabinet.

11 You all just got a lot richer, "'You all just got a lot richer,' Trump tells friends, referencing tax overhaul," CBS News, December 23, 2017.

12 richest one tenth of one percent of Americans now owns, Robert Reich, "The danger of dynastic wealth," *Chicago Tribune*, September 18, 2017.

12 carry water for America's growing aristocracy of the ultra-rich, "Trump tax plan puts ultra-rich before the middle class," *Chicago Tribune*, September 27, 2017.

13 open up our libel laws so when, "Donald Trump pledges to curb press freedom through libel laws," *Guardian*, February 26, 2016.

13 The real scandal here is that classified information is illegally given out by 'intelligence' like candy, Donald J. Trump, Twitter, February 15, 2017, retrieved at twitter.com/realdonaldtrump/status/831853862281699331.

13 arrested the rapid march of our government toward monarchy, Thomas Jefferson to James Monroe, October 19, 1823, retrieved at www.loc.gov /resource/mtj1.054_0046_0046/?st=text.

13 To undo a mistake is always harder than not to create one originally, Eleanor Roosevelt, "Undo the Mistake of Internment," retrieved at www.nps .gov/articles/erooseveltinternment.htm.

14 Mr. President, look at us. This is America, "Protesters mass at airports to decry Trump's immigration policies," CNN, January 29, 2017.

14 The broad historical causes which shaped these decisions, *Korematsu v. United States*, 584 F. Supp. 1406 (N.D. Cal. 1984), retrieved at law.justia .com/cases/federal/district-courts/FSupp/584/1406/2270281.

14 You met with Trump and you call that resistance, "Nancy Pelosi leaves press conference after being shouted down by undocumented immigrants protesting talks with Trump," *Mercury News*, September 18, 2017.

15 Immigrant youth has been at the forefront protesting, Sandy Valenciano, "Why California Undocumented Youth and I Interrupted Nancy Pelosi's Dream Act Press Conference," *Huffington Post*, September 19, 2017.

15 Get that son of a bitch off the field right now, "Donald Trump blasts NFL anthem protesters: 'Get that son of a bitch off the field,'" *Guardian*, September 23, 2017.

16 NFL players who #TakeAKnee are sons of Justice, Dr. Rev. Barber, Twitter, September 23, 2017, retrieved at twitter.com/revdrbarber/status /911769272229203968.

16 Rooted in the experiences of Black people in this country, #BlackLives-Matter, retrieved at hudsonvalleyblmcoalition.org/home/about.

16 Protest is patriotic, John Legend, "The NFL Protests Are Patriotic," *Slate*, September 24, 2017.

16 Black Lives Matter is not a trend, "Black Lives Matter leader: 'In the fight of our lives against fascism,'" *Berkeley News*, October 6, 2017.

16 Reproach and censure in the strongest possible terms are necessary, "Members of White House presidential arts committee resigning to protest Trump's comments," *Washington Post*, August 18, 2017.

17 We are chained and pinioned in our moment, Bernard DeVoto, "The Second Step," *Saturday Review of Literature*, February 5, 1938.

17 History, as nearly no one seems to know, James Baldwin, "Unnameable Objects, Unspeakable Crimes," in *The White Problem in America* (Johnson Publishing, 1966).

19 The narrative that Stono represents has always been, Jack Shuler, *Calling Out Liberty: The Stono Slave Rebellion and the Universal Struggle* (University Press of Mississippi, 2011).

20 Wherever the wealthy by the influences of riches, Howard Rock, *The New York City Artisan, 1789–1825: A Documentary History* (SUNY Press, 1989), p. 8.

20 A long habit of not thinking a thing wrong, *Common Sense*, Paine, *Collected Writings*, p. 5.

21 Ojibwe legends speak of a time when our people, Winona LaDuke, "Uranium Mining, Native Resistance, and the Greener Path," *Orion Magazine*, January 23, 2009.

21 The revolt against brutality begins with a revolt against the language, Rebecca Solnit, "Call climate change what it is: violence," *Guardian*, April 7, 2014.

21 Change is often unpredictable and indirect, "How Rebecca Solnit Became the Voice of the Resistance," *New York Times*, August 8, 2017.

22 we will mourn the loss of biodiversity and natural resources, The Emissions

Gap Report 2016, UNEP Synthesis Report, retrieved at wedocs.unep.org /bitstream/handle/20.500.11822/10016/emission_gap_report_2016.pdf.

22 The spirit of resistance to government is so valuable, Thomas Jefferson to Abigail Adams, February 22, 1787. Retrieved at www.loc.gov/item /mtjbib002565.

22 I had to give strong consideration to the cause, "How 2 Guys, A Lobster Boat, And A District Attorney Just Made Climate History," *ThinkProgress*, September 10, 2014.

1: We the People, Resist

23 The Constitution itself. Its language is "we the people," Frederick Douglass, "The Constitution of the United States: Is It Pro-Slavery or Anti-Slavery?" Glasgow, Scotland, March 26, 1860. Retrieved at www.blackpast .org/1860-frederick-douglass-constitution-united-states-it-pro-slavery-or-anti-slavery.

23 the dark power of words, Patrick Healy and Maggie Haberman, "95,000 Words, Many of Them Ominous, From Donald Trump's Tongue," *New York Times*, December 5, 2015.

24 universal empire is the prerogative of the writer, Thomas Paine, "American Crisis II," Paine, *Collected Writings*, p. 100.

24 In establishing American independence, David Ramsey, *The History of the American Revolution, Vol. II, 1789* (reprinted Applewood Books, 2011), p. 319.

24 Experts in authoritarianism advise to keep a list, Amy Siskind, *Medium*, November 20, 2016. Retrieved at medium.com/@Amy_Siskind/week-1-experts-in-authoritarianism-advise-to-keep-a-list-of-things-subtly-changing-around-you-so-aa8738496f9.

25 corporations have no consciences, no beliefs, no feelings, John Paul Stevens, *Citizens United v. Federal Election Commission*, January 21, 2010, retrieved at www.supremecourt.gov/opinions/09pdf/08-205.pdf.

25 The 'resistance' decided to pretend the loss, "Inaugural shows 'The Resistance' is an attack on democracy," *New York Post*, January 20, 2017.

25 most incendiary and popular pamphlet of the entire revolutionary era, Gordon Wood, *The American Revolution: A History* (Modern Library, 2002), p. 69.

26 Gratitude, I am sensible, is seldom to be found in a community, Thomas Hutchinson, *Thomas Hutchinson's Strictures upon the Declaration of the Congress at Philadelphia* (London, 1776), p. 31.

26 motley rabble of saucy boys, John Adams, "Adams' Argument for the Defense: 3–4 December 1770," retrieved at founders.archives.gov/documents /Adams/05-03-02-0001-0004-0016.

28 he did not simply change the meaning of words, Eric Foner, *Tom Paine and Revolutionary America* (Oxford University Press, 2005), p. xxxi.

28 moral father of the Internet, Jon Katz, "The Age of Paine," *Wired*, May 1, 1995.

29 We, therefore, beseech your Majesty, "Petition to the King; July 8, 1775," *Journals of the Continental Congress*, retrieved at avalon.law.yale.edu/18th_century/contcong_07-08-75.asp.

29 Never can true reconcilement grow, *Common Sense*, Paine, *Collected Writings*, p. 27.

29 Attached to your Majesty's person, family, and government, "Petition to the King; July 8, 1775," *Journals of the Continental Congress*, retrieved at avalon .law.yale.edu/18th_century/contcong_07-08-75.asp.

30 Lest this declaration should disquiet the minds of our friends and fellow-subjects, "A Declaration by the Representatives of the United Colonies of North-America, Now Met in Congress at Philadelphia, Setting Forth the Causes and Necessity of Their Taking Up Arms," July 6, 1775, retrieved at avalon.law.yale.edu/18th_century/arms.asp.

30 It is the good fortune of many to live distant, *Common Sense*, Paine, *Collected Writings*, p. 26.

31 A mastery irresistible performance, quoted in Phillip Papas, *Renegade Revolutionary: The Life of General Charles Lee* (NYU Press, 2014), p. 130.

31 working a wonderful change in the minds of many men, George Washington to Lieutenant Colonel Joseph Reed, April 1, 1776, retrieved at founders .archives.gov/documents/Washington/03-04-02-0009.

31 To argue with a man who has renounced the use and authority of reason, Paine, "American Crisis V," Paine, *Collected Writings*, p. 151.

32 America is best seen through the eyes of an immigrant, Alfredo Véa, quoted in Jeff Biggers, "Dear Gov. Jan Brewer: Wax On, Wax Off, Or, Welcome to Arizona, Now Go Home," *Huffington Post*, July 26, 2010.

32 neither the city's merchants as a body, nor any established elite, R.A. Ryerson, "Political Mobilization and the American Revolution: The Resistance Movement in Philadelphia, 1765 to 1776," *William and Mary Quarterly*, Vol. 31, Issue 4 (October, 1974), p. 565.

33 There is something exceedingly ridiculous in the composition of monarchy, *Common Sense*, Paine, *Collected Writings*, p. 10.

34 I think the game will pretty well be up, George Washington to Lund Washington, December 10–17, 1776, retrieved at founders.archives.gov /documents/Washington/03-07-02-0228.

34 these are the times that try men's souls, "American Crisis I," Paine, *Collected Writings*, p. 91.

35 Without the pen of the author of *Common Sense*, John Adams, quoted in Jill Lepore, "A World of Paine," *Revolutionary Founders: Rebels, Radicals, and Re-*

formers in the Making of the Nation, edited by Alfred F. Young, Ray Raphael, Gary Nash (Vintage, 2011), p. 89.

35 The ever memorable 19th of April gave a conclusive answer to the questions of American freedom, June 14, 1775, *Maryland Journal & the Baltimore Advertiser,* quoted in Mary Ellen Snodgrass, *American Colonial Women and Their Art: A Chronological Encyclopedia* (Rowman & Littlefield Publishers, 2017), p. 180.

36 would be tyrants if they could, Abigail Adams to John Adams, March 31–April 5, 1776, retrieved at www.masshist.org/digitaladams/archive /doc?id=L17760331aa.

36 We hold these truths to be self-evident: that all men and women are created equal, "Declaration of Sentiments and Resolutions, Woman's Rights Convention, Held at Seneca Falls, 19–20 July 1848," retrieved at ecssba .rutgers.edu/docs/seneca.html.

36 Your celebration is a sham, Frederick Douglass, "The Meaning of July Fourth for the Negro," in Philip Foner, *The Life and Writings of Frederick Douglass, Volume II Pre-Civil War Decade 1850–1860* (International Publishers Co., Inc., 1950), p. 675.

36 he has waged cruel war against human nature itself, "Declaring Independence: Drafting the Documents, Jefferson's 'original Rough draught' of the Declaration of Independence," retrieved at www.loc.gov/exhibits /declara/ruffdrft.html.

37 He [the King] has excited domestic insurrections amongst us, "In Congress, July 4, 1776. The unanimous declaration of the thirteen United States of America," retrieved at www.loc.gov/resource/bdsdcc.02101/?st=text.

37 How far life, liberty, and the *pursuit of happiness* may be said to be unalienable, Thomas Hutchinson, "Strictures upon the Declaration of the Congress at Philadelphia in a Letter to a Noble Lord, London," 1776, retrieved at oll.libertyfund.org/pages/1776-hutchinson-strictures-upon-the -declaration-of-independence.

38 the strange Absurdity of their Conduct whose Words, Wheatley, *Poems,* p. 204.

38 How is it that we hear the loudest yelps for liberty, Samuel Johnson, quoted in John T. Lynch, *Samuel Johnson in Context* (Cambridge University Press, 2011), p. 356.

38 the colonists are by law of nature freeborn, as indeed all men are, white or black, James Otis, "The Rights of the British Colonies Asserted and Proved," 1763, retrieved at oll.libertyfund.org/pages/1763-otis-rights-of -british-colonies-asserted-pamphlet.

39 one of the first Signs of the Decay, George Mason to George Washing-

ton, December 23, 1765, retrieved at founders.archives.gov/documents /Washington/02-07-02-0270.

39 slow Poison, which is daily contaminating the Minds and Morals of our People, George Mason, quoted in Douglas A. Blackmon, *Slavery by Another Name: The Re-Enslavement of Black Americans from the Civil War to World War II* (Doubleday, 2008), p. viii.

39 That all men are born equally free and independent, George Mason, Virginia Declaration of Rights, 1776, retrieved www.archives.gov /founding-docs/virginia-declaration-of-rights.

40 What right had they to say, *We, the people*, Patrick Henry, Virginia Ratifying Convention, June 4, 1788, retrieved at press-pubs.uchicago.edu /founders/documents/preambles14.html.

41 inconsistent with the principles of the revolution, Luther Martin, "The Debate in the Convention of 1787 on the Prohibition of the Slave-Trade," from the Madison Papers, Vol. III, p. 1388, retrieved at www.nytimes.com/1860 /11/24/news/the-debate-in-the-convention-of-1787-on-the-prohibition-of -the-slave-trade.html?pagewanted=all.

41 The augmentation of slaves weakens the states; and such a trade is diabolical in itself, George Mason, Debate in Virginia Ratifying Convention, June 15, 1788, retrieved at press-pubs.uchicago.edu/founders/print_ documents/a1_9_1s14.html.

42 Well, the first thing I want to say is: Mandate my ass, Gil Scott-Heron, "B Movie," *Reflections*, 1981, retrieved at www.discogs.com/Gil -Scott-Heron-Reflections/master/7702.

42 The cause would have suffered in my hands, quoted in John Epps, *The Life of John Walker, M.D.* (J. Haddon and Co., 1832), p. 142.

42 Like King Solomon, who put neither nail nor hammer to the temple, Maria Stewart, "An Address at the African Masonic Hall," 1833. Retrieved at www.blackpast.org/1833-maria-w-stewart-address-african-masonic-hall.

43 The greatest in the United States Constitution is its first three beautiful words, Donald J. Trump, Remarks by President Trump to the 72nd Session of the United Nations General Assembly, September 19, 2017, retrieved at www.whitehouse.gov/the-press-office/2017/09/19/remarks -president-trump-72nd-session-united-nations-general-assembly.

43 the democratic idea of American exceptionalism, Harvey Kaye, "Dangerous Idea: American Exceptionalism," Wisconsin Public Radio, retrieved at archive.ttbook.org/book/dangerous-idea-american-exceptionalism.

43 my country is the world, and my religion is to do good, *Rights of Man*, in Foner, *The Complete Writings of Thomas Paine, Volume 2*, p. 414.

43 Where liberty is not, there is mine, Thomas Paine, quoted in Moncure

Daniel Conway, *The Life of Thomas Paine* (reprinted by Cambridge University Press, 2011), p. 14.

44 as a free people, subject to no one, Jean Soderlund, *Lenape Country: Delaware Valley Society Before William Penn* (University of Pennsylvania Press, 2014), p. 12.

44 silly intention of an Insurrection amongst the Finns, E. A. Louhi, *The Delaware Finns or the First Permanent Settlements in Pennsylvania, Delaware, West New Jersey and Eastern Part of Maryland* (Clearfield, 2001), p. 138.

44 the best model that hath ever existed in the democratical form, James Boswell, *An Account of Corsica* (Dublin, 1768), p. 116.

45 placing himself at the head of a democratic government, Voltaire, *The age of Louis XIV: to which is added, an Abstract of the age of Louis XV* (Fielding and Walker, Paternoster Row, 1781), p. 289.

45 had a liberal character rare in a period when the rule of absolute monarch, Dorothy Carrington, "The Corsican Constitution of Pasquale Paoli," *The English Historical Review*, Vol. 88, No. 348 (July 1973), p. 481.

45 First Captain General of the liberty tree, quoted in Alfred Young, *Liberty Tree: Ordinary People and the American Revolution* (NYU Press, 2006), p. 339.

45 The Corsicans are not so remote from us as the Americans are from you, *The Public Advertiser,* January 17, 1769, retrieved at franklinpapers.org /franklin/framedVolumes.jsp?vol=16&page=019a.

45 Two great and powerful Nations are employing their Forces, "A Horrid Spectacle to Men and Angels," American Philosophical Society, January 17, 1769, retrieved at franklinpapers.org/franklin/framedVolumes .jsp?vol=16&page=018a.

46 By reason of Long Bondage and hard Slavery, Massachusetts Archives Collection. v.186-Revolution Petitions, 1779–1780. SC1/series 45X, Petition of John Cuffe, retrieved at dataverse.harvard.edu/dataset.xhtml?id=2692258.

46 History is a prophet who looks back, Eduardo Galeano, *Open Veins of Latin America: Five Centuries of the Pillage of a Continent* (Monthly Review Press, 1997), p. 8.

47 I do not arise to spread before you the fame of a noted warrior, William Apess, *On Our Own Ground, The Complete Writing of William Apess*, edited by Barry O'Connell, (University of Massachusetts Press, 1992), p. 277.

48 Upon the banks of the Ohio, a party of two hundred white warriors, William Apess, *Eulogy on King Philip: as pronounced at the Odeon, in Federal Street* (Boston, 1836), p. 58.

48 While the son of the forest drops a tear and groans over, William Apess, *A son of the forest and other writings* (University of Massachusetts Press, 1997), p. 114.

48 How inhuman it was in those wretches, to come into a country, Apess, *Eulogy*, p. 8.

49 Assemble all nations together in your imagination, Apess, *On Our Own Ground*, p. 157.

49 What, then, shall we do? Apess, *Eulogy*, p. 53.

50 Look at the disgraceful laws, disenfranchising us as citizens, Philip Gura, *The Life of William Apess, Pequot* (University of North Carolina Press, 2015), p. 113.

50 I say, then, that a different course must be pursued, Apess, *Eulogy*, p. 59.

51 Congratulations, Donald Trump, You Just Reignited the DAPL Resistance, Rebecca Bengal, "Congratulations, Donald Trump, You Just Reignited the DAPL Resistance," *Vogue*, January 24, 2017.

51 We are expendable people. We always have been, Rebecca Bengal, "Congratulations, Donald Trump, You Just Reignited the DAPL Resistance," *Vogue*, January 24, 2017.

51 By granting the easement, Trump is risking our treaty rights and water supply, "Trump Executive Memorandum on DAPL violates law and tribal treaties," January 24, 217, retrieved at standwithstandingrock.net /trump-executive-order-dapl-violates-law-tribal-treaties.

52 Your blood will mix with ours, and will spread, with ours, over this great island, Thomas Jefferson to Hendrick Aupaumut, December 21, 1808, retrieved at founders.archives.gov/documents/Jefferson/99-01-02-9358.

52 Tribal nations across Turtle Island have been emboldened by the resistance movement, Winona LaDuke, "Winona LaDuke on New Ways to Keep Pipelines Out of the Great Lakes," *Yes! Magazine*, January 31, 2017.

53 Five years after American colonists declared their independence from England, Jack Ferrell, "Rebellion at the Mission: The Yuma Revolt of 1781," *Western Voice*, March 13, 2014.

54 why should not the remaining Indians in this Commonwealth be placed, William Apess, *Indian Nullification of the Unconstitutional Laws of Massachusetts Relative to the Marshpee Tribe: or, The Pretended Riot Explained* (Press of Jonathan Howe, 1835), p. 83.

54 Resolved, That we, as a tribe, will rule ourselves, and have the Constitution, quoted in Daniel R. Mandell, "'We, as a tribe, will rule ourselves': Mashpee's Struggle for Autonomy, 1746–1840," in *Reinterpreting New England Indians and the Colonial Experience* (Colonial Society of Massachusetts, 2003). Retrieved at www.colonialsociety.org/node/1407.

55 a talented, educated, wily, unprincipled Indian, professing with all, quoted in Gura, *Life of William Apess*, p. 94.

55 In my mind, it was no punishment at all, Apess, *Indian Nullification*, p. 65.

56 The red children of the soil of America address themselves to the descendants of the pale men, quoted in *Reasoning Together: The Native Critics Collective* (University of Oklahoma Press, 2008), p. 249.

57 We're seeing an unfair court system in place in North Dakota that is persecuting, *Democracy Now!*, October 20, 2017.

2: Let Your Motto Be Resistance

58 Let your motto be resistance! Resistance! Resistance! Henry Highland Garnet, speech at the National Negro Convention, Buffalo, NY, 1843, retrieved at www.blackpast.org/1843-henry-highland-garnet-address-slaves-united-states.

59 You come against me with hatred and oppression and violence, Antonia Blumberg, "Activist Bree Newsome Reveals Staggering Faith During Confederate Flag Action," *Huffington Post*, June 30, 2015.

60 Thank you President Trump for your honesty & courage to tell the truth, John Bowden, "David Duke thanks Trump for blaming 'alt-left' for Charlottesville," *The Hill*, August 15, 2017.

60 The first time I heard it I said 'You have to be kidding,' Sabrina Siddiqui, "Donald Trump strikes muddled note on 'divisive' Black Lives Matter," *Guardian*, July 13, 2016.

60 Racism and murder are unequivocally reprehensible, A Statement from Denise Morrison, August 16, 2017, retrieved at www.campbellsoupcompany .com/newsroom/news/2017/08/16/statement-denise-morrison-president-ceo-campbell-soup-company.

61 Many of those people were there to protest the taking down of the statue of Robert E. Lee, Jennifer Schuessler, "Historians Question Trump's Comments on Confederate Monuments," *New York Times*, August 15, 2017.

61 On July 9, 1776, upon hearing the Declaration of Independence read for the first time, Bree Newsome, "Go ahead, topple the monuments to the Confederacy. All of them," *Washington Post*, August 18, 2017.

62 reverence for the characteristic rights of freemen, Washington's Inaugural Address, 1789, retrieved at www.archives.gov/exhibits/american_originals /inaugtxt.html.

63 Nothing better can be said in favor of a trade that is the most shocking, Otis, *Rights of the British Colonies 1764*, retrieved at press-pubs.uchicago .edu/founders/documents/v1ch13s4.html.

63 I do hereby further declare all indented servants, Negroes, or others, quoted in Alan Gilbert, *Black Patriots and Loyalists: Fighting for Emancipation in the War for Independence* (University of Chicago Press, 2012), p. 10.

64 Delivering up Negroes to their former masters, quoted in David Olusoga, *Black and British: A Forgotten History* (Pan MacMillan, 2017), p. 157.

64 When we contemplate our abhorrence of that condition, to which the arms

and tyranny of Great Britain were exerted to reduce us, Pennsylvania—
An Act for the Gradual Abolition of Slavery, 1780, retrieved at avalon
.law.yale.edu/18th_century/pennst01.asp.

65 The law made rendition essentially a private matter, Eric Foner, *Gateway to
Freedom: The Hidden History of America's Fugitive Slaves* (Oxford University
Press, 2015). p. 39.

66 In case it shall be found that any of my Slaves may, George Washington to
Tobias Lear, April 12, 1791, retrieved at founders.archives.gov/documents
/Washington/05-08-02-0062.

66 You will permit me now, Sir (and I am sure you will pardon me for doing it),
Tobias Lear to George Washington, April 24, 1791, retrieved at founders
.archives.gov/documents/Washington/05-08-02-0099.

67 I wasn't going to be her slave, "Ona Judge Staines, the Fugitive Slave
Who Outwitted George Washington," February 5, 2014, retrieved at
www.newenglandhistoricalsociety.com/ona-judge-staines-fugitive-slave-
outwitted-george-washington.

67 Whilst they were packing up to go to Virginia, I was packing to go, quoted
in Erica Armstrong Dunbar, *Never Caught: The Washingtons' Relentless Pursuit of Their Runaway Slave Ona Judge* (Atria, March 2017), retrieved at
longreads.com/2017/03/06/the-slave-who-outwitted-george-washington.

67 escape has been planned by some one who knew what he was about,
George Washington to Oliver Wolcott Jr., September 1, 1796, retrieved
at www.encyclopediavirginia.org/Letter_from_George_Washington_to
_Oliver_Wolcott_Jr_September_1_1796.

67 She has many changes of good clothes, of all sorts, *The Pennsylvania Gazette*, May 24, 1796, retrieved at commons.wikimedia.org/wiki
/File:Oney_Judge_Runaway_Ad.jpg.

68 thirst for complete freedom, quoted in Gary B. Nash, *The Forgotten Fifth:
African Americans in the Age of Revolution* (Harvard University Press, 2006),
p. 62.

69 black silk shorts, ditto waistcoat, ditto stockings, shoes highly polished,
quoted in Jesse Holland, *The Invisibles: The Untold Story of African American
Slaves in the White House* (Globe Pequot Press / Lyons Press, 2016), p. 53.

69 Card-playing and wine-drinking were the business, *The Granite Freeman*,
Concord, New Hampshire, May 22, 1845.

70 This woman is yet a slave. If Washington could have got her and her child,
"A Slave of George Washington!" by Benjamin Chase, *The Liberator*, January 1, 1847.

70 Ages to come will read with astonishment that the man, Edward Rushton,
"Expostulatory Letter to George Washington ... on his continuing to be a
proprietor of slaves" (Liverpool, 1797), p. 22.

70 I regret that the attempt you made to restore the Girl, George Washington to Joseph Whipple, November 28, 1796, retrieved at founders.archives .gov/documents/Washington/99-01-02-00037.

71 What if I am a woman, Maria Stewart, *Maria W. Stewart, America's first Black Woman Political Writer: Essays and Speeches*, edited by Marilyn Richardson (Indiana University Press, 1987), p. 22.

72 read and re-read until their words were stamped in letters of fire upon our soul, quoted in Peter J. Hinks, *To Awaken My Afflicted Brethren: David Walker and the Problem of Antebellum Slave Resistance* (Penn State University Press, 1996), p. 154.

72 Methinks I heard a spiritual interrogation, Maria Stewart, "Why Sit Ye Here and Die?" 1832, retrieved at www.blackpast.org/1832-maria-w-stewart-why-sit-ye-here-and-die.

73 Is it blindness of mind, or stupidity of soul, or the want of education, Maria Stewart, "An Address at the African Masonic Hall, 1833," retrieved at www.blackpast.org/1833-maria-w-stewart-address-african-masonic-hall.

73 Let our girls possess what amiable qualities of soul they may, Maria Stewart, "Why Sit Ye Here and Die?"

73 The first Black feminist-abolitionist in America, William Andrews, *Sisters of the Spirit: Three Black Women's Autobiographies of the Nineteenth Century* (Indiana University Press, 2008), p. 22.

73 O woman, woman! upon you I call, ed. Richardson, *Maria W. Stewart*, p. 55.

74 Look at the suffering Greeks! Their proud souls revolted, ed. Richardson, *Maria W. Stewart*, p. 53.

74 I am among the millions who have experienced the shock, Fania Davis, "This Country Needs a Truth and Reconciliation Process on Violence Against African Americans—Right Now," *Yes! Magazine*, July 8, 2016.

75 The whole history of the progress of human liberty, Frederick Douglass, *Frederick Douglass: Selected Speeches and Writings*, edited by Philip Foner (Chicago Review Press, 2000), p. 367.

76 bondage to a tyranny more brutal than that imposed, George Wallace, Speech by George C. Wallace, "The Civil Rights Movement fraud, sham and hoax," July 4, 1964, retrieved at www.let.rug.nl/usa/documents/1951 -/speech-by-george-c-wallace-the-civil-rights-movement-fraud-sham-and-hoax-1964-.php.

77 hope to a beleaguered populace mired in colonial dependency, John Egerton, *Speak Now Against the Day* (Knopf, 1994), p. 11.

78 I set up the office of the Southern Christian Leadership Conference, quoted in Belinda Robnett, *How Long? How Long?: African-American Women in the Struggle for Civil Rights* (Oxford University Press, 1997), p. 166.

79 was enough to terrify any person, what had not the soldiers then to fear? Mitch Kachun, *First Martyr of Liberty: Crispus Attucks in American Memory* (Oxford University Press, 2017), p. 16.

80 A great-great-grandson of Crispus Attucks, Martin Luther King, Jr., *Why We Can't Wait* (Beacon Press, 2010), p. ix.

80 It took the indiscriminate murder of a man of color, Amy Goodman, *Democracy Now!*, March 5, 2015.

81 I am aware that there are those who consider the non-resistance, William Whipper, quoted in C. Peter Ripley, *The Black Abolitionist Papers: The United States, 1830–1846* (University of North Carolina Press, 1991), p. 243.

81 Among the diversity of opinions that are entertained in regard to physical resistance, Henry Highland Garnet, *A Memorial Discourse* (J. M. Wilson, 1865), p. 46.

82 inflammatory, treasonous, poisonous and a flight of fancy, *Liberator*, quoted in Martin B. Pasternak, "Rise now and fly to arms: The life of Henry Highland Garnet," Dissertation, University of Massachusetts Amherst, 1981, p. 87.

82 token of gratitude and a memento of the battle for liberty at Christiana, Jonathan Katz, *Resistance at Christiana: The Fugitive Slave Rebellion, Christiana, Pennsylvania, September 11, 1851: A Documentary Account* (Crowell, 1974), p. 261.

84 get my property, William Parker, "The Freedman's Story," *The Atlantic*, March 1886.

84 The perilous times, so often predicted, are upon us, quoted in Gordon Barker, *Fugitive Slaves and the Unfinished American Revolution: Eight Cases, 1848–1856* (McFarland, 2013), p. 92.

84 redemptive violence, Parker, "The Freedman's Story."

85 Parker and his noble band of fifteen at Christiana, Frederick Douglass, *The Portable Frederick Douglass* (Penguin, 2016), p. 289.

85 If Washington and Attucks opened the Revolution of the past, quoted in Earl Ofari Hutchinson, *Let Your Motto Be Resistance: The Life and Thought of Henry Highland Garnet* (Beacon Press, 1972), p. 44.

3: Enemy of the People

86 One of the first rights of a freeman is to speak or to publish his sentiments, quoted in James Tagg, *Benjamin Franklin Bache and the Philadelphia Aurora* (University of Pennsylvania Press, 1991), p. 49.

87 Vice President–elect Pence, we welcome you and we truly thank you, Christopher Mele and Patrick Healy, "'Hamilton' Had Some Unscripted Lines for Pence. Trump Wasn't Happy," *New York Times*, November 19, 2016.

87 changing the language of musicals, Ben Brantley, "Review: 'Hamilton,' Young Rebels Changing History and Theater," *New York Times*, August 6, 2015.

87 It is not "freedom of the press" when newspapers and others, Donald J. Trump, Twitter, August 14, 2016, retrieved at twitter.com /realdonaldtrump/status/764870785634799617?lang=en.

88 The FAKE NEWS media (failed @nytimes, Donald J. Trump, Twitter, February 17, 2017, retrieved at twitter.com/realdonaldtrump/status /832708293516632065?lang=en.

88 hostile foreign governments or subversive organizations, Michael Grynbaum, "Trump Calls the News Media the 'Enemy of the American People,'" *New York Times*, February 17, 2017.

88 Donald Trump is demonstrating an authoritarian attitude, Grynbaum, "Trump Calls the News Media the 'Enemy of the American People.'"

88 object is to throw things into confusion that he may ride the storm, Alexander Hamilton, "Objections and Answers Respecting the Administration," August 18, 1792, retrieved at founders.archives.gov/documents /Hamilton/01-12-02-0184-0002.

89 There is nothing lighthearted about it whatsoever—it is an incitement, Brian Stelter, "Trump punches CNN in a juvenile tweet," CNN, July 2, 2017.

89 My use of social media is not Presidential, Donald J. Trump, Twitter, July 1, 2017, retrieved at twitter.com/realdonaldtrump/status/8812817550I 7355264?lang=en.

89 The alternate domination of one faction over another, George Washington, Washington's Farewell Address 1796, retrieved at avalon.law.yale .edu/18th_century/washing.asp.

89 We respect the important role that the press plays and will give them respect, but it is not unlimited, Lois Beckett and Sabrina Siddiqui, "Jeff Sessions bows to Trump pressure and launches crackdown on leakers," *Guardian*, August 4, 2017.

90 use of surveillance powers to target journalists and news organizations, U.S. Sen. Ron Wyden to Attorney General Jeff Sessions, October 10, 2017, retrieved at www.wyden.senate.gov/download/?id=28F1E0B4-F15B-4A88-8 22F-23D7C1D34FC3&download=1.

90 We have to all adopt certain civil habits that enable others to enjoy, Adam Liptak, "Amid Protests at Trump Hotel, Neil Gorsuch Calls for Civility," *New York Times*, September 28, 2017.

90 Justice Gorsuch should have known better than to sign up, "Neil Gorsuch speech at Trump hotel draws protests," CNN, September 28, 2017.

91 This is the kind of statement one expects to hear from a despot, not from

an American president, Brian Stelter, "Trump hits a new low in attacks on the free press," CNN, October 5, 2017.

91 With all of the Fake News coming out of NBC and the Networks, Donald J. Trump, Twitter, October 11, 2017, retrieved at twitter.com /realdonaldtrump/status/918112884630093825?lang=en.

91 This madcap threat, if pursued, would be blatant and unacceptable intervention, Hayley Miller, "Donald Trump Goes After the Free Press Yet Again," *Huffington Post*, October 13, 2017.

92 Network news has become so partisan, distorted and fake, Donald J. Trump, Twitter, October 11, 2017, retrieved at twitter.com/realdonaldtrump/status /918267396493922304?lang=en.

92 Are you recanting of the Oath you took on Jan. 20 to preserve, Ben Sasse, Twitter, October 11, 2017, retrieved at twitter.com/BenSasse/status /918296123269189632.

92 I will be announcing THE MOST DISHONEST, Donald J. Trump, Twitter, January 2, 2018, retrieved at twitter.com/realdonaldtrump/status /948359545767841792

93 has long stood as a beacon for independent media around the world, "In response to Trump's fake news awards, CPJ announces Press Oppressors awards," Committee to Protect Journalists, January 8, 2018. Retrieved at cpj .org/blog/2018/01/press-oppressor-awards-trump-fake-news-fakies.php.

93 to give the news impartially, without fear or favor, Adolph Ochs, "Without Fear or Favor," reprinted in *New York Times,* August 19, 1996.

93 the future of race relations, Gene Roberts and Hank Klibanoff, *The Race Beat: The Press, the Civil Rights Struggle, and the Awakening of a Nation* (Random House, 2017), p. 6.

94 In social media posts, our journalists must not express partisan opinions, "The Times Issues Social Media Guidelines for the Newsroom," *New York Times*, October 13, 2017.

95 Of those men who have overturned the liberties of republics, *The Federalist Papers*: No. 1, retrieved at avalon.law.yale.edu/18th_century/fed01.asp.

95 His Highness, the President of the United State and Protector of the Rights of the Same, "Title for the President, [May 11] 1789," retrieved at founders.archives.gov/documents/Madison/01-12-02-0095.

95 You are afraid of the one—I of the few, John Adams to Thomas Jefferson, December 6, 1787, retrieved at founders.archives.gov/documents/Jefferson /01-12-02-0405 .

95 the malice and falsehood of Satan, Abigail Adams, quoted in Jeremy Duda, *If This Be Treason: The American Rogues and Rebels Who Walked the Line Between Dissent and Betrayal* (Globe Pequot Press / Lyons Press, 2016), p. 28.

96 If all printers were determined not to print anything till, Benjamin Franklin, *Benjamin Franklin: His Life As He Wrote It* (Harvard University Press,
1990), p. 94.

96 The right of the people of the United States to listen to the sentiments
of their representatives, Richard N. Rosenfeld, *American Aurora: A
Democratic-Republican Returns: The Suppressed History of Our Nation's Begin-
nings and the Heroic Newspaper that Tried to Report It* (St. Martin's Press,
2014), p. 13.

96 no editor did more to politicize the press in the 1790s, Gordon Wood, *Empire of Liberty: A History of the Early Republic, 1789–1815* (Oxford University
Press, 2009), p. 253.

96 The refuse, the sweepings of the most depraved, quoted in Richard M.
Rollins, *The Long Journey of Noah Webster* (University of Pennsylvania
Press, 1990), p. 80.

97 who willfully or ignorantly misrepresent the design of a law, *Federal Gazette*, October 13, 1792.

97 Jay was burned in effigy, guillotined in effigy, hanged in effigy, from Maine
to Georgia, George Walter Prothero and Ernest Alfred Benians, reprinted
in *The Cambridge Modern History* (University Press, 1969), p. 320.

97 America realigned with a despotic rather than a republican state, quoted
in James Tagg, "The Limits of Republicanism: The Reverend Charles Nis-
bet, Benjamin Franklin Bache, and the French Revolution." *Pennsylvania
Magazine of History and Biography*, 1988, 112 (4), p. 539.

97 Profession costs nothing and it will be remembered that the present administration, *Aurora*, December 17, 1796.

98 The part I acted in the American revolution is well known, Thomas Paine
to George Washington, 1796, retrieved at thomaspaine.org/major-works
/letter-to-george-washington.html.

99 old, querulous, Bald, blind, crippled, Toothless Adams, quoted in David
McCullough, *John Adams* (Simon and Schuster, 2001), p. 500.

100 To write, print, utter or publish, or cause it to be done, or assist in it, Sedition Act 1798, An Act in Addition to the Act, Entitled "An Act for the Punishment of Certain Crimes Against the United States," retrieved at avalon
.law.yale.edu/18th_century/sedact.asp.

100 Truth will out! William Duane, "The foul charges of the Tories against
the editor of the *Aurora* repelled by positive proof and plain truth, and his
base calumniators put to shame" (Philadelphia, 1798), retrieved at archive
.org/details/truthwilloutfouloobachrich.

101 they spliced the Stamp Act and Direct Tax together as parts of a single
program, Paul Douglas Newman, "Fries's Rebellion and American Polit-

ical Culture, 1798–1800," *Pennsylvania Magazine of History and Biography* (January 1995), p. 37.

101 a continual grasp for power, quoted in Jon Meacham, *Thomas Jefferson: The Art of Power* (Random House, 2012), p. 317.

101 first citizen who suffered in resisting tyranny, quoted in Rosenfeld, *American Aurora*, p. 526.

101 I know not which mortifies me most, Thomas Jefferson to John Taylor, November 26, 1798, retrieved at founders.archives.gov/documents /Jefferson/01-30-02-0398.

102 audacious calumnies against the government, Alexander Hamilton to Josiah Ogden Hoffman, November 6, 1799, retrieved at founders.archives .gov/documents/Hamilton/01-24-02-0007.

102 any alternative between an abandonment of the constitution and resistance, Bache, *Aurora*, July 3, 1798.

102 The Lexington Kentucky *Gazette* summoned organized resistance, Douglas Bradburn, "A Clamor in the Public Mind: Opposition to the Alien and Sedition Acts," *The William and Mary Quarterly*, Third Series, Vol. 65, No. 3 (July 2008), p. 565.

103 Let him say what the government is, if it be not a tyranny, Thomas Jefferson, "Resolutions Relative to the Alien and Sedition Acts," November 10, 1798, retrieved at press-pubs.uchicago.edu/founders/documents/v1ch8s41.html.

103 direct resistance to certain laws of the Union, Alexander Hamilton to Jonathan Dayton, October–November 1799, retrieved at founders.archives .gov/documents/Hamilton/01-23-02-0526.

103 These are the facts which no perfidious artifices can evade, nor impudence deny, James Smith, "The Aurora and the Alien and Sedition Laws," *The Pennsylvania Magazine of History and Biography*, vol. 77, issue 2, April 1953.

104 If they have a sense of honor left, Benjamin Franklin Bache, 1769–1798.

104 No terror, no force, no menace, no fear, quoted in Susan Dunn, *Jefferson's Second Revolution: The Election Crisis of 1800 and the Triumph of Republicanism* (Houghton Mifflin Harcourt, 2004), p. 172.

105 possibly the least democratic election in American history, Jill Lepore, "Party Time: Smear Tactics, Skulduggery, and the Début of American Democracy," *The New Yorker*, September 17, 2007.

105 The changes in administration, which in every government and in every age have most generally been epochs of confusion, Margaret Bayard Smith to Susan B. Smith, March 4, 1801, in *The First Forty Years of Washington Society; Portrayed by the Family Letters of Mrs. Samuel Harrison Smith (Margaret Bayard)* (Scribner's Sons, 1906), p. 26.

106 a bunch of people into a mass detention whether or not they had any in-

volvement in unlawful activities, Colin Moynihan, "The Ongoing Legal
Battle Over the 'Black Bloc' Inauguration Day Protest," *The New Yorker,*
June 21, 2017.

106 Today's verdict reaffirms, Sam Adler-Bell, "Jury Acquits First Six J20 Defendants," *The Intercept,* December 21, 2017.

107 In a republic, light will prevail over darkness, truth over error, James
Madison to James Monroe, December 4, 1794, retrieved at www.loc.gov
/resource/mjm.05_0799_0804/?sp=2&st=text.

108 In every revolution, the people at large are called on to assist and promised
true liberty, ed. Young, et al., *Revolutionary Founders,* p. 10.

108 This specific case and this specific warrant are pure prosecutorial overreach,
Julia Carrie Wong and Olivia Solon, "US government demands details on all
visitors to anti-Trump protest website," *Guardian,* August 15, 2017.

108 assesses it is very likely some BIEs are influenced by a mix of anti-authoritarian,
Jana Winter and Sharon Weinberger, "The FBI's New U.S. Terrorist Threat:
'Black Identity Extremists,'" *Foreign Policy,* October 6, 2017.

108 Black identity extremism is the FBI's latest tactic to criminalize black ac-
tivists and justify increased police presence in black communities, Kirsten
West Savali, "Janaya Khan, Black Lives Matter Leader, Dismantles FBI's
Fraudulent 'Black Identity Extremist' Report," *The Root,* October 17, 2017.

108 an unprecedented level of hostility towards protesters, Adam Gabbatt,
"Anti-protest bills would 'attack right to speak out' under Donald Trump,"
Guardian, May 8, 2017.

109 The freedom of Speech may be taken away, George Washington to Officers of the Army, March 15, 1783. Retrieved at founders.archives.gov
/documents/Washington/99-01-02-10840.

109 nothing but capital against labor, a rich man's war, quoted in Michael
Helquist, *Marie Equi: Radical Politics and Outlaw Passions* (Oregon State
University Press, 2015), p. 173.

110 the majority of southern draft resisters opposed conscription, Jeanette
Keith, "The Politics of Southern Draft Resistance, 1917–1918," in *Other
Souths: Diversity and Difference in the U.S. South* (University of Georgia
Press, 2008), p. 119.

111 Your honor, I ask no mercy, I plead for no immunity, Eugene Debs, *Writings and Speeches of Eugene V. Debs* (Hermitage Press, 1948), p. 439.

111 The question in every case is whether the words used are used in such
circumstances, *Schenck v. United States,* March 3, 1919, Opinion, Holmes,
retrieved at www.law.cornell.edu/supremecourt/text/249/47.

112 Oh, it's very easy to attend a civic lunch, listen to a number of complimentary speeches from well-mannered and admiring people, Helquist,
Marie Equi, p. 155.

112 I'm going to prison smiling, Helquist, *Marie Equi*, p. 190.

112 That, at any rate, is the theory of our Constitution. It is an experiment, *Abrams v. United States*, November 10, 1919, Dissent, Holmes, retrieved at www.law.cornell.edu/supremecourt/text/250/616.

113 by any jury that has been sufficiently inflamed by a district attorney, H. L. Mencken, *Mencken Chrestomathy* (Vintage, 1982), p. 258.

4: To Undo Mistakes

114 O ye that love mankind! Ye that dare oppose, Paine, *Common Sense*, in Foner, *The Complete Writings of Thomas Paine, Volume 2*, p. 36.

114 banished from our land that religious intolerance, Thomas Jefferson, "First Inaugural Address," March 4, 1801, retrieved at avalon.law.yale.edu/19th _century/jefinau1.asp

115 And shall we refuse the unhappy fugitives from distress that hospitality, Thomas Jefferson, "First Annual Message to Congress," December 8, 1801, retrieved at avalon.law.yale.edu/19th_century/jeffmes1.asp

115 open to receive not only the Opulent and respectable Stranger, George Washington to Joshua Holmes, December 2, 1783, retrieved at rotunda .upress.virginia.edu/founders/default.xqy?keys=FOEA-print-01-02-02-6127.

115 all men have a natural and inalienable Right to worship almighty God, Jonas Phillips to George Washington, September 7, 1787, retrieved at founders .archives.gov/documents/Washington/04-05-02-0291.

116 This new world hath been the asylum for the persecuted lovers of civil and religious liberty, Paine, *Common Sense*, in Foner, *The Complete Writings of Thomas Paine, Volume 2*, p. 23.

116 Not one third of the inhabitants, even of this province, Paine, *Common Sense*, in Foner, *The Complete Writings of Thomas Paine, Volume 2*, p. 23.

117 You are not an American, Thomas Paine to James Madison, May 3, 1807, retrieved at thomaspaine.org/letters/other/to-james-madison-may-3-1807.html.

118 Our citizenship in the United States is our national character, "American Crisis XIII," in Paine, *Collected Writings*, p. 351.

118 The restrictions either previously or now were never, ever, ever based on race, religion, or creed, Michael Shear, "New Order Indefinitely Bars Almost All Travel from Seven Countries," *New York Times,* September 24, 2017.

118 A total and complete shutdown of Muslims entering the United States until our country's representatives, Donald J. Trump, Statement on Preventing Muslim Immigration, December 7, 2015, retrieved at web.archive.org/web /20170508054010/www.donaldjtrump.com/press-releases/donald-j.-trump -statement-on-preventing-muslim-immigration.

119 What I do for this country? They put the cuffs on, Michael Shear, Nich-

olas Kulish, and Alan Feuer, "Judge Blocks Trump Order on Refugees Amid Chaos and Outcry Worldwide," *New York Times*, January 28, 2017.

119 violates their rights to Due Process and Equal Protection guaranteed by the United States Constitution, Ariane de Vogue, Eli Watkins, and Alanne Orjoux, "Judges temporarily block part of Trump's immigration order, WH stands by it," CNN, January 29, 2017.

119 The Constitution prevailed today, Jaweed Kalem, "'No one is above the law,' Washington attorney general says," *Los Angeles Times*, February 9, 2017.

119 That's right, we need a TRAVEL BAN for certain DANGEROUS, Donald J. Trump, Twitter, June 5, 2017, retrieved at twitter.com/realdonaldtrump /status/871899511525961728?lang=en.

120 plainly discriminates based on nationality, Vivian Yee, "Judge Temporarily Halts New Version of Trump's Travel Ban," *New York Times*, October 17, 2017.

120 In the first month of its enforcement, Sam Levin, "Tears, despair and shattered hopes: the families torn apart by Trump's travel ban," *Guardian*, January 8, 2018.

120 Rather than repeat the failures of the past, this Court should repudiate them, Chris Fuchs, "Children of Internment Resisters Attack Travel Ban in Supreme Court Brief," MSNBC, September 20, 2017.

120 The court has a chance to make sure that one, it doesn't repeat the mistake that they made earlier, Chris Fuchs, "Children of Internment Resisters Attack Travel Ban in Supreme Court Brief," MSNBC, September 20, 2017.

121 torn from their homes, farms and places of business to be imprisoned together in large groups, *Toyosaburo Korematsu v. United States*, 140 F.2d 289 (9th Cir. 1943), retrieved at law.justia.com/cases/federal/appellate-courts /F2/140/289/1567033.

121 We have no common race in this country, Eleanor Roosevelt, "Undo the Mistake of Internment," retrieved at www.nps.gov/articles/eroosevelt internment.htm.

122 I'm sorry, this is wrong, Lorraine Bannai, *Enduring Conviction: Fred Korematsu and His Quest for Justice* (University of Washington Press, 2015), p. 18.

123 exclusion goes over 'the very brink of constitutional power,' *Korematsu v. United States*, December 18, 1944, Dissent, Murphy, retrieved at www.law .cornell.edu/supremecourt/text/323/214.

124 I am ready, willing, and able to bear arms for this country, quoted in Peter Irons, *Justice at War: The Story of the Japanese-American Internment Cases* (University of California Press, 1993), p. 153.

124 There were riots, sit-down strikes, work stoppages and other episodes of unrest at the camps, "Center shatters myth of 'quiet' Japanese Americans imprisoned in camps," UCLA News Room, September 15, 2015.

125 high government officials suppressed, altered and destroyed evidence in order to influence the outcomes of these cases at trial, quoted in Bannai, *Enduring Conviction*, p. 164.

126 Mr. Korematsu's name will always be familiar to legal scholars and historians, teachers and government officials, "An Old Wrong Redressed," *Washington Post*, October 8, 1983.

126 provide for a public education fund to finance efforts to inform the public, 50 USC 4201, retrieved at uscode.house.gov/view.xhtml?req= granuleid:USC-prelim-title50-section4201&num=0&edition=prelim.

126 Civil disobedience has also been a time-honored community occupation, as a quick reading of American history will show, William Sloane Coffin, *The Collected Sermons of William Sloane Coffin: The Riverside Years, Volume 2* (Westminster John Knox Press, 2008), p. 152.

127 Because the US Government takes the position that aiding undocumented Salvadoran and Guatemalan refugees, quoted in Linda Rabben, *Sanctuary and Asylum: A Social and Political History* (University of Washington Press, 2016), p. 133.

128 Welcoming Leonor into our space and really inviting her to make this her home, Doug Livingston, "Area church uses national playbook for giving sanctuary to undocumented immigrants," *Akron Beacon Journal*, October 21, 2017.

128 Families were kept apart because a husband or a wife or a child had been born in the wrong place, President Lyndon B. Johnson, "Remarks at the Signing of the Immigration Bill, Liberty Island, New York, October 3, 1965," retrieved at www.lbjlibrary.org/lyndon-baines-johnson/timeline /lbj-on-immigration.

128 When Mexico sends its people, they're not sending their best, "Here's Donald Trump's Presidential Announcement Speech," *Time*, June 16, 2015.

128 to ensure the public safety of the American people in communities across the United States, Executive Order: "Enhancing Public Safety in the Interior of the United States," January 25, 2017, retrieved at www.whitehouse.gov/the-press-office/2017/01/25/presidential-executive-order-enhancing-public-safety-interior-united.

129 We need policy and legislation, but ultimately, sanctuary comes from the people, Marion Renault, "Woman facing deportation given sanctuary in Columbus church," *Columbus Dispatch*, September 6, 2017.

129 shall not arrest, detain, extend the detention of, transfer custody of, or transport anyone solely on the basis of an ICE, Annie Rose Ramos, "Small

Georgia Town Limits Cooperation with Immigration Agents," MSNBC News, May 4, 2017.

130 crime rates are lower when localities stay out of the business of federal immigration enforcement, Gene Demby, "Why Sanctuary Cities Are Safer," NPR, January 29, 2017.

130 splitting up families and cutting funding to any city—especially Los Angeles, "'Sanctuary cities' endangered by Trump order threatening to cut federal funds," *Guardian*, January 25, 2017.

130 Every year, too many Americans' lives are victimized as a result of sanctuary city policies, Sari Horowitz, "Sessions makes sweeping attack on Chicago's sanctuary city policy," *Washington Post*, August 16, 2017.

130 not cave to the Trump administration's pressure because they are wrong morally, Lynn Sweet, "AG Jeff Sessions bashes Rahm Emanuel in sanctuary city speech," *Chicago Sun-Times*, August 16, 2017.

130 but to actually transform our city's policies to stop targeting us for imprisonment, Sarah Lazare, "A National Sanctuary Campaign Is Rising to Defy Trump's Nightmare White Supremacist, Xenophobic Agenda," *AlterNet*, January 26, 2017.

131 violates a fundamental constitutional principle of separation of powers, Ed Kilgore, "Judge Rules Trump's Sanctuary-Cities Order Flagrantly Unconstitutional," *New York Magazine*, November 21, 2017.

131 a wall of justice—against President Trump's xenophobic, Ben Adler, "California Governor Signs 'Sanctuary State' Bill," NPR, October 5, 2017.

132 dark chapter in our state's history, Patrick McGreevy, "Gov. Brown repeals unenforced sections of Prop. 187," *Los Angeles Times*, September 15, 2014.

132 California was not part of this nation when its history began, Katy Steinmetz, "California Prepares to Resist the President in Uncertain Times," *Time*, February 2, 2017.

5: Cities of Resistance

133 To The States, or any one of them, or any city of The States, Walt Whitman, *Leaves of Grass*, 1900, p. 173.

133 Resistance alone will not deliver us, Valarie Kaur, February 7, 2018, retrieved at valariekaur.com.

134 The great question of the seventies is, shall we surrender to our surroundings, Richard Nixon, "Annual Message to the Congress on the State of the Union," January 22, 1970, retrieved at www.presidency.ucsb.edu/ws/?pid=2921.

134 It forcibly thrust the issue of environmental quality and resources conservation, Gaylord Nelson, "Earth Day '70: What It Meant," retrieved at archive.epa.gov/epa/aboutepa/earth-day-70-what-it-meant.html.

134 irreparable harm to the public interest, *Sierra Club v. Morton*, 405 U.S. 727 (1972), retrieved at supreme.justia.com/cases/federal/us/405/727/case.html.

134 The critical question of "standing" would be simplified and also put neatly, *Sierra Club v. Morton*, 405 U.S. 727 (1972), retrieved at supreme.justia.com /cases/federal/us/405/727/case.html.

135 cannot long survive if it destroys the social good on which it depends— the ecosphere, Barry Commoner, *Making Peace with the Planet* (Pantheon, 1990), p. 20.

136 We are suffering from a disordered and lawless form of humanism, Barry Commoner, in interview with Claude Lévi-Strauss, *Psychology Today,* Vol. 5, No. 12, pp. 39, 80 (May 1972).

136 The Oil Party will be covered by the national media, and for this reason, "Anti-Nixon 'Oil Party' Protest Planned for Sunday Afternoon," *Harvard Crimson*, December 15, 1973.

137 The People should never rise, without doing something to be remembered, from the diary of John Adams, December 17, 1773, retrieved at founders .archives.gov/documents/Adams/01-02-02-0003-0008-0001.

137 a primary contributor to the global warming that we see, Doina Chiacu and Valerie Volcovici, "EPA Chief Pruitt Refuses to Link CO_2 and Global Warming," *Scientific American*, March 10, 2017.

137 has spent more than $350 billion over the past decade in response to ex- treme weather and fire events, Lisa Friedman, "Congressional Auditor Urges Action to Address Climate Change," *New York Times,* October 23, 2017.

138 closely coordinated with major oil and gas producers, electric utilities and political groups, Coral Davenport and Eric Lipton, "The Pruitt Emails: E.P.A. Chief Was Arm in Arm With Industry," *New York Times*, February 22, 2017.

138 I like what Donald Trump has done here as president, Rebecca Leber, "Did Trump's EPA Chief Just Say His Mission Is to Dismantle the Agency?" *Mother Jones*, July 17, 2017.

138 national efforts to reduce environmental risk, "Our Mission and What We Do," Environmental Protection Agency, retrieved at www.epa.gov /aboutepa/our-mission-and-what-we-do.

138 I think that measuring with precision human activity, Alex Guillen and Emily Holden, "What EPA Chief Scott Pruitt promised—and what he's done," *Politico*, November 19, 2017.

139 Over the past century, human activities have released large amounts, Jeff Biggers, "Call It What It Is: Climate Cover-Up, Not Climate Denial," *Huffington Post*, March 9, 2017.

139 tweeted climate change skepticism 115 times, Dylan Matthews, "Donald

Trump has tweeted climate change skepticism 115 times. Here's all of it," *Vox*, June 1, 2017.

140 Very recent research does suggest that persistent winter, Erik Ortiz, "Why climate change may be to blame for dangerous cold blanketing eastern U.S.," NBC News, January 5, 2018.

141 Scientific evidence for warming of the climate system is unequivocal, "Climate Change 2007: Synthesis Report," Intergovernmental Panel on Climate Change, retrieved at www.ipcc.ch/publications_and_data/ar4/syr /en/spms1.html.

141 there is general scientific agreement, Shannon Hall, "Exxon Knew About Climate Change Almost 40 Years Ago," *Scientific American*, October 26, 2015.

141 The level of complete corruption from the fossil fuel industry, "Watch Bill McKibben Talk Climate Change Battle on 'Real Time,'" *Rolling Stone*, March 4, 2017.

142 They're trying to deconstruct and dismantle the basic protections, Justin Worland, "Inside Scott Pruitt's Mission to Remake the EPA," *Time*, October 26, 2017.

142 Removing climate change resources from the EPA website, "Removing Climate Change Resources from EPA Website 'Offensive and Dangerous,' Science Group Says," Union of Concerned Scientists, October 20, 2017.

142 that the world is being carried to the brink of ecological disaster not by a singular fault, quoted in Michael Egan, *Barry Commoner and the Science of Survival* (MIT Press, 2007), p. xiii.

142 We have unleashed a mass extinction event, Sydney Pereira, "How to Save Humanity: 15,000 Scientists Urge Action," *Newsweek*, November 13, 2017.

143 those spectacles of misery that poverty and want present to our eyes in the towns and streets of Europe, Thomas Paine, *Agrarian Justice*, 1797, retrieved at thomaspaine.org/major-works/agrarian-justice.html.

143 Now the forests are removed, the land covered with fields of corn, orchards bending with fruit, *Portable John Adams*, p. 14.

143 A change in our climate ... is taking place very sensibly, Thomas Jefferson, *Notes on the State of Virginia*, 1804, retrieved at xroads.virginia.edu/-hyper /jefferson/ch07.html.

144 a country, in a state of nature, covered with trees, Hugh Williamson, *Observations on the Climate in Different Parts of America Compared with the Climate in Corresponding Parts of the Other Continent, to which Are Added, Remarks on the Different Complexions of the Human Race, with Some Account of the Aborigines of America* (New York, 1811), p. 24.

145 The old process of selective remembering and willful forgetting of the history of the Revolution, Alfred Young and Harvey Kaye, *Liberty Tree:*

Ordinary People and the American Revolution (New York University Press, 2006), p. 300.

145 The Revolution has a different meaning if you start here, Erick Trickey, "The Story Behind a Forgotten Symbol of the American Revolution: The Liberty Tree," *Smithsonian*, May 19, 2016.

145 Timber production soared from one billion board feet in 1840, Whit Bronaugh, "North American Forests in the Age of Man," *American Forests*, Summer 2012.

146 I contend that the narrow measure of Iowa's woodland, Thomas MacBride, "The Proceedings of the Iowa Academy of Science" (Des Moines, 1898).

146 Nowadays almost all man's improvements, Henry David Thoreau, "Walking," *The Atlantic*, May 1862.

147 social activism and his defense of nature, Laura Dassow Walls, *Henry David Thoreau: A Life* (University of Chicago Press, 2017), p. xviii.

147 The greater part of what my neighbors call good I believe in my soul to be bad, Henry David Thoreau, *Walden* (Houghton, Mifflin, 1894), p. 19.

147 Under a government which imprisons any unjustly, Henry Davis Thoreau, "Resistance to Civil Government (Civil Disobedience)," *Civil Disobedience and Other Essays* (Dover, 1993), p. 9.

147 This winter may find climate activists spending as much, Bill McKibben, "How to Save the Planet From President Trump," BillMoyers.com, December 1, 2016.

147 Signing orders to move forward with the construction of the Keystone XL and Dakota Access pipelines in the Oval Office, Donald J. Trump, Twitter, January 24, 2017. Retrieved at twitter.com/realdonaldtrump/status/8239508 14163140609?lang=en

148 adequately consider the impacts of an oil spill on fishing, Valerie Volcovici, "Federal judge orders more environmental analysis of Dakota pipeline," *Reuters*, June 15, 2017.

148 We have named the site of our resistance, LaDonna Brave Bull Allard, "Why the Founder of Standing Rock Sioux Camp Can't Forget the Whitestone Massacre," *Yes! Magazine*, September 3, 2016.

149 use of military-style equipment and excessive force, Catherine Thorbecke, "Showdown Looms at Dakota Access Pipeline," ABC News, December 3, 2016.

149 The U.S. government is wiping out our most important, LaDonna Brave Bull Allard, "Why the Founder of Standing Rock Sioux Camp Can't Forget the Whitestone Massacre," *Yes! Magazine*, September 3, 2016.

150 We are speaking publicly to empower, "We 'Acted from Our Hearts': Activists in Iowa Admit to Repeatedly Sabotaging Dakota Access Pipeline," *Democracy Now!*, July 25, 2017.

150 This is something people have got to understand, Andy Davis, "Five 'grannies' face trial for protesting pipeline along Mississippi River," *Press Citizen*, April 17, 2017.

151 I was arrested, along with about 30 other water protectors, Miriam Kashia, "Why I was arrested for trespassing," *Milwaukee Journal Sentinel*, February 21, 2017.

151 We will be developing not a camp, but a village, Mikki Halpin, "Standing Rock Sioux Tribe Historian LaDonna Brave Bull Allard on DAPL Protests and Seventh Generation Activists," *Teen Vogue*, April 26, 2017.

152 the US experienced a historic year, Alexander C. Kaufman, "2017 Shatters Records with $306 Billion in Damages from Climate-Linked Disasters," *Huffington Post*, January 8, 2017.

152 I can assure you that we will follow the guidelines of the Paris Agreement, Lauren Gambino, "Pittsburgh fires back at Trump: we stand with Paris, not you," *Guardian*, June 1, 2017.

152 I know President Trump is trying, Melanie Mason, Evan Halper, and Patrick McGreevy, "Gov. Brown unveils plan for global climate summit, further undercutting Trump's agenda," *Los Angeles Times*, July 6, 2017.

152 The cause of America is in a great measure the cause of all mankind, Thomas Paine, *Common Sense* reprinted in *Thomas Paine: Collected Writings: Common Sense / The Crisis / Rights of Man / The Age of Reason / Pamphlets, Articles, and Letters* (Library of America, 1995), p. 5.

153 catastrophes and disasters, "As Catastrophic Flooding Hits Houston, Fears Grow of Pollution from Oil Refineries & Superfund Sites," *Democracy Now!*, August 28, 2017.

154 The urban metabolism currently operates as an inefficient, Herbert Giradet, *Creating Regenerative Cities* (Routledge, 2015), p. 8.

154 The concept of a regenerative city could indeed, Jeff Biggers, "Cities and States Lead on Climate Change," *New York Times*, November 30, 2016.

155 It only took two nanoseconds, Elizabeth Shogren, "As Trump Retreats, States Are Joining Forces on Climate Action," *YaleEnvironment360*, October 9, 2017, retrieved at e360.yale.edu/features/as-trump-retreats-states-are-stepping-up-on-climate-action.

155 In the Trump era, cities have to lead the way, "NYC Delivers First-Ever City Plan to Meet the Goals of the Paris Climate Agreement," City of New York, October 3, 2017. Retrieved at www1.nyc.gov/office-of-the-mayor/news/634-17/nyc-delivers-first-ever-city-plan-meet-goals-the-paris-climate-agreement.

157 4 percent annual growth rate of the soil carbon stock, Jeff Biggers, "Iowa's Climate-Change Wisdom," *New York Times*, November 20, 2015.

157 better stewardship of the land could have a bigger role, "Regreening the

planet could cut as much carbon as halting oil use—report," *Reuters*, October 17, 2017.

158 Dull, inert cities, it is true, Jane Jacobs, *The Death and Life of Great American Cities* (Random House, 1992), p. 448.

159 Representing the largest coal-producing state in the nation, Jeff Biggers, "From Selma to Coal River Mountain: Ken Hechler's Century of Hellraising Leadership Marches On," *Huffington Post*, November 20, 2013.

161 Naturally, we are compelled to ask the question, "Eulogy for the Reverend James Reeb by the Reverend Dr. Martin Luther King, Jr., in Brown Chapel, Selma, Alabama, March 15, 1965," retrieved at www.beaconbroadside.com /broadside/2015/03/martin-luther-king-jrs-eulogy-for-james-reeb.html.

162 I don't mind being poor, Jeff Biggers, "Reason to Believe in Environmental Justice: Coalfields Hero Judy Bonds," *Huffington Post*, December 15, 2010.

162 the youngest generation's constitutional, Ephrat Livni, "Kids around the world are suing their governments for ruining the planet," *Quartz*, December 16, 2017.

Index

Democracy Now!, 57, 80
Democratic Republicans, 94, 96–97, 102
Denman, William, 121
DeVoto, Bernard, 17
Dewey, John, 12
Dine (Navajo), 159
Direct Tax, 100–101
DisruptJ20, 105, 107–8
Dixon, Brandon, 86–87
Donne, John, 52
Donnelly, Ann M., 119
Douglass, Frederick, 23, 36, 73, 75, 80–82, 83, 84, 85, 162
Douglass, William, 134–35
Dreamers/Dream Act, 14–15, 129
Duane, William, 13, 103–5
Duke, David, 59–60
Dyer, Mary, 126
Dyson, James Ian, 58–59

Earth Day, 134
Earth Justice, 162
Egerton, John, 77
Eisenhower, Dwight D., 34
Emancipation Proclamation, 85
Emanuel, Rahm, 130
Enduring Conviction: Fred Korematsu and His Quest for Justice (Bannai), 122–23
Energy Transfer Partners (ETP), 51, 148
environmental movements, 6–7, 20–22, 133–51, 158–63; regenerative cities, 152–58; "We Are Still In" coalition, 155
Environmental Protection Agency (EPA), 28, 133–34, 137–42, 151, 159, 161
Environment and Natural Resources

Division, U.S. Department of Justice, 138
EPA. *See* Environmental Protection Agency (EPA)
Equi, Marie, 109–13
Espinal, Edith, 128, 129
Espionage Act of 1917, 109, 110, 112
ESPN, 94
ethnic and religious discrimination, 122–32; refugees, 127–28; Sanctuary Movement, 127–31
ETP. *See* Energy Transfer Partners (ETP)
"Eulogy on King Philip" (Apess), 47–51
Everett, Edward, 46
Executive Order 9066, 125
Exxon, 141

Fairfax Resolves, 39
fake news, 12, 60, 87–94, 95, 100
Farmer, James, 77
Faulconer, Kevin, 156
FBI. *See* Federal Bureau of Investigation (FBI)
FCC. *See* Federal Communications Commission (FCC)
Federal Bureau of Investigation (FBI), 108
Federal Communications Commission (FCC), 91–92
Federal Gazette, 97
Federalist Papers (Hamilton), 95
Federalists, 94–97, 99, 101, 102–3, 104, 105
Ferguson, Bob, 119
Ferguson, Missouri, 74, 80
Ferrell, Jack, 53
Fischer, David Hackett, 144
Foner, Eric, 28, 65

Author photograph by Miriam Alarcón Avila

JEFF BIGGERS is an award-winning historian, journalist, and playwright. He is the author of several books,
including *The United States of Appalachia*, *State Out of the
Union*, and *Reckoning at Eagle Creek*, winner of the Delta
Prize for Literature and David Brower Award for environmental reporting. His last book, *The Trials of a Scold*,
was long-listed for the PEN/Jacqueline Bograd Weld
Award for Biography. He is the founder of the Climate
Narrative Project, an arts and advocacy initiative for
schools and communities. Visit jeffbiggers.com.